Brave in the Broken

My Journey from
Despair to Hope:
What the Stars
Showed Me about
Resilience

Katerina Karaindrou

WESTBOW
P R E S S®
A DIVISION OF THOMAS NELSON
& ZONDERVAN

WestBow Press books may be ordered through booksellers or by contacting:

WestBow Press
A Division of Thomas Nelson & Zondervan
1663 Liberty Drive
Bloomington, IN 47403
www.westbowpress.com
844-714-3454

ISBN: 978-1-6642-2736-1 (sc)
ISBN: 978-1-6642-2737-8 (hc)
ISBN: 978-1-6642-2735-4 (e)

Library of Congress Control Number: 2021905304

Print information available on the last page.

WestBow Press rev. date: 4/29/2021

Contents

The House Up On The Mountaintop

It's quiet
in this house up on the mountaintop,
a snug, brick-built house with but one window
in its warped wooden door.
Through the window's shattered glass, Light
bravely and beautifully breaks in.
In the center of its single room stands a dilapidated redwood table.
Around it, two chairs; and above it, a dusty and
dusky lamp, whose Light abounds.
A young girl is sitting at that table, tasting grace, and trusting it
as she patiently waits for the guest of the second chair.
Sitting at that table, she lays down her burdens, lays down her pain.
She places her anxious heart on Light's hands as
it shines above and extends beyond her.

Down at the edge of the mountain, that same
girl is making her way to the house.
Only, in this different moment in time, a scarf has replaced her hair,
hurt has found refuge in her eyes, and fear
has stripped her of her innocence.
How frail, scarred, and weary she is as she courageously
trudges toward the mountaintop.
Yet even in the rising, raging wind and the depth
of the darkness up ahead and all around,

trusting in the Light she cannot yet see, she
boldly continues her resilient ascent.
Broken on the mountain foothills, she cannot see how beautiful she is.
And, perhaps, what makes her beautiful is not
her fragile, fractured appearance
but the boundless courage in her heart that
holds her shattered soul together
as she stays brave,
even when the mountain seems unmovable, even
when the path feels too steep to climb.
And, perhaps, what makes her beautiful is the
boldness of the faith that rises within her
as she graciously battles the overwhelming darkness surrounding her,
as her walls come crashing down, as her knees begin to fail.
Yet despite the darkness, there is still a house up on the mountaintop,
And that same girl, in a different moment
in time, is there, waiting for her.

One is fighting for the other, fueled by love and grace,
and oh, how beautiful it is
when Light bridges brave and broken,
with the sound of a knock on the door of peace,
as the girl who was once trudging up the hill of hardship
finally arrives at the house up on the mountaintop.
And oh, how beautiful it is
when the two girls sit at that table in the arms of Light,
and the house becomes a home.

Prologue:
The Broken Question

"Dad's going to pick up the car from the parking, and then he's coming to pick *us* up, so we can go home, OK?" Mom asks.

I nod. I can't speak. I've been on very high dose chemo for the past five days, and the taste of the medicine, combined with the extreme nausea prevents me from speaking, eating, or even swallowing.

Mom's phone rings. "Yeah, OK. We're coming right down. Should I bring the bags first? Katerina's very weak. She needs help with her wheelchair. OK, all right," Mom says and hangs up the phone.

She leaves the hospital room to pack our bags in the car downstairs. For a moment, I am alone in the room. Lying there, not able to even lift my head up, I close my eyes and take a deep breath. I am pretty dizzy and very nauseated. Chemo has stolen every inch of life from me. As I lie there powerless, I stare at the ceiling, squeeze my chemo teddy bear, and break down crying.

Mom soon returns. When she sees me crying, she rushes in the room and hugs me. "What happened?" she asks me. "What's the matter? Are you OK? You want some Zofran maybe?"

I shake my head signing no. I take a paper box that the nurses have given me to throw up in, grab the pen that's resting on the table next to my bed, and begin writing. "I can't do this anymore."

My mom reads the note, and I feel her heart break. She hugs me and tells me, "I know. But hey, chemo two is out of the way. You are almost halfway there."

I know what she is saying isn't true. I know a have a long, long road ahead of me.

"Dad's waiting in the car. When we go home, you'll see. You'll feel better," Mom says.

Home? What home?

My name is Katerina, and this has been my life for the past couple of months. In January 2018, I was diagnosed with a very rare and malignant form of bone cancer. I decided to write this book so that I could share with you my thoughts and experiences throughout this journey. Don't worry if you are confused. We'll take the story from the beginning.

Part I

Chapter 1

The Physics Class Incident and the C Word

It was Monday, December 11, 2017, and my mom had just come back from a long day at work. She walked in my room and asked me how my day had gone.

"It was good. We have a language midterm this Tuesday," I told her. "But, Mom, my knee hurts so much. Today at school I couldn't walk up the stairs or bend it to sit in the chair."

"Why? Did you get tired at school? Did you overdo it in the gym?" my mom replied.

"Maybe. I don't know. It hurts a lot, but it usually goes away after three or four days. It's the same pain I've been having for the past eight months."

"OK. Maybe put some ice on it, and if it doesn't get better, we can go to the doctor."

Tuesday, December 12, 2017, was when the first strike hit. I woke up six minutes late to get ready for school. My knee was in so much pain. I tried to sit up in the side of my bed. I pushed my hands against the bed, pressed my feet to the ground, and tried to get up. But I couldn't. I fell down. My knee was shaking. I tried to pick myself up, but all my efforts were in vain. My knee started trembling until it collapsed. I got very scared. *Wow, this is the first time something like this has happened. Maybe it is a broken bone*, I thought. My knee had been hurting for almost nine months now, but the pain always came and went after a few days—like waves that calmed after some time.

My mom came downstairs quickly and told me that we were going to the hospital. She helped me get up. I was in so much pain. At the hospital, they gave me a white plastic wristband with my name on it and rushed me to the emergency room. After waiting for ten minutes, crying because of the pain, I went in for an x-ray.

The x-ray came back inconclusive. A doctor came in and started pushing and pressing on my knee. He said it was a clear fracture. He diagnosed me with a stress fracture in the knee. A stress fracture is a small crack in a bone, or within the bone, and it is caused by overuse and repetitive activity. I held back a few tears and went home to rest. We were planning to go to France for a ski trip, but the doctor told me that I would need a full leg cast to stabilize my knee. Skiing was clearly off the table.

We left the hospital, went to a store, and bought the cast. I still remember that pain.

At school the next day, everybody was asking me what had happened, and I casually replied, "It's just a broken knee." But it was difficult explaining that my knee was broken without my having done anything.

"So what? Did it just break?" most people would ask. Even the teachers thought there was something off with my diagnosis.

"Yeah, pretty much," I said.

On Friday, December 22, 2017, we went on vacation to a Greek village in the mountains. It was fun, but I couldn't really do anything—or walk. I rented a camera to have something to work on. Photography is one of my biggest passions. It allows me to express myself and show people how I view the world. A camera is the brush I use to paint the world any color I want and draw anything I imagine. I was huge on gear too. But in case you don't already know, camera gear is super expensive. Thus, I started saving up to someday get my own camera.

After a couple of days, we left for France. We ended up going on that ski trip after all. Amalia, my twin sister, and Thanos, my older brother, along with Philip and his younger brother, our friends from school, and their parents all went skiing, and I just stayed in the hotel and watched movies.

After we got back, my knee was worse, and the pain didn't stop. We decided to go to the doctor. We arrived from France on a Sunday. That Monday, I didn't go to school. I couldn't.

Little did I know what the next day would be like.

On Tuesday, January 9, 2018, I woke up in pain. Later that day, my dad took me to the hospital. There, I met another doctor, the best in his field. Dr. Vasilis was friends with my dad, and my dad trusted his medical opinion fully. Little did I know when I met Dr. Vasilis how much he would change my life. He examined me, checked to see if my knee was warm, and reviewed my MRI. He, along with one of his colleagues, explained that the diagnosis I had previously been given was wrong. False. I didn't have a stress fracture. I had something serious—way more serious.

The doctors were vexed and worried. My situation was rare. Different signs indicated different things, and that made it extremely difficult for them to understand the problem and give me an accurate diagnosis. They said they needed to run some more tests—immediately.

They sent me right away to another hospital, and even though there was no availability for an appointment, the hospital squeezed me in. It was urgent. Dr. Vasilis talked to my dad alone for a while. I was worried sick already. Little did I know what the next few days would be like.

When I got to the radiology clinic, I saw my mom, who had left her office to come and talk with the doctors. That alone meant the situation was serious. I was still in the dark. My parents were looking at each other and then looking at the doctor and then glancing back at me. That look in their eyes—I'll never forget it. I knew it wasn't good. Both of my parents kept saying everything was OK, but I wasn't so sure of that anymore.

Waiting was the hardest part. After some time, I went in for my first test of the day. I took a new radiography and skeletal scintigraphy. The results were sent to the doctor before we got them. He contacted my parents. The results were not good.

The next day, a team of doctors who worked with Dr. Vasilis reviewed the results of my scans. That was the first time I heard it. I was not ready. I had come across it online, but never, not in a million years, did I believe it could be a possibility. But I was wrong.

"The bone scan is negative, but the MRI is inconclusive. We need to do a biopsy to confirm and rule out the possibility of some malignancy," one doctor said.

"Wait. What?" I said. I looked at my dad.

His eyes were puffy and red. He was trying to hold back the tears. It was like he knew things were not good.

"Malignancy?" I asked with a trembling voice.

"It's going to be all right. It's nothing serious. I promise," my dad said with a stuttering voice and cracked a smile.

I looked over at the doctor, and tears flooded my eyes. He said we needed to do the open, surgical biopsy as soon as possible, just in case.

As I was walking out of the room, I just stopped. My mom thought it was because of the crunches or the pain. But no. I just couldn't do it anymore. I couldn't hold it together. I just stopped there, in the middle of the hallway, and took a breath—a very, very deep breath. Yet I still felt as if I were suffocating. I started breathing rapidly and deeply. My mom turned around and hugged me.

That was when I burst into tears—so, so many tears. I knew all the people sitting and waiting in the hallways were looking at me. I felt it, but I didn't really care. I was numb. I couldn't process it. I didn't know why I was crying. I hadn't yet believed I could have cancer. I was shaking. I didn't know how to react, what to think, or how to deal with such information. It was just my subconscious reacting. I was crying every twenty steps, and everyone was staring at me.

They scheduled the biopsy for the next day, Thursday, January 11.

Sign of Courage 1

About a month before the whole knee situation had begun, I'd been seeing the same dream again and again. I thought it was weird, but I didn't really connect the dots—not until that day at the hospital. In the dream, I was diagnosed with cancer. Everyone thought I was going to die, yet somehow I didn't. And the next image in the dream was me standing in front of Tsolainio, which is one of our school buildings, holding a book. Then I woke up. Always. I had seen the exact same dream around ten times. It was unreal. Was it a coincidence? Was it just my body subconsciously warning me that something was wrong? Was it God preparing me for what was to come? I'll leave that up to you to decide. Don't choose your answer yet. Remember the question. And make your choice after reading the rest of the story. Trust me.

After we left the hospital, my mom and I headed home, and my dad left for work. On the way back, I was crying. My mom was too. We stopped at a church near our house. We walked in to pray. I always believed in God and loved him, but this time I didn't have the strength to trust him. I hadn't yet learned how to. I mean, malignancy? I couldn't understand it. It didn't make sense to me. I was always nice and helped people and did the best I could in everything. This just didn't make sense to me. Little did I know, though, that I would understand it all in the end. The story soon gets interesting.

We walked in the church and sat in the front row to pray. I closed my eyes and asked God to save me, to help me, to heal me. I prayed with all the power of my heart; every bone in my body was begging God to make this go away. It was a desperate cry, a plea, the most honest and raw prayer I had ever said to him since losing my grandpa few years ago. Before going home, I said, *But, God, let your will be done. I know you know best. I will try to trust you. I believe you have a plan for my life, much better than my own. Give me strength to trust you.*

And God listened. He listened, and He whispered to me that the purpose of this all would be revealed to me in the most profound ways. I couldn't hear Him though. My cry was louder than the voice of hope during that time. It *had to* be though. There's purpose behind everything. Hope and pain would fight again soon.

That night was one of the toughest. I switched off all the lights. It was completely dark—that's how I felt. It was completely quiet—that's how I needed to feel. I needed to quiet all the voices in my head, all the fears, all the unanswered questions. I put on my headphones and listened to some music. I closed my eyes and tried to cry. I needed to let it all out, but I couldn't. I couldn't cry, the tears didn't run down. I felt numb; I felt nothing and everything at the same time. I tried to cry again, silently. My throat hurt, and my stomach was so tight. I don't know what I was feeling. Since I couldn't let my feelings out by crying, I decided to write them down. This is what I wrote that night:

January 10, 2018

I feel so alone. Like nobody knows my sadness. Nobody knows the demons in my mind. I'm so scared. Actually, I'm not scared. I'm overwhelmed. I don't know how I'm supposed to deal with this. Tomorrow is surgery day. They need to do a biopsy. Mom says it's nothing to worry about. That things will be fine. I'm not so sure of that. The doctors whispered. They gave each other that look, and they spoke with "code" terms. "Code" terms for cancer. I know it. I probably have cancer. I cannot comprehend this. It seems like this big bubble of "overwhelment," if that's even a word. One day it's cancer, one day it's not. First, they said a fracture, then osteomyelitis, now cancer ... I don't know how to handle this. I know God's with me, but I try to feel his presence, and even though I know he's here, I can't sense it. I do believe everything happens for a reason. I'm crying all the time. I need a sign from God. Something to tell me that it's all under control. I'm not scared to die. I'm scared of the suffering. I want someone to talk to. I don't want to stress my parents with my thoughts and make them even more scared and sad. Their child might die. I don't want to talk to Ami about this. She's hurting so much already. My negative thoughts will just make her sadder. I need to stay strong for my family. But I'm so weak. You should have seen the look on their faces in that room with the doctors. My dad was holding my mom's hand tightly and holding back the tears. Their divorce didn't matter anymore. Their child was dying, and they were in this together. They were torn today. But they didn't want me to know. How could they do it? How could they hide their pain? My parents were suffering in that room. I could see it in their eyes. If only you saw their eyes. I'll never forget that look in their eyes, the pain it hid, the fear it masked. I saw them struggling, trying to convince themselves that it's going to be all right. I don't want to leave just yet. I don't want to die. But I might be. I might be dying. I

don't want to let myself believe that. I need to get some sleep. I have surgery in four hours.

Lying there, in silence, tears on my pillow, I couldn't help it. Fear and pain felt like a tear in my heart. Tears wet my face. I couldn't take it. The agony was unbearable. Nobody knew; nobody could help.

God, can you hold me close tonight? Get me through the night. Save me from this fear. I am not gonna make it myself. In these moments of pain and suffering, be there for me. Help me feel you by my side. Give me peace. Quiet the voices of fear in my mind. Please give me the strength to endure this, to make it through another day. I'm broken. Unsay the doctor's spoken words. Help me find hope in the hopeless. I don't know how to face this. I want to live. I'm not ready to die—not yet.

The next morning on January 11, after getting only four hours of sleep, I was awoken by my mom to get ready for surgery. She helped me change into fresh clothes and brush my teeth. I wasn't allowed to drink or eat anything. My sister, Amalia, came downstairs to my room with a big smile and a tired look on her face.

"Are you ready?" she asked.

"I guess," I said with a quiet voice.

I got dressed, and then my mom helped me pack a hospital bag—the first of many. On the drive to the hospital, we weren't talking. It was so early. Dark outside. My stomach was tight. I was nervous.

At some point Amalia, looking at me, cracked a smile, and said, "Hey, don't worry. Everything's gonna be all right."

I don't know why, but this phrase got stuck in my mind. Everybody kept telling me the same thing, but it was only in that very moment, by that person, that it really touched me. And until this day, these words stay with me, that half-asleep, subtle smile as she told me that it was going to be okay. I'll always remember that.

When we got to the hospital, I went up for pre-op tests. Soon I was asked to change into a hospital gown and bid my parents and sister goodbye. As the doctors rolled me in the elevator, I could see my dad, mom, and sister with tears in their eyes, smiling and waving as the elevator door was closing. Amalia broke down. She looked so worried. I was shaking. I started crying too. The elevator door closed, and we went down to the OR floor. I had to be brave. But I couldn't. I didn't know how. I was broken. Fear was winning this fight. But—spoiler alert—bravery and fear fight again in the future. And that next fight, I'm telling you, is going to be more exciting. Let's get back to the story though.

Before being wheeled into the OR, I met with Dr. Vasilis, who introduced me to the anesthesiologist and gave me a tight hug to stop the tears from flooding my eyes. As they moved me to the operating table, I felt my whole body shaking.

"OK, you got to stop trembling, so we can start," the anesthesiologist said and smiled.

I laughed. Yeah right, if only I could control it. Eventually the drugs kicked in, and next thing I remembered was waking up with blurry vision in the OR. A doctor came in and asked me if I could try to move to the bed next to me. I couldn't see, but I told him that I could. Two other surgeons helped me change beds. Dr. Vasilis came into the OR and told me that everything had gone great.

All I said was, "Thank you." I fell asleep again. And the next time I woke up, my family were all by my side.

After the biopsy I was in a lot of pain, but it was manageable. All I cared about was getting out of that hospital. After five to six hours, I was finally discharged, and we went home. My mom rented out a wheelchair so I could move around the house and go to school. I was on four different pain meds, taking nine to ten pills a day. For someone who had just learned how to swallow pills like three days before, I call that a whole lot of progress.

Sign of Courage 2

I stayed home on Friday but decided to go to school on Monday. During physics class, another student walked in to make an announcement. He said that there was an eleven-year-old boy from another city in Greece who had been diagnosed with bone cancer above the right knee. He said no treatment seemed to be effective, and the boy's parents had set up a fund so they could seek another treatment in the United States. The teacher encouraged us to help as much as we could.

"This is what you all should pray never happens in your life," he said. "These situations are extremely difficult and very serious."

As I was listening to him speak, my hearing became more and more silent, dull, distant. My vision grew blurry, my breathing faster, my pulse stronger. I was having a panic attack. I started sweating and crying. I was sitting in the front row of the class, so I couldn't let out my tears. I also couldn't go out because I couldn't walk. The lesson hadn't even officially started. I didn't know what to do. I put my head down low, hid my face with my hair, and silently cried during that whole lesson. I could feel people looking at me, chatting about me. I saw the teacher stare at me, wondering what was wrong.

After the class finished, people started gathering around me, asking me what was wrong.

The teacher came up to me and said, "Hey, Katerina, what happened? Are you okay?"

I couldn't speak. I just burst into tears—a loud cry, desperate.

The teacher went to get me some water. Some kids left for the next class. A friend of mine, Ourania, stayed with me.

After I calmed down a little bit, I told her and the teacher, "The bone cancer that little boy has… This is probably what I have too." I burst into tears again. "I don't want to die," I whispered.

Ourania hugged me. I saw her eyes. They were red. She wanted to cry too. I was causing my friends and family so much pain.

Soon after, the school psychologist came down and asked me if I was OK and if I wanted to talk. I didn't. I had no words to say. Just tears to cry. I then called my dad to come pick me up. I didn't want people to know about this. I didn't want anyone else to know I was sick. But with me crying in class like that, I knew the news was about to spread; people would soon find out. When my dad picked me up, I told him about what had happened. His eyes became red again.

I always observe people's eyes. Expressions and words can mask feelings and pain; they can act strong and be reassuring that things will be okay. But eyes can't. Eyes don't lie. Instead, they get red and swollen and watery and start tearing up like the sky on a rainy fall day.

I didn't want people to notice *my* eyes. My expressions and words were saying, "I got this. I'm strong enough. It's all going to work out." My eyes, though, were crying out, "Save me. Pull me out. I'm drowning. I am not going to make it."

But I masked that pain with tears, blamed it on the shock, the surprise. I didn't want to accept my pain because, once I accepted it, this would become real. This would become real life, and I didn't want that to happen. I didn't want to let myself believe that there was the slightest possibility of me having cancer.

After that physics class incident on Monday, I decided to stay home the next few days. I was clearly not ready to deal with whatever this was. Lots of people messaged me asking me what had happened. I just said I got a bit upset, but it was nothing serious, and I was fine. Still pretending the problem wasn't there.

On Wednesday I also stayed home. It was results day. The hardest part was the waiting—the uncertainty, the fear, the what-if. You try to prepare yourself. Some people choose to "think positively"; some others prefer the "realistic approach." I tried both. Neither worked. You can never prepare yourself enough for something like this.

Sign of Courage 3

On our way to the hospital, I was casually on my phone. Suddenly, an article popped up. It was from a support group page, where people shared their stories of going through difficult illnesses. The title of the article was, "A Message from an Angel." As I read the first words of the text, I started shaking. I couldn't believe it. This couldn't be a coincidence.

"Dear Amalia," were the first words the author had used to write this article eleven years ago. "I was diagnosed with a bone sarcoma in the right knee, in January 2006." The resemblance between the author's circumstance and mine was undeniable and unexplainable. My sister's name was Amalia, it was January, and I was heading to an oncologist to find out whether I had a bone sarcoma in the right knee. That really seemed to be a message from an angel.

The article went on to talk about the fact that the author had endured a lot but was about to lose the fight. I couldn't make sense of why I'd stumbled on this article that morning, but I knew there had to be a reason for it.

My parents, Amalia, and I all went to the hospital to meet with an oncologist. As we walked into his office, I felt an unexpected calmness in the atmosphere. It was so strange, considering that both the article I'd previously read, and the physics class incident had brought up a lot of fear and worry. I can't really describe or explain it. It was just this strange and sudden feeling of calmness.

As we sat down, the oncologist introduced himself and said that he had the biopsy results back. "I am afraid it *is* indeed a malignant sarcoma."

Those were his words. Knowing my history with crying, you would expect me to burst into tears, to panic, to feel shocked. My mind was running, going at a hundred miles per hour—fear, disbelief, the dream, the article, the physics class incident. Yet in that moment, all I said was, "okay."

That was it. No tears, no sadness, no pain in that moment. Just a calm, "okay." A brave "okay". Remember this word. It transforms in the future.

We talked for a while. I asked about the course of treatment, the risks, and all the FAQs of cancer patients. Treatment included lots of chemotherapy and multiple surgeries. The oncologist said treatment would take about ten to twelve months, but he advised us to seek that treatment abroad because of how rare and aggressive this sarcoma was.

The news was devastating. And yet I was calm. I was at peace. I looked outside the window, and the sky was beautiful. There were light rays falling from the sky down to earth. The colors were gorgeous. I'll never forget that sunset—neither the one in the sky nor the sunset of peace I felt in me that afternoon when I got the news. Denial? Shock? Underestimating the problem? I don't think so. I'd rather explain that "sunset feeling" as peace—a strange peace, calmness. It was almost certainty—certainty that I was going to be OK, even if nothing about the situation was. Even though I had been shaking from fear a few moments before, I was now at peace. It was so strange, almost poetic. Faith and fear had fought yet again. And that one was on faith, on the trust that things would work out, even if there was a what-if haunting my mind.

That sunset feeling was like a sign for me. It was a sign that acted as a testament to the fact that, amid bad news, in the very midst of hardships and challenging times, there would be a strange, unexplainable, yet undeniable peace. When most would lose hope and strength, I would be supplied with a sunset feeling, a sense of peace. It was a testament to the fact that, through faith, I would get through it. Faith would be the anchor of hope for me that, ironically and yet perfectly magically, would propel me and push me forward against all currents and waves that try to drown me as I cross the ocean of cancer and climb to get to the top of the mountain of this battle. And you know what they say about the top of the mountain. It has the best view. The view is so incredible, it is like a thousand sunset feelings all at once. At the time, I didn't realize it, but I now know that that sunset feeling was a confirmation that God was going to be there with me every step of the way and was going to transform all fear and hurt into peace—into sunset feelings.

Remember that sunset feeling. It's a really important detail. You'll see why.

Chapter 2

How Do You Say Goodbye?

After we left the oncologist's office, I remember feeling relieved. We finally had an answer, and we could finally start attacking whatever this was. But I was also numb. I hadn't yet processed what had just happened. The rest of my family was already home, waiting to hear the news. During the car ride, everybody was quiet. Silence was deafening. Everybody was sinking in their own thoughts.

Eventually my dad spoke out. "OK, look. I don't want you to worry. We will go to the best doctors, and you will be fine. Everything will be fine. Most likely, you and Mum will go to the States for your treatment, and me and Amalia will stay here and visit you as much as possible."

"Wait, what?" I said.

My fear after that incident during physics class was becoming a reality. For a moment, fear paralyzed me. I was speechless, trying to process.

"What about school? I can't just stop in the middle of the year. And what about you and Ami? I can't do this without you guys," I said, and my voice cracked.

"I know, sweetheart. It's a very difficult time for all of us as a family, but mostly for you," Mum said. "But we have to stick together as a family. The most important thing right now is getting you well. So, if we have to go to the States for that, we will."

To be honest I don't really remember what happened after. We got into an argument about where I should have the treatment. I wanted to do everything here. Home. But little did I know what home truly was. I needed the support system so much. But my parents disagreed. I understand that they wanted to make sure I received the best possible treatment and care, but I really wanted to stay home.

It was such a strange feeling. One moment, I had everything, and the next, I had a very aggressive form of cancer that had been growing in my leg for months—a cancer that would soon kill me if I didn't do anything about it. And the only thing I *could* actually do about it was receive a treatment that had more side effects than the cancer itself, for more than a year, in a foreign country, without some of the most important people in my life by my side. This realization hurt more than words can explain. It was like getting your heart ripped out of your chest and thrown against a wall. I couldn't understand why this was happening. Why now?

On Thursday January 18, the next day after I was diagnosed, I decided to go back to school. I don't quite remember what that morning felt like, what I was thinking, or even how I was feeling. I just remember, after I arrived late to class thanks to my wheelchair, a few of my friends who knew about my leg approached me and asked how I was doing. I told three of my friends—Miltiadis, Ourania, and Olga—that it was cancer and that I would probably need to go to the States for treatment for about a year. One of them started crying. People started staring at us and whispering. By the end of class, six more people found out. And by the time the bell rang for the first break, half of my class knew.

After the break, one teacher walked in and saw a group of students around me, a few of whom were crying. She asked one of my classmates what was that all about and found out about my diagnosis. She approached me and asked me. It took every part of me, every cell in my body to find the strength to keep it together and not burst into tears when she asked me how I was handling the situation. I had to be brave. Another teacher teared up when she found out. I was always one who caused people to smile; seeing how many people cried because of me hurt me so much. I knew deep down that this was not my fault, but I could not ignore the pain that I was causing. My heart broke into a trillion pieces every time students from other classes came to ask me about my leg. I had to comfort them and assure them that everything was going to be okay, even though I, myself, doubted that. I had to smile and tell them that I'd be back in a year, even though I, myself, feared that I might never get to see them again.

The news spread so quickly. More than fifty people knew by the end of the day. I honestly still don't know how I kept it together that day. I had to put up this mask, this shield of strength, because, if I was open about my feelings, I knew I wouldn't get through the day. I didn't even know what those feelings were, which was another reason I couldn't be honest about them. I guess I was still numb. I still hadn't understood or processed the situation.

Everybody kept telling me how strong I was, but strong was the last thing I felt. I tried to participate as much as I could in class. I knew I would have to give up school soon. And that day, I tried my hardest to hold onto that part of my life. My education was something *I* had control over. It was *my* responsibility and *my* choice to either study or not. I thought that maybe, if I just tried extra hard enough, maybe cancer didn't have to steal this part of my life too.

As the days went on, I started skipping school more often. I had no strength to go—neither emotional nor physical. And that broke me. I had to watch my life fall apart and be OK with that. Day by day, tear by tear, I had to lose a part of me, a part of my life, and still seem strong for the people around me. I didn't want to cause them any more pain. Every time I went to class, I was reminded of what I would miss out on. I was reminded how "not normal" I would look during the chemo. And I hated remembering those things.

It also seemed pointless after some time. Juggling all the thoughts this diagnosis had created made me consider the possibility that I might not make it out. And if that were the case, sitting in class, acting as if everything was normal seemed pointless.

I was so conflicted. On the one hand, I wanted to spend my potentially last days home in the best and most creative way possible. On the other hand, though, I wanted to spend them as normally as possible. Either way, I wanted to do things that would make the voices in my head shut off. But there weren't many things that could do that. I wouldn't call it denial, but I definitely tried to ignore the diagnosis. I was hoping that maybe, just maybe, if I forget about it, it would go away.

Wednesday, January 24, 2018

Today was my last day of school. Maybe the last day I'll ever get to go to school. Maybe I'll never get to sit in a classroom again and joke with my friends or laugh when we're not supposed to or complain about homework or stay up late studying or spend the recess doing class assignments or study for a test or be a normal fourteen-year-old. Maybe this is it. I should be sad, scared, anxious ... But I don't think I am any of that. I'm numb. I can't feel, I can't process. I've given up, but I'm still acting as if I have the strength to deal with this. I'm doing it for my family. I have to be brave. I don't want them to worry. But the truth is, I don't have any strength left. I don't know how I'll endure this. I don't want to have to go through this. I feel alone. I know God is by my side, holding my hand as I cry. But I can't feel him near. I feel completely alone. I have so many people who care about me, and yet I've never felt more alone in my life. I'm numb, frozen. Nobody knows these holes in my heart. Nobody knows these thoughts in my mind. I'm scared I won't survive. Oh, God, hold me. I'm the real definition of drowning. I feel like ... Actually, I don't know what I feel like. This is too much. I can't take it. I'm lying still in this bed, but my heart is beating out of my chest, my mind is racing, and voices are telling me how this will take over me. I can't see the end of this nightmare.

This was my journal entry of that day.

The last day of school was very emotional. It was a sad, miserable day, yet it was filled with so much love, so much hope. It fascinates me how opposites always go together. It's in the darkest sky that stars shine the brightest. I find this so meaningful and purposeful. Only if the sky is dark enough can you see the stars. Only when you're hopeless can you take a chance and hope. Only when you're scared can you let go of the fear and place your trust in something greater than you and your problem. Only when you're broken, tired, and worn out can you allow love to mend the pieces of your heart together. It's through adversity that you evolve. It's through fear that you learn to trust. It's through pain that you learn to endure. It's through sadness that you learn to hope. And it's through loneliness that you learn to love. Only when it's dark can you see life's stars, life's secrets, life's beauty.

That day at school, my friends surprised me with a goodbye party and many cards, hugs, and kind words. But the most meaningful gift they gave me was a little red notebook, in which they each had written their goodbye letter for me. Love's in the details. When they gave it to me, I was so emotional. But I was still numb. I wanted to cry so badly, but I held back the tears. They had done so much for me, and I didn't want to remember this day as a crying day but, rather, as a hopeful day full of laughter and smiles.

When that final bell rang, my heart skipped a beat. *This is it*, I thought. I was heartbroken. I didn't want to leave. I wished time would stop. I wish I could freeze this moment. How could I let go?

I hugged my friends one by one, and they all took me outside in my wheelchair. Each time I hugged someone, I wondered if that would be the last time I did so. I tried to remember the feeling each hug gave me—the motivation and the support. We took a group photo, and then my mom picked me up and drove me home. I'm trying to figure out a metaphor to put into words what that felt like, but I just can't. Time was moving, and as much as I wanted it to stop, I knew the only way out was through.

Many people are standing and knocking at a door that's already open. I was one of them. I tried to convince myself that, if I just knocked on the door a little while longer, maybe what was standing behind it would change. But I couldn't see clearly. I thought I knew what cancer hid, why it was standing behind the door, but I didn't. It's in the process that you learn to see the result. Life is oftentimes understood in review.

On Thursday, January 25, we left for Germany. Just for two days though. We flew there, so I could meet my oncologist. It was decided. I would do all my treatments in the university hospital in Essen, a city in northwestern Germany. Dr. Thanos, a neurosurgeon and my dad's best friend, helped us out so much during this time. He stepped up and researched different cancer centers that specialized in sarcomas; learned about doctors; and, overall, took on the load of all the planning, removing the burden from my parents. They were broken. This was too much for them. I'm so grateful for Dr. Thanos, not only for his help but also because he was the only one whose humor made me laugh every single time. We had already become best friends. So anyway, this was the plan; my mom and I would move to Essen for a year and a half, and Amalia and my dad would visit as often as they could.

Upon arriving in the hospital in Essen, we met with Prof. D, an oncologist who specialized in sarcomas. She talked to us about the chemotherapy drugs, the protocol, and the side effects, and she answered all our questions.

Dr. Thanos came with us to Germany so he could help us out. At night in the hotel room, we had a talk. I asked him more about the type of cancer I had and about the chemo, the chance of survival, and more. I asked him things that I was afraid to ask my oncologist in front of my parents. I knew he wouldn't sugarcoat it, and I truly needed to hear the raw truth to prepare myself to deal with what was coming. He told me that this sarcoma was very rare and aggressive. But he also promised that I would win.

The next day, we returned home to Athens. We had to prepare to leave again in about ten days, pack our things, and say our goodbyes. How can you find the strength to do that? That's the question I couldn't get out of my head. This was the last full week I had to spend at home, the last week to be as normal as possible, the last week to spend quality time with the people I loved.

I spent the next few days just lying around, doing more tests, and seeing friends and family. I also had a second surgery that Tuesday, to freeze and save some ovarian tissue, since the chemo would most likely affect that as well. I thought it was just going to be a painless procedure, but I was so wrong.

Although it was a very quick surgery, the anesthesiologists gave me too much anesthesia, as we later found out. Normally, in general anesthesia, they give you a paralytic, along with other drugs that make you sleep and not remember. In my case, the rest of the meds were weaned off, but the paralytic was partially still in my system. As a result, when I woke up in the recovery room, I could not breathe. I was awake but paralyzed. I felt as if I was suffocating. I started panicking. It was as if I was drowning. That was the first time I feared I was going to die.

I tried to tell my mom that I couldn't breathe, but the doctors couldn't do anything about it. They put me on high oxygen and tried to calm me down. Every second was torture. Imagine the unbearable agony of not being able to breathe while being fully conscious of the fact that, even though you try to take a deep breath, you just can't. It was a nightmare. I closed my eyes, giving in to the influence the anesthesia still had on me. I hoped that, once I opened them again, I would be home, able to breathe.

But not even a few seconds later, I abruptly opened them; my soul jumped up, and I tried to sit up, in vain since I could not move. I was desperately grasping for air, trying to fill my lungs. I was helpless. It was traumatizing. It was torture. Agony.

After a while, the medication started wearing off. I still felt as if I couldn't breathe, but I could now speak.

"I can't breathe," I told my mom and then fell back asleep.

"They put you on oxygen, honey. Try to relax," she told me.

"No, Mom," I said. "I can't breathe. I can't. Breathe."

I was in agony. I was suffocating. I was drowning, sinking, desperately trying to keep my head above water, to catch a breath, to survive. Every time I took a breath, I inhaled less and less air. As I exhaled, I felt my lungs collapse, a tight feeling rushing through my chest. It was pure agony. I don't know exactly how long this lasted for. It felt like hours. Every second felt like eternity. Trauma, fear, and anxiety rushed through my body as I realized that I couldn't breathe, as my lungs hurt from trying to grasp for air. I'll never forget that. I was so scared for what was coming. I was sure for a moment that I wouldn't survive.

I want to be honest with you in this book. I've had dark thoughts—a lot. But the thing about the night is that it's temporary. It can only last for so long. The sun always rises. No matter how dark it gets, how long it takes, the sun always rises in the morning; light always shines. And during the night, when it gets too dark, that's when stars can be seen; that's when the light of day can make its appeal in a transformed version that reflects and shines through the details of the darkness, through the little things, through the insignificant moments, through the stars. That's what the stars of suffering are all about. They are moments of hope amid pain, agony, and fear.

On Wednesday, January 31, I went to the hospital for some last CT scans to look for metastasis. The pain from the tumor was unbearable. I had to be transferred to another hospital in the middle of the night to receive pain medications intravenously. While in the hospital, I had a mental breakdown. I couldn't do it. There was no way—not in a million years—that I would ever be able to pull this off, to endure, to get through chemo, to not see my family and friends for months.

My mom was there to keep me company. Love's in the details. Dr. Vasilis was there too. He held my hand and told me to *be brave*. Little did I know what this phrase would soon symbolize. God's in the details. And so is hope.

Thinking of the future was just like staring at a tsunami that was heading directly at me and wanting to run with everything in me but not being able to. That's what this diagnosis felt like. Everywhere I looked, I could only see pain and hopelessness. Desperation was worse than fear. But as I was lying there in the hospital bed, Dr. Vasilis held my hand and told me that the only way out was through. What a profound moment that was.

As I thought about it, I realized that, during the day, you don't know stars exist, yet you fear the night. But as the sun sets and light fades, the stars appear. *First* the sun sets, and *then* the stars appear. *First*, it's got to get dark, and *then* can you see the stars. *First* fear paralyzes you, and *then* you learn to trust unconditionally. *First* you experience pain, and *then* you find its hidden purpose. As the sun is setting, you don't know that the stars will appear. When you're alone at 3:00 a.m. crying, you can't see the smiles the future holds. When your heart is broken and loneliness creeps in, you can't see the love you'll feel later. When fear knocks on the door of your mind and moves in, you can't see the courage you'll soon find. You think that what's coming is just darkness. But if you choose to go through it, face it, and fight it, not only do you witness a magical, colorful sunset as the day comes to an end, but you also see the trust you placed come to life, in the form of constellations of stars that light up the night sky. But *first*, the sun sets, and darkness comes, and *then* the stars shine.

Let's say it's a snowy day outside, and your driveway is covered in snow. But you have places to be and errands to run. The only thing you can do is clear out the driveway and get rid of the snow that's blocking your way. You go to the garage and look for tools that will help you clear out the snow. The first tool you see is a grass cutter, but you know you have a shovel somewhere in the house. Will you go look for the shovel? Or will you just take the grass cutter and hope it does the trick? That place you have to go to—that's your destination. It's the next thing you want to do in your life. And the snow that blocks your way is a problem—a disease, a financial setback, a loss, or anything else you might have to deal with. Now, in order to get to where life needs you to be, to fulfill your destiny, you need to clear out the snow, deal with the problem.

Your tools in the garage symbolize the different coping techniques you can use to help you face and deal with the problem. The shovel represents an attitude of gratitude and hopefulness and the grass cutter an attitude of bitterness and hopelessness. Which are you going to choose? Sure, the grass cutter is the most easily accessible. It's *easy* to be bitter about a problem, a sickness, a loss. It's *easy* to say, "Why me?" It's *easy* to want to give up, to get discouraged and think, *Oh I'll never make it to where I need to be. I'll never clear out the snow in time.*

But is *easy* a good enough reason for you to choose the grass cutter? What about efficiency? Clearly the grass cutter will not help you move out the snow. You know that already. You just try to fool yourself into thinking it might because it's comfortable and convenient.

It's comfortable to be miserable about a problem. Your hope isn't challenged, and your faith isn't tested, because you choose not to have any. That's why you're comfortable with the grass cutter, even though you already know it's not going to help you achieve your goal, clear out the snow, get better, break the addiction, or move through whatever the obstacle is. You choose to stay discouraged, bitter, upset, and hopeless because it's *easier*; it takes less courage, less faith, and less risk.

You see, with the other option, there's always the risk that you'll choose to go look for the shovel, but you won't end up finding it. There's always the risk that you'll choose to be optimistic and hopeful and to believe and trust that your loved one will survive or that you'll break the addiction or beat the cancer, but it's still not going to happen. And if you hope for something and it doesn't end up happening, you get more hurt than if you hadn't hoped to begin with. If an airplane takes off and crashes halfway through the trip, the result is more damage and pain than if it hadn't taken off at all. There's always that risk with hope. That's why, even though you know the grass cutter won't help, you still choose it. That's why, even though you know being disappointed and discouraged and bitter won't help you, you still choose to give up the fight.

But what if you ended up finding the shovel after all? What if you chose to take that risk and it worked out? Yes, there's a possibility that the plane crashes, but there's also a possibility that it won't. Yes, there's a possibility that the shovel is lost or broken, but there's also a chance that it's not. And it if it's not, you get to clear out the snow completely, which then allows you to get to your destination.

There is a chance that you'll start hoping and being optimistic and ambitious and have faith and place your trust but still not get well or not get the promotion or lose your loved one. But there's also a chance that your being hopeful will actually *help* you get better, give you *strength* to break the addiction, or boost your *determination* to get that job you wanted.

So, isn't that possibility of things actually working out *enough* for you to just want to *try* and go look for the shovel? Isn't the *sole* possibility that the shovel will help you clear out the snow *enough* for you to go look for it?

For me, it was. Just the possibility of my beating the cancer was enough of a reason for me to take the risk of choosing to be hopeful. I knew it was more challenging. If you hope, you have more to lose. But at the same time, if you hope, you have more to win. And that was a risk I was willing to take.

The time had come—I had to say goodbye. I had to find a way to say goodbye, not just to my family but to my whole life. Letting go is a tricky subject. It's very difficult to let go of something you love and are used to, because then you become exposed to change, vulnerable to pain and prone to hurt.

But here is where it gets tricky. That negative change is the most ideal and perfect situation for God to show up and create beauty from ashes. Sometimes negative change can lead you to *positive* change. Sometimes being lost is the only and most perfect way for you to find the right path. And what's interesting is that the path you *thought* was right, before you got lost, turns out to be the wrong path after all. The situation you were in *before* the negative change occurred, *before* the cancer formed, *before* that loved one passed away, *before* your hope was crushed, *before* your heart was broken turns out to *not* be helping you reach your destiny or grow as a person. Growth comes from dirt, from pain. And this is what ties everything together—letting go.

By letting go of something positive, something that has great value, you instantly allow negative change to come into your life. And, at the same time, you trust that it will be transformed into positive change that will take you to new levels and open doors for you that you couldn't even imagine. So, you let go with the trust that something better will come.

Letting go of my life before cancer was like a declaration that I would win this battle, and my life after enduring this trial would be way better and more meaningful. It also meant I was accepting my situation, accepting the new reality. But to make that declaration, I needed to believe it. And being still in shock and denial, I had doubts and voices that kept telling me "what if …." But letting go is having faith. And I knew I wanted to be able to do that; I wanted to be able to trust God's plan and timing. So, I knew I *had* to let go. As difficult as it was, letting go was the only way to move toward being healthy again. The only way out was through, and letting go was a crucial part of that process.

As I thought about it more, I realized that growth is always in reach. You can't grow until you reach out of your comfort zone, your normalcy. However, to reach for something new, you first must let go of the old. To reach for hope, I first had to let go of doubt. To reach for trust, I had to let go of fear. And to reach for a stronger and more mature version of myself, I had to let go of my life before the cancer.

If you think about it, it's just like wakeboarding. While you're wakeboarding, you're holding on to the grip, and the boat pulls you and gives you speed. But if you fall, you have to let go of the grip; if you don't, the boat will just keep pulling you, and you'll hit against the waves and get hurt. The boat driver might be yelling out, "Let go." But if *you* don't beat your fear and panic in that moment, you'll keep being pulled by the boat and rocked by the waves. When you finally gather up the courage and let go of the grip, you fall into the depths of the sea. For a moment, you're scared of drowning. But your life vest keeps you above water, no matter how deep the ocean is or how strong the waves are. So long as you're wearing that life vest, you'll never drown.

As I was wakeboarding through life, cancer came my way, and I lost my balance. I was so scared to let go of the grip, of my life before getting sick, of the person I was before the wave of this diagnosis hit me. But I had forgotten that I was wearing a life vest this whole time. God was not going to let me drown. He wasn't going to leave me alone. Not letting go would keep me from reaching, from growing, from surviving. It was easy to live in the past when I couldn't see my future. It was easy to hold onto life before this sickness, when I didn't know how life would be during treatment or whether I would get to live all that long in the first place. But I realized that, even though I didn't know what tomorrow held, I could rest because I knew who held it.

Car makers understand this principle well. Isn't it significant how the rear-view mirror is so small compared to the windshield, which is so big? What's in front of you is much more important and bigger than what's behind you. Life after cancer, the person adversity would shape me into would be so much more significant than the person I used to be before getting sick.

I knew I had to keep my eyes on the windshield, on the future. I knew I had to let go of the grip and fall into the ocean. I knew I had to let go of fear so I could reach for hope and strength. But *how* do you let go? *How* do you say goodbye? "Have a great year"? "I love you"? Which words could summarize all the feelings and thoughts, the confusion, the nostalgia, the pain, and the hope?

People always told me, "It's a see you soon, not a goodbye." But how could they be so sure of that? When I said my goodbyes, I didn't know whether they would be the last ones.

That night, as I was thinking of all these things, my sister called me up to the kitchen. She said she wanted to give me a gift that I could always have with me to remember her and get strength from. She reached in her pocket and took out a small box and gave it to me. I opened it, and tears flooded my eyes. It was one of those necklaces that you could write your name on. This one was a silver necklace that said "fighter."

"This is to remind you to always be a fighter. So even when it gets hard and painful, promise me you won't give up, you won't stop fighting," my sister said.

I held the necklace. "I promise," I told her and teared up.

I was moved by her thoughtful gift. My heart was full of love and gratitude that I had her in my life. I wore the necklace and hugged her as tight as ever. "Now, you're always going to be with me, throughout everything I go through in Germany," I told her.

We figured it was only appropriate to have a last family dinner the eve before we left for Essen. So, on Sunday, February 4, my aunt cooked some delicious food and we all got together to celebrate and say goodbye, to hope and let go, to love and miss, to appreciate and expect, to share our fears and choose to believe. My parents, family, and three of my friends gathered around the table that night and talked about life, fear, and school. We made plans for going to college, promises that we'd all gather every year to celebrate, and plans for a huge welcome home party with ponies. That was an inside joke.

It's funny because we didn't plan to dine together. Victoria, Ivy, and Aimiliana, three of my closest friends, came over to say goodbye, and they ended up staying longer. My godfather happened to pass by our house and stopped to give me a hard drive full of movies to watch while in the hospital. My dad came over to look for apartments to rent in Essen with my mom. And just like that, perfectly coincidently, we all sat around that table to properly spend my last night home as a family. I felt so much love around that table. I was so grateful for what I had, the people in my life, their love, and their sacrifice. Yet I was just as sad, because I knew what I was letting go of.

I saw life happen right before my eyes, and I knew that, this time the following week, nothing would be the same. As I smiled and raised my glass to toast, I knew that this time the following week, month, and season, nothing would be the same. I knew that *that* smile would not exist; *that* joy would be a memory; and *that* person, *me*, who was then full of life and hope, would be a pale, bald, bed-bound, weak, skinny sick person—someone I wouldn't even be able to recognize. I knew that, but *I raised my glass anyway*. I chose to believe there was a purpose behind this all. I chose to be grateful for every moment in time I got, knowing that nothing was a given, and everything was temporary. I chose to be brave—just like

Dr. Vasilis told me to. "You can do this," I whispered to myself. "Just stay brave".

After dinner and after everyone left, my aunt and sister called me into my sister's room. Amalia gave me a letter, her goodbye letter. This was too much for my heart to take. I didn't want to leave without her. "Letting go—I have to let go," I kept telling myself. I started reading the letter and felt a lump in my throat and tears in my eyes. This was another perfect example of how stars shine in darkness, love is felt in pain, and purpose is revealed behind adversity. Her letter hugged my heart and placed its broken pieces back together. My aunt gave me two jars and a card in the shape of a rainbow. Just the fact that she gave me her most valuable asset—her time—by making me this, meant so incredibly much to me. One of the jars was big and had thirty-one little papers with thirty-one hopeful messages—one for each day of the month. The other one was much smaller, and it was empty.

"This jar is for negative feelings, sadness, and tears. Promise me you'll keep it empty, or empty it out every night," she told me.

Love's in the details.

My grandma gave me an envelope with a card and a letter inside. I opened the letter and teared up. I recognized it immediately. *I* had written that letter to my grandpa when he was admitted in the ICU a couple months before he died. He had started losing hope and was getting tired of trying. So, I had written him that letter with words of encouragement. It had helped him so much. And now, it was helping *me*. It was so surreal. I was writing to *him* four years ago, exactly what *I* needed to hear *now*—as if I knew what I would need to say to myself in four years' time.

Purpose. It's all about hidden purpose. His *suffering*, which lasted so long, was going to be my greatest source of *strength*. His *fight* for life was going to give *life* to *my* fight. If there was one thing my grandpa taught me, it was resilience. Keeping on fighting when all odds say you wouldn't. It was his *adversity* that became *my* biggest *lesson*. Find purpose behind pain. It's all about purpose. Little did I know four years ago how what I wrote for *him* in the car on my way to school on a crumbled little piece of paper was going to be a profound, endless source of hope for *me*.

What you give always comes back. When you give selflessly, you receive in ways you could not have imagined things that you did not expect. All I'd wanted back then was to make him feel better for a short period of time. Little did I know, though, that by helping *him*, I was ultimately helping *myself*. Giving. Grace. This alliteration has great purpose. Just like struggle does. It also has profound transformation power. His pain had the power to be transformed into a source of help for me.

Hopefully, *my* pain would be transformed into something greater and bigger than me too. It would mean something. It would affect someone. How what you go through affects other people, how it can be used to serve *your* purpose, reveals *its* purpose. Meaning. Purpose. Words that can truly be understood only in the context of pain and adversity. Just like stars— only visible in darkness.

That night, I lay in bed to sleep, but my mind was running. Thoughts, fears, random ideas, funny memories, and imaginary scenarios collided. *It's really happening*, I thought to myself. I can't explain how overwhelming that realization was.

Chapter 3

And So It Begins

The next morning, we woke up super early to go to the airport. My whole family was there—my parents, my grandparents, my aunt, even Dr. Vasilis (he's family too). In the airport, we cried a lot, took many group photos, hugged each other more tightly than ever, and made a promise that the next time we would all gather would be to celebrate.

You know that feeling where your whole body is kind of shaking and your stomach is tied up and every breath physically hurts because you just want to burst into tears? Well, that's exactly how I was feeling that morning. As the hurt grew stronger, our hugs became tighter.

Amalia rolled me in my wheelchair until bag control. In the airport, there was a specific corner. Once you turned left, you had to let go. I called it the goodbye corner. I dreaded the moment I had to make the turn. Before leaving, I hugged my grandparents, my aunt, and Dr. Vasilis. He gave me a bag with his professional camera and three different professional lenses. He told me to take as many photos with it as I could and try to capture the positive side of this journey. He said that, through these cameras, he would be with me, and he promised that he would visit.

I was so overwhelmed and emotional. God had brought this incredible person into my life in my lowest moment to give me strength in my faith and help me persevere through this challenge. I don't think it was a coincidence that Dr. Vasilis loved photography too. God is the details. In times of hurt and pain, I looked for God and tried to find Him in big things, in a good medical report, in a turnaround of a negative situation.

But sometimes, as I was looking for God in big things, I missed His whispers through little details. I had to close my physical eyes, and see life through the eyes of my heart, letting faith be the lens of the camera I used, and hope be the prism that would enable light to reflect and enter my field of view, impacting my perception of the situation.

Right outside the security check, I hugged Amalia to tell her goodbye. I had been trying to gather all my strength to say goodbye, but when I hugged her, I just broke. I broke down crying because I knew, this time next week or month, I would need to hug her again, but I wouldn't be able to. I tried to lock this memory in my mind so that I could remember the feeling of her hug, which I knew I would soon need. I wanted to remember the comfort her hug gave me, how it took away all fear, and how it sheltered me from pain. A simple hug and yet it was so powerful.

"I love you. Stay safe ok?" I told her, crying.

"I'll be there with you always. And I promise I'll visit as soon as possible," she said.

It was something about these words that tore my heart and ripped apart the armor that I had been trying to put up. At that moment a thought crossed my mind. *What if I don't see her again? What if something happens and she can't come, or the chemo does something to me?* When I said my last goodbye, I died a little bit inside.

"We have to go," Dad said.

As I pulled back, I held my sister's hand tightly. I didn't want to let go. But I had to. But *why?* As I let her hand slip through mine, I felt my heart break. All I could think in that moment was how she was going to be all alone that night. I wouldn't be there to joke about school or argue about English homework. And there was nothing I could do to make it right, to change it.

Oh, God is it ever going to get easier? Hold her close tonight. I won't be there to. Stay close to her; help her feel your presence. We're apart, but let her know she's not alone. I love her more than she could ever know. Oh, is it ever going to get better? Please just hold her close tonight, God. Keep her safe. Stay near.

We started moving toward the gate.

I placed my hands in the side handles on the wheelchair and tried to move in it toward the "goodbye corner." But I froze. My heart was heavy. I felt paralyzed. Fear had paralyzed me—fear of change, fear of risk, fear of suffering. And then suddenly God came down to that messy place in my mind and gave me the strength and courage to turn the corner. He took that step of faith *with* me.

We sat in our seats and waited for the plane to board. I always get a window seat. I've traveled a lot of times, and every single one of them, I get the window seat. I love looking out in the clouds. For a moment, I am reminded of how small our world is, how small my problems are, and how much bigger than me their purpose is.

As the plane started moving toward the takeoff lane, I looked outside the window. I saw the most beautiful clouds I'd ever seen in my life. There were massive holes in the sky and huge light streaks leaking from up above. It was unreal. The horizon was full of these holes in the clouds. The strength and opacity of those light rays that were coming through was so great; I had never seen anything like that before in my whole life. The light was shining through them and taking on different shades of gold as the plane moved closer to it. My heart felt full. All its broken pieces were suddenly mended. Hope had saved me. I knew in that moment that, no matter how bad it got, I would always have God by my side. This was a confirmation that on the horizon there was hope; there was something greater than me, something more powerful than pain, and something more purposeful than hurt. Trusting that God had seen my tears, had heard my prayers, and would never leave me or abandon me gave me comfort. I wouldn't fight alone. God would give me peace and hope. He would shine through darkness like that light ray shining through the clouds outside the airplane window.

Since it was the first time we were going to Germany, my dad had come with us too, to help us settle in and to buy things for the house like, plates, blankets, and everything else, while my mom took care of me.

When we arrived in Germany, we checked in at the hotel we would be staying at for the next two weeks until all the papers for the apartment we rented were signed. The first two days were filled with doctors' appointments, scans, more consults, more scans, other tests, and—you guessed it—even more appointments.

I was scheduled for a port placement surgery. We decided to go to Cologne, a nearby city, the day before the operation to forget about the stress that came with it. Cologne was beautiful. We went exploring, and it was snowing. Snow absorbs sound. It could somehow quiet all the voices of fear in my mind. We went to a great café, and I enjoyed time with my parents. We visited the cathedral and took photos with Dr. Vasilis's camera. I felt like he was with us too.

After we got back, I went in for the surgery the next day and ended up staying in the hospital for about four days, because of low blood pressure and low red blood cells. I was sharing a hospital room with a two-year-old girl who had just started chemo. She was with her mom and aunt. *Her name was Amalia.*

God's in the details. Love is too.

My mom connected with her mom. I could tell it gave her so much strength that "Amalia" was there. It gave *me* strength too. I had her in the necklace around my neck, in memories in my mind, and in the article that morning of the biopsy. And now, she was here in the hospital bed next to me; she was always with me somehow.

My mom had been trying to convince me to cut my hair before chemo started so that I would not have to deal with waking up to strands of hair on my pillow. So, a couple of days after we arrived in Essen, my mom and I went to the hair salon in the hospital. The lady working there didn't understand English, so we had to call up my dad, who speaks German, to talk to her on the phone. He explained that I was starting chemo next week, and I wanted to cut my hair to prepare for it.

With that, the lady put my hair up in a ponytail, took the scissors, and cut the whole thing off.

Seeing myself with short hair hurt so much. After we got back to the car, I burst out crying. I had never cried so much in my life—not even when I was diagnosed or lost my grandpa or after the surgery in my abdomen. That day, I cried more than I had ever cried before. It wasn't because of having shorter hair but because of what having my hair cut symbolized. Hair is hair. It means nothing. But it also makes cancer real. It makes this a reality. It makes fear louder. It makes pain stronger.

Remember when I was telling you about sitting and knocking at a door that was already open? Well, having my hair cut for chemo, I was pushed through the door without being ready to go through it on my own. It was as if life was just pushing me around, forcing me to take steps when I didn't have the strength to. But that's how you grow; this is how you find that strength that you need—by being forced to escape your comfort zone and rely on things greater than you and your adversity.

My parents heard me cry but said nothing. At the time, I was so sad that they didn't say anything to help me. I remember feeling so alone. I remember not wanting to even try to get through this because of how alone I felt. But that was just a cloud; it would pass. Right now, when I look back, I hurt *more* for my parents. Hearing their kid cry for more than forty-five minutes straight and knowing that nothing they said would fix things was probably one of the most painful and heartbreaking feelings in the world. Yet they were so brave, so strong. I wonder how they did it. They sacrificed their own feelings for me. They chose to be stronger and to not break down—for me. That's what love is. That's what love looks like.

After I calmed down, my mom suggested going to IKEA to buy things for the apartment. She knew how much I loved IKEA. She wanted to offer me a reason to smile. When we got there, I didn't want to get out of the car. I didn't want to be in a wheelchair. I didn't want to accept my reality, my new self. But my dad convinced me to.

We had a talk in the car, just the two of us. He opened up, and for the first time, I saw him cry. He let himself be vulnerable and told me how he hated seeing me cry and hated the fact that there was nothing he could do to make me feel better. I'll always remember that conversation. It is a testament to the fact that, during the very moments of pain, you can find the most love. Many times, pain stems from love, love that can't be expressed. I also realized that, when people open up, when they're honest and upfront about their feelings, they connect more easily. So, with that talk, my dad convinced me to go to IKEA after all. He said that, since we all were sad, the least we could do was distract ourselves with fun things, like an IKEA shopping spree.

Two minutes in, and I'd already put ten things in our cart, mainly picture frames to put up all the photos I'd taken with me to decorate my new room and make it feel like home. I wanted to put up photos of my family next to my bed so that I could always go to bed after the worst days and wake up in the morning knowing that they were next to me. I also chose a couch for our apartment. I picked out a big three-sectional gray couch. Little did I know what this couch would end up symbolizing.

Going to IKEA with my parents helped me forget about the present for a moment and picture my future. As I was moving around the aisles in my wheelchair, I was not a sick kid about to begin chemo; I was a mom who had a stable job and was picking out things for my new house and three kids. It enabled me to be someone else, to be the future me. And I hadn't been able to see my future at the time—because I had accepted that I might not have one.

After shopping, we sat at the restaurant there to grab a bite to eat. It was a fun end to a pretty horrible day. Have you ever noticed that, when you smile or laugh after you have cried, a simple smile brings you so much more happiness than it used to? Well, I felt the same way. Every difficult moment made the happy moments or the future even more joyful and the beautiful times even more beautiful.

The next couple of days were spent in between the hospital and the hotel room. I was really missing my family. I was really missing home.

I was with my aunt and Amalia on FaceTime, and we were talking. I remembered that time when I'd hugged Amalia at the airport and the thought I'd had. This time the previous week, I had been with her, but now she was on the other side of my iPhone screen. That really hit me. The journey was about to begin. The storm was about to hit. And I needed a little extra help to help me get motivated before the big fight.

And here's what happened.

I was talking with Dr. Vasilis on WhatsApp, and he told me he would call me during his break in between surgeries so we could talk about how I was doing psychologically. When he called, I was sitting down in the hotel lobby with my parents. My dad was working, and my mom and I were playing with cards.

I got on the phone with him and told him, "I can't do this. I don't think I have the strength to. I cry every hour. I feel so helpless, and everything seems negative"

"I know," he said. "But I also know how to take all that pain away. Close your eyes and count down from ten. Loudly," he added.

I closed my eyes and started counting down. "Ten, nine, eight, seven, six—"

And suddenly, as I said number six, I felt someone's hand on my shoulder. I turned around, surprised. I couldn't believe what I was seeing.

It was Dr. Vasilis, standing there with a bright smile that lit up the room. I ran (in the wheelchair) to hug him. And in his arms, I burst out crying. My heart had been aching for so long, but being in his arms gave me so much hope and made me feel safe. Like a guardian angel, he always showed up when I needed it the most.

"I told you I knew how to take all that pain away," he said. "Let's remember number six. That's when it all got better. Let's remember that, for when times get tougher. It only takes four seconds for complete pain to be turned into indescribable joy."

I'll never forget these words—or number six. As I looked away, I saw Amalia and my aunt walk in the front door. I couldn't believe that they were here too. I took a moment to catch my breath and realize what had just happened. I rushed to hug them, and tears made my vision blurry. A smile lit up my face, and my cheeks started hurting from laughing so much. For a moment, a thought passed my mind. *Wow, I had forgotten what laughing felt like.* I hugged my sister and remembered her hug again. It gave me so much love and comfort. I was so far from home, yet I had never felt closer to it.

That night, we all went out for dinner. We drove up to a different town in a remote restaurant in the middle of a forest next to a very big lake. It was dark, but you could still tell the scenery was beautiful. It's the little moments that ultimately give you the purest form of joy and comfort, and it's in them that you can find life's purpose and meaning.

In the restaurant, we sat at a big table next to a fireplace. It was beautiful. I sat next to Dr. Vasilis. We talked about how I could find things to be hopeful for amid everything going on.

"Once we start attacking this tumor, the pain will go away; you'll start feeling better, and you'll have more things to be excited about or happy over," he said at one point.

He was the only person who could make me *want* to start chemotherapy. His words restored hope in me and made me very optimistic about a future that I often doubted I would even get to have.

At the restaurant our waitress was Greek. God's in the details. He knew I was really starting to miss home, so He was bringing home to me. Little did I know that, through that, He was also teaching me what home was really all about. You'll see what I mean.

The next morning, we all had breakfast together in the hotel. The hotel itself was pretty awesome; the rooms had the comfiest beds and pillows I had ever slept in, and the hotel also offered the best oatmeal ever for breakfast. Joy was in the details.

As we were enjoying each other's company, we discussed starting chemo, losing my hair, and going shopping for the apartment. We concluded it would be better if I just shaved all my hair off once the chemo started to prevent going through the emotional struggle of having to watch it all fall out. After breakfast, we all sat at the hotel lobby and talked. The hotel had a photo booth area, so we decided to take a few family photos. I kept a copy of every photo we took, because I wanted to put them all up in my new room.

Dr. Vasilis had to leave that morning, because he had an operation scheduled for the following day. He is an orthopedic surgeon, so most of his time is spent in the operating room. Before he left, we all sat together for a while. He showed my sister and me a video from one of his latest operations that was actually of a knee replacement surgery, which would be a part of my tumor removal operation in the summer. It was difficult to watch at first, but both my sister and I found it super fascinating and interesting in the end. Before he left, he hugged me and promised me he would visit again as soon as he could. He told me that he would always be there for me and that he was only one text and *four seconds* away.

Amalia and my aunt stayed in Essen for two more days. Those days were spent around the city, hanging with each other, and enjoying the time we had together.

A few days after they left, on Tuesday, February 13, I was admitted to the hospital for my first ever block of chemotherapy. That day, I was very nervous. I dreaded the moment I would have to be hooked up to the medical machines through which the drugs would be administered. After drawing blood and poking my chest with a 17 needle to access the port, the doctors started me on saline. They gave me an antiemetic to prevent nausea and an injection to prevent the chemo from damaging my reproductive system.

After about two hours and a liter of saline, they finally started me on the actual chemotherapy drug. The first one on my regimen was Vincristine. This is known to cause problems to your peripheral nervous system, so they told me to let them know if I felt any numbness or tingling sensations in my extremities. The medicine itself came in a small, clear plastic bag with a red cup attached to the line in the chest.

"Good luck," my nurse told me with a German accent and a big smile on her face, after confirming for the third time my full name and date of birth.

I smiled. "Thank you," I replied. "To be honest, I could use the luck."

Now, *she* smiled. For a brief instance, I felt like nothing had changed, like I used to feel before this storm of cancer hit, back when I made everyone smile. I looked around. That feeling disappeared as I tasted the horrible metallic taste of the medicine that had started entering my bloodstream. I looked around again. I remembered my camera theory.

My camera theory is an attitude about life that I decided to adopt when Dr. Vasilis gave me his camera and lenses. When I looked around, life looked dull. But behind dullness, behind desperation, behind pain, lies great potential. There is potential for love to be expressed, for bonds to be strengthened, for courage to emerge, and for hope to rise. Sometimes hope is best expressed when it runs down our face in the form of tears and consists of pain and heartache that have been transformed. I knew, in that moment, that I could seize and take advantage of that potential. I knew I could transform dullness if I just switched up the lens through which I looked and captured life.

I made it my goal, in that very instant, to make someone smile every single day for the rest of my life—whether that someone was myself; my mom, dad, or sister; or a stranger I saw down the street. Life is about just that. Sharing smiles. When you share smiles, a light shines. That doesn't mean the darkness doesn't exist, but it sure means that you have a bright light of love and grace and kindness guiding you and sheltering you from the uncertainty and fear of the darkness. I decided, therefore, to start capturing life through the lens of kindness and smile sharing.

As I was thinking of ways to do that, the chemo started to affect me. "It tastes like glue mixed with metal and gas," I told my mom.

She smiled.

Mission accomplished, I thought to myself.

"I love the accuracy level of your description," she said sarcastically.

I giggled.

That day, my mom stayed with me at the hospital, and my dad went back to the hotel to pack all our things up and move them to the apartment we'd rented. The Vincristine infusion took about an hour. When it was finished, the machine started beeping. We called the nurse, and she unhooked the plastic bag and started me on more saline and some other medications.

Not even ten minutes had gone by, and another nurse came in to start me on the second drug of the day, Ifosfamide. This one came in a much bigger bag and was ten times the dosage of the previous medication. Just a minute after the infusion started, I got extremely dizzy all of a sudden and could not even hold my head up. I lowered the back of my bed and lay down. A few minutes in, and my whole body was trembling, just like when you have an extremely high fever. My body's temperature changed all the time; I was getting hot flashes every two minutes. My veins in my arms started burning. That's when I realized. This was going to be so much harder than I'd thought. I was planning on watching a movie, but I could not even turn in my bed because of the extreme dizziness.

I closed my eyes and thought to myself, *OK, you've got to hold on. This is what you were waiting for. This pain is good. The suffering is good. Because it's the only way. Hold on. It's the only way. The only way out is through. You're walking through the door. This is you taking the step. Hold on. You got this. God's got you. He's not leaving you. Keep it together. Do this for your family. Endure this for them. They are worth it. They are worth every chemo and every hot flash, and every pain. Do this for them. Do this for you. For the life you dream of. Do this for who you have the potential to become. Hold on tight.*

As I kept repeating these things to myself, I fell asleep. When I woke up, there was a nurse in the room who wanted to measure my weight and blood pressure. I woke up in pain and feeling more nauseated than I had ever felt in my life. I looked down at the IV line coming out of my chest and saw an orange liquid leaving a small plastic bag and entering my bloodstream. My mom told me that was the last chemo drug of the day.

"I don't think I can get up. I feel very dizzy and nauseous," I told her.

"I know, sweetheart, but you have to. Just for a moment. The nurse needs to do this, to make sure you're OK. You can sleep all you want in just a moment," she told me in a calm voice.

As she helped me sit up by the side of my bed, I noticed her eyes. My vision was blurry, and I couldn't really understand what was going on around me, but I *did* notice her eyes. I saw her hurt in them. Fear. Pain. Despair. She hated seeing me like this.

"It's okay, Mom," I told her and tried to smile. "It's all going to be okay. I promise."

She placed her hand in mine and held it real tight. She smiled and teared up.

The nurse measured my blood pressure and told me that it was lower than they expected and that she would let the doctor know. My weight was elevated because of the many liters of fluids I had gotten since that morning.

That night was a long one. At around 9:00 p.m., a nurse brought my mom a bed to sleep in. It was one of those beds that folds in three. I hated the thought that she would have to spend most days of this year sleeping in that bed.

"You wanna change beds?" I asked her.

"No, no. Are you kidding me? Get some rest. Don't worry about me," she replied.

Love is in the details. That's what love really looks like.

That night, I tried to sleep but couldn't. Normally, I would have watched a movie, but the dizziness had not subsided. The nausea had also started getting worse. After some time, the machine started beeping again. Day one was officially done. That sound gave me so much strength. It was finally over. *Only four more days to go, and chemo one is out the way,* I thought to myself.

The nurse came in and unhooked the last drug, which I found out was called Doxorubicin; it was supposed to be the most effective and aggressive of them all. People usually call it the Red Devil, and I think that name is pretty accurate. I also found out that, before I'd taken the doxo, I'd also been given another drug called Etoposide. This was supposed to be most effective in sarcomas, so I was feeling grateful for the fact that it existed and for being able to get it.

I lay in bed that night feeling restless. Powerless. Lifeless. I was so tired from all the drugs. I had never felt so sick in my life. *You almost have to die in order not to die,* I thought to myself. That was a realization that I couldn't understand. I could not see how all that suffering could make me better. It only made me feel sicker and more helpless than ever.

I stared at the clock that was hanging in the wall above the door of the room. Time was moving so slowly. It made the suffering worse. Every second was another second that I lost my strength to endure the pain.

The next morning, my dad came to spend the day with me, while my mom went home to take a bath and bring an extra set of clothes. Day two was pretty much the same—more chemo, more nausea, more dizziness, more trembling, more pain, more antiemetics, diuretics, and analgesics. But there was also more exhaustion, more endurance, more acting stronger than I felt, more crying in my parents' arms, more desperation, more praying, and more hugs. Even my tears smelled like the chemotherapy. It was heartbreaking to watch and emotionally drenching to go through.

Amalia tried talking to me on FaceTime, but I was too dizzy to engage in a conversation. I really tried to. I wanted her to see me as okay as possible. I wanted her to see me strong, because I knew that it would break her heart to know that I was in pain, emotionally or physically, and not be able to be there for me or do anything about it. That's why I told my mom to not tell her that I was tired of going through the therapy or that I'd had a few breakdowns and tears of desperation.

At night, my mom told me that a friend of mine, Miltiadis, had texted her asking her how I was and wishing me luck with the chemotherapy. My heart was full. It gave me strength to keep fighting that night—for my friends, for my family, for those who needed me to be here. I had to be brave for them. They were worth every tear and every punch that the drugs gave me as they brutally killed everything inside me.

That night, I wasn't very conscious of everything going on, and I couldn't really think clearly. But I needed to talk to God.

God, today, I'm on my knees. This is so much harder than I thought it would be. I can't think clearly. I'm in so much pain. I can't really feel you near. I am weak, sick, dizzy. I'm not myself. But I'm trying to trust you. It's challenging and difficult. But hope lasts. Give me faith. God, as I fall asleep tonight, send an angel to watch over me at night. Make the chemo work. Make it kill the cancer. Give me peace to fall asleep and make time go by faster, so that before I even know it, I am back home. I am not losing hope, God. But I am getting tired. I feel powerless. Hold me near. Keep me safe. I need to make it, God. My family needs me. I can't leave them. Please, make the chemo work. I'll endure the nausea. It's OK. I just need it to work. It has to work, God. Stay close to my sister as she falls asleep tonight without me near. Keep my family safe as they fall asleep tonight with hurt and fear of tomorrow. And please, hold me close tonight, as I endure, as I cry, as I run out of strength.

I'll never forget that prayer—the vulnerability, the connection, the love, the trust.

Day three was by far the worst. I threw up so many times I lost count. I had to change clothes three times and remove my cast because I threw up on them. The nurses gave me more meds and did everything they could to help me feel more comfortable. I hadn't eaten or drank anything in the last three days, so everybody was just trying to make me eat something. One doctor who examined me even suggested eating a Popsicle to help me with the taste.

"Maybe during the next block," I told her and smiled.

I was feeling terrible and didn't want to even be *near* food. You can imagine how much I suffered when the parents of the kid I was sharing a room with during this hospitalization decided to get traditional Turkish street food and eat it in the room with all the windows closed. I think that contributed to how nauseated I was that day. But if I'm being honest, it's such a funny memory to look back at amid a terrible situation.

The next two days were still very difficult. But on day four, I received an email that changed my mood completely. It was from my Mr. A, my French teacher at school. He wanted to check in on me and make sure I was OK. He wished me a quick recovery and encouraged me to keep fighting. I was so moved. It meant so much to me. I really felt stronger just by reading that email. There were people who needed me here—not just my family but also my friends and other people too. I couldn't give up. I couldn't lose this fight. I finished chemo one motivated and ready to conquer this cancer.

On day five, I was texting Dr. Vasilis, telling him how relieved I was to finally be discharged from the hospital. In that moment, the doctors of the ward walked in my room and told us that the news wasn't so good.

"I am afraid the chemotherapy already affected your bone marrow more than we had expected. Your red blood cells are extremely low from day five of the cycle. Unfortunately, you are very anemic, and we cannot discharge you. You will need to get a blood transfusion and stay overnight for monitoring," one really friendly doctor said.

"Will she be able to be discharged tomorrow?" my dad asked, after seeing the worry and disappointment in my eyes.

"We don't know. It is possible, if her counts increase to the minimum with the transfusions. But we can't know for sure. It could potentially take a few days. I am really sorry," she replied.

I was very sad. We had booked tickets to go meet two of my favorite actors from a show I used to watch a lot, who were on a European tour in Düsseldorf, only about an hour away. I was really hoping to be discharged so that I could make it to that event. I also wanted to just go to the apartment and stay in bed all day to recover. If I'm being honest, I didn't really care where I went, I just wanted to *not* be in the hospital.

I called Dr. Vasilis and told him the news. He wasn't surprised. He said he had noticed I was already a little bit anemic, so he'd anticipated the chemotherapy to affect my bone marrow a lot.

"But, hey, there's always a good side to everything," he said. "This only proves how strong these drugs are, right? Well, that's what we want, isn't it? We want them to be as strong as possible, so that they absolutely destroy every last cancer cell in your body. So, consider it a good thing when you experience these side effects. It just means the drugs are doing their thing, so that, soon, you can do *your* thing *too* and be back at school and go skydiving with me or take amazing photographs of volcanos."

I smiled. *Volcanos.* He never failed to restore hope in my life. He truly was a source of light in that utter darkness.

Later that day, I got three bags of blood. My dad was talking with Dr. Thanos on the phone. He's the funny one. He never fails to make me laugh. No matter how sad I am, his jokes and humor always break that sadness away. My dad put him on speaker. He started speaking in German with the funniest accent ever.

"What I just said is that you now have been infused with German blood. You are now one of us," he said and laughed.

I smiled.

The next morning, the doctor woke me up early to draw blood and examine me. I was too weak to ask her about being discharged. I was lifeless; even sitting up was exhausting. I was a wreck. My body had completely given in to the drugs. Everyone always told me that the first chemo would be the easiest and that the more I did, the worse they would get. If that was what the easiest felt like, I didn't want to even *try* to do the rest. But I knew I had to. The only way out was *through*.

Later that day, I finally got discharged.

"You will probably need to come back in a couple of days," the doctor told me after signing the discharge papers. "Your blood counts are at the minimum, and they are expected to fall rapidly. You have to measure your temperature every hour once you start to not feel well. If you have a temperature of 38°C for two consecutive measurements or one measurement higher than 38.5°C, you need to come to the emergency room immediately. The most common infection could be catastrophic with your immune system."

I didn't really understand everything she was saying, since I was still loopy from all the drugs. The doctor gave my parents more information about expected side effects and emergency situations. She was so cooperative and really helped my mom, who was very worried. I hated seeing her worry. I wished I could take care of myself, so she wouldn't have to go through all that, but I couldn't even lift my head up or sit up without needing help. And this was just the first chemo. After we were given all the necessary information, my parents helped me sit in my wheelchair and took me to another room to remove my port needle.

A nurse approached me and put on her gloves to start the process. "It's going to be a bit cold," she told me in a German accent and then sprayed an antibacterial solution around my port.

Before removing the needle, she flushed it and added heparin to prevent blood clots. The port flush tasted disgusting. That same metallic gluey taste. I was so ready to leave the hospital.

As we got out, my dad brought the car from the parking lot, and we drove to the new apartment. I was excited to see it but had no energy to even keep my head up. As soon as we entered, I went straight to bed, as I was extremely dizzy from the chemotherapy. My mom had organized the room and the closet and had prepared everything for me. Love's in the details.

I lay in bed and felt a cold wind rush through my body. I was cold. My heart was cold. The room was too. It didn't feel like home. It was miserable and lonely. I associated this room with being sick. It was depressing. The minutes wouldn't go by. I didn't even have the energy to consciously be sad or scared. I would burst into tears all the time. Hopelessness. My body was just done. I didn't even have enough physical strength to turn and twist in my bed. My knee hurt a lot too. The pain from the tumor kept me up at night. My whole leg felt as if it was on fire. I could feel the tumor aggressively pressing on my bones.

I spent the next three days in bed and didn't even get up to eat. I had been over a week without eating. I knew I needed nutrients, but the nausea made any food consumption impossible. So did the pain. And the numbness. And the hurt. I had started experiencing more side effects. And by that time, even the little energy left in me was gone.

A day later I started running a fever and was rushed to the ER. I spent the next two weeks in the chemo ward while being treated for many infections. I was sharing a room with a two-year-old girl, her mom, and her sister. They were extremely loud, playing music out loud, arguing, screaming, shouting, and overall not being very respectful. That added to the emotional stress that I was under and made the whole situation much worse.

A few days in, my mom left the hospital for a little while to go by the apartment and bring me an extra set of clothes. At some point during that time, a nurse walked in and asked me how I was feeling. I told her I was OK, but halfway through the sentence I broke down and started crying. I was emotionally and physically exhausted. I was utterly hopeless. Pain had taken over.

Not for long, however. The nurse that I was talking to sat by me on my bed, held my hand, and asked me what was wrong.

"I just want to go home. That's all. I want to go home."

"You will," she told me. "Soon you'll go home."

Home? What home? Nothing felt like home anymore.

What does it mean to feel at home? Discovering home was a whole other journey that I had embarked on without even knowing it. I would find out, however—in the most unexpected way. You'll see.

Chapter 4

Breathe in and Hold Your Breath

So here we were now.

Today, I finished my second round of chemotherapy. It was through. We had to change rooms twice, which is very uncomfortable when you're dealing with extreme nausea. My mom's been struggling seeing me at this state daily. I wish she didn't have to go through all that. If only I could take all the pain away from my family. Dad has been visiting for every round of chemo. Ami will be coming to spend a few days with me in Essen soon. I'm so excited to hug her again.

This protocol I am in is called VIDE. If you haven't heard of it before, it is important to note that it's one of the most aggressive and heavy treatment protocols ever. The drugs are so toxic they affect your nerves, heart muscle, skin, nails, digestive tract, bone marrow, kidneys, reproductive system, bones, and hair follicles—basically everything. Even when I got discharged after the first chemo block, I was back at the hospital with a very high fever, neutropenia, and terrible mucositis, which is basically sores all over your mouth and digestive tract. Mucositis prevented me from eating, drinking, swallowing, and even talking. To communicate I had a little notebook where I wrote down things I wanted to say.

If I'm being honest, however, there were some funny bits during these two past blocks of chemo too. The hospital offered three meals throughout the day, and every morning a lady came in and asked me what I wanted to eat. It was always an either-or question. As you can imagine, I get very nauseated from the drugs, which resulted in anorexia. So, during these two rounds of chemo, my mom would always pick for me. After the first chemo, she realized that there was no way I was eating hospital food, so she started picking for herself instead. There was nothing wrong with the food itself; to the contrary, it seemed nice. But me being very sensitive to smell, I couldn't even be in the same room with it. It made the nausea so incredibly worse. Consequently, every time my mom wanted to eat, she would go to the playroom / waiting room area.

Before the first chemo block, my mom brought groceries from home and made me a sandwich with cream cheese and turkey breast. I haven't eaten cream cheese ever since. I soon realized that everything I ate during chemo I wouldn't be able to eat after chemo. The taste of the medicine affected my taste buds so much and changed the flavor of every food— even water.

It was time to think strategically. I decided that I would eat certain foods during chemo that I wished I could stop eating, and I would never eat foods I really liked and would like to eat when I got well. During the second chemo, my mom and I were prepared. The morning of the second infusion day, she made me pancakes in the hospital kitchen.

Here's the thing; I love pancakes. But me thinking smart, I figured that it would do no harm if I stopped eating them when I got well—*if* I got well. I always have to correct myself. During the third day, she made me some pasta with red sauce. It tasted great, but it also made the nausea worse. When I got out of the hospital, she made me chicken with teriyaki sauce and French fries—always French fries. I found out that Germany produces the best and sweetest potatoes ever. Ironic, since they are French fries. Haha. Bad joke; I'm sorry. Enough food talk. Let's get back to the story.

Another kind of funny moment during chemo involved my sensitivity with clothes and pillows. I decided I wanted to distance myself from the chemo as much as possible. During the first block, I was wearing clothes I really liked and ended up throwing up on them. Therefore, during the second chemo I was more prepared. My mom went to Primark, a store with very affordable clothes and got me what I named "chemo clothes." Very original name, I know. These chemo clothes would only be worn during the chemo and would be donated if they were in good condition after I was done with the treatment. I also decided that I didn't want to bring my favorite teddy bear to chemo sessions, because I didn't want to associate it with being in the hospital and being sick. Instead, I picked out another one and named it "chemo buddy." Even more original, I know. Chemo buddy would be my best friend during the treatments. What was special about it was that it used to be Amalia's favorite, but she gave it to me when we were little. So, in a way, it made me feel as if Amalia was there with me during the chemotherapies, holding my hand and letting me know it was going to be okay—just like that morning before the biopsy.

Another thing I found helped me during these therapies was having my own pillowcase. Before moving into our apartment in Essen, we'd gone to IKEA to pick out things for the house. When it came to pillows, we got only small and long ones. Unfortunately, the pillowcases we had could not fit the pillows of the hospital. Therefore, we also packed my chemo pillow every time I was hospitalized.

Some other kids who I shared a room with were far more extra on the packing issue. Some would bring blankets and huge pillows and toys and room decorations. *We* tried to keep it as minimal as possible to make the transportation easier. We still ended up with four different bags and a suitcase though. It was funny walking in the hospital with so much stuff. It looked as if we were permanently moving in.

It never compares to what we looked like when we first came to Germany though—three people, five suitcases, and three bags. That's all I'm saying.

When writing this book, I contemplated about how much I wanted to include. I decided I wanted to be very candid about my feelings and experiences. I want to be honest and raw and show you the reality of childhood cancer but, at the same time, how meaningful of a situation it can become when it acts as a soil in which unconditional love and hope can grow.

I never realized before how powerful this experience could be. It brings people closer, and it reflects the hidden amount of love and strength people have locked inside them. Going through tremendous physical suffering leads to unimaginable emotional struggle. However, that suffering can be transformed into an opportunity, a soil for life's flowers to grow in, a night sky for life's brightest stars to shine in. Such a negative and difficult situation is ideal for something magically meaningful to emerge.

The day after we were discharged, Dad left again to go home. It was me and my mom again. I knew she wanted to be there for me, but I was heading for a big crash emotionally, and I wanted to try and reduce the casualties. I was mentally exhausted, and I didn't want to let her into my thoughts and feelings, not while they were still negative, still full of fear and hopelessness. I didn't want to hurt her or to add to the pain she was already experiencing.

Instead, I cast out all my fear and doubts to God every time I prayed. Praying for me was like a therapy session. I opened up to God, told Him how I felt, what I was afraid of, and what hurt me the most. Most of the time when I prayed, I broke down crying. It was such a powerful and significant moment. It was simultaneously a casual conversation with a best friend and a desperate cry to a Savior. It was so meaningful to me that, in that moment, negative emotions coexisted with positive ones. In that conversation with God—that therapy session and vulnerable moment of prayer—fear coexisted with trust, doubts coexisted with hope, and desperation coexisted with patience. However, the most significant revelation was not the coexistence of these opposing forces but, rather, the presence, *despite* the contrast and the battle between them, of peace. Maybe that's proof of the power of a sunset feeling—a moment of peace amid the battle between fear and hope, doubt and faith, joy and sorrow. As the day turns to night, as light and darkness fight against each other, a beautiful sunset is created.

Overall, I was still in denial, ignoring the diagnosis, doing everything I could to not be the girl with cancer. I didn't talk to many people from school; being in the hospital made it impossible. I'd stopped doing schoolwork. I didn't even have the strength to open a water bottle, much less pick up a book or do homework. I also didn't really want to keep up with my class.

I think what was stopping me was a voice of fear. Every time I thought about school, a wave of fear beat me down. What if I chose to study, but I didn't ever make it back to school? What if I chose to hope, but I didn't ever see that hope take root? Studying was a declaration that I was not yet brave enough to make—*yet*. There was purpose behind timing.

Sometimes I thought to myself that nothing mattered, time had stopped, and I was stuck. I was stuck suffering. I was stuck in a body that wouldn't let me be who I wanted to be or do what I want to do. I was stuck in this place of desperation, lifeless and disconnected. I looked at myself in the mirror, and I didn't even recognize myself. This was the saddest thing of all, what broke my heart into millions of pieces. I was a wreck that had sunk, and I was trying to swim. But the storm was so much stronger than me; the waves pushed me down and I felt like I was drowning. And many times, I even wondered if trying to swim was even worth it.

And then it hit me, always. The storm was stronger than me, but God was stronger than the storm. And just like that, I'd spot a lighthouse, and its light would reveal pieces of the broken boat I was unable to see during my darkness. The light would guide me toward them, and I could finally get a grip, grab a hold of them, rest, and let the storm pass and the tides push me toward the lighthouse. That's what the storm does. Eventually, it pushes you toward the lighthouse. This season of darkness, cancer was my storm. But the lighthouse guided me toward things I could hold onto—people, notions, thoughts—things I could rest upon, catch my breath, and grab a hold of hope and patience.

God never promised we wouldn't face storms. But He *did* promise we wouldn't face them *alone*. He *did* promise that He would be *with* us every step of the way, and even if we don't see or feel Him, He'll be working behind the scenes for our good. He'll be making the storm lead us toward the lighthouse. The proof of God is not in the absence of pain and suffering. The proof of God is in our ability to endure and make it through.

After a few days of being home, I started developing most of the side effects of the chemo. I was nauseated, my bones hurt, my eyes burned, and my whole GI tract was full of sores and blisters.

"It's starting," I told my mom.

"Don't worry, hon. We'll deal with that when the time comes. For now, just take your meds, use the mouthwash, eat as much as possible to boost those white blood cells, and try not to think about it," she replied.

She went into my room and asked me to come in and take a look at something. She told me to sit on the bed and went to the kitchen to bring a "surprise from home," as she said. When she came in, she was holding a few envelopes, a big card, and a box. She handed me over the card, and as

I reached out to grab it, I saw what it was. My hands started shaking, and I tears filled my eyes. The card was from my classmates from French class. It was full of photos of me with them. There was something about seeing myself then, with them, seeing myself smile. I hadn't seen that in so long. I didn't recognize me—not because I had hair or because I was up eight kilograms but because I was smiling. In all the photos, I was smiling. And I hadn't seen my face with a smile in so long. My mum rushed to hug me and asked what was wrong. I told her I just missed everything.

As I read the card, my heart became so full. I felt motivated again—just like that. I felt like I wanted to swim, to fight, to endure. This felt likes the sign I was asking God to give me. This simple card was one of those pieces of the boat that the lights guided me toward, that helped me stay in the fight a little longer. Seeing myself with a smile sure broke my heart because it was something I never did these days, but it also filled me up with motivation, determination, and strength to do everything in my power to get that smile back.

As I saw the hope that this card had given me, I asked my mom to bring me the "box of memories" as we called it. It was a box in which I kept all the cards, gifts, and pictures I'd taken from home before I'd left. Usually, I didn't look at it. I didn't read the cards, because they made me miss home and that life even more. But now I felt like I needed to get courage. I saw that little red notebook my friends had given me. I saw the cards, the "open when" envelopes from Ourania, and the goodbye letter from Amalia. That letter meant so much to me. I couldn't imagine how difficult it was for my sister to write—submerging her pain and staying strong for me. I find it so significant that the best and most meaningful expressions of love come out in moments of pain.

The day closed with me still nauseated, in pain, and weak. But as the sun set and darkness came, I knew I was filled with light, and I was sure I'd make it through the night, through the darkness. I had found my light again. I had found the light that was trapped in that box of memories, the light of hope and love. And I knew that, even if I lost it again, I'd always be able to find it in that box, in the people close to my heart. As my friend Ourania told me, "Distance means nothing, when someone means so much."

The next day, the side effects from the chemo took over. I'd reached the point where it was painful to speak, eat, and swallow, and I was running a fever.

"OK, let's keep track of your temperature, and let's hope we won't need to go in again," my mom told me.

I knew I would have to go back to the hospital in a few days. I was trying to be positive and brave. I think when people hear those two words, they get confused. Being positive doesn't mean that every day is good, that everything is great, and that you're always hopeful. It just means that, even on dark days, even when it gets a little too hard to hope, even when you feel like God is silent, even on *those* days, you recognize and deeply believe that there *are* better days ahead, that the pain and hurt are temporary, that this cloud of darkness is just a season.

On the other hand, being brave doesn't necessarily mean having the strength to go on. It doesn't mean that life is not difficult, that it doesn't just get a little too much somedays, or that you have unlimited strength to fight. It just means that you *choose* to fight *even* when you *don't* have the strength to. It means that you choose to go on and that you show up and you keep showing up, even though you know that the odds are against you. Making the *choice* to be brave is the very thing that gives you that *true strength*.

A hopeful and optimistic attitude is not something you can find or develop easily. It takes a lot of courage and determination. It's a constant battle between fear and faith, doubt and trust, and desperation and hope. But most importantly, it's a *choice*. It's a choice you have to make every morning. This is the choice that will determine how you fight the battle and how you deal with the problems and negativity of each day.

A few days later, my grandma visited me in Essen. I was very excited to spend time with her. One morning, I was on the phone with Dr. Vasilis, and I was really struggling with the side effects and feeling discouraged and hopeless. That's why he had called me. We talked about being brave.

After we hung up, he sent me a text. "I'll see you in a few hours," he wrote.

What?

Just two hours later, the doorbell rang. My mom opened the door, and I instantly teared up. It was Dr. Vasilis. He had been at a medical conference in Brussels, and because I was so tired and worn out, he'd decided to drive to Essen and see me. He was like a guardian angel God had sent to make me brave. I rushed and hugged him tightly. We then spent some time talking about everything that was going on. We talked about the treatment; fear; and, most importantly, being brave. He showed me a Bible verse on his phone.

"Therefore, do not worry about tomorrow for tomorrow will worry about itself. Each day has enough trouble of its own" (Matthew 6:34).

"That's what you're going to tell yourself, whenever you find yourself worrying and stressing about the future. We'll take it a day at a time, okay?" Dr. Vasilis told me.

"Okay," I replied, full of courage.

We then sat around the dining table and had lunch together. Before eating, Dr. Vasilis said a prayer. I'll never forget that moment. During that prayer, he also asked God to take the nausea away and make me *brave*. Love's in the details. We all were in tears. But soon after, these tears were replaced by smiles as we talked about photography, going home, traveling, food, and so many other things.

After lunch, Dr. Vasilis had to leave because he had to drive back to Brussels to catch his flight. He was performing a surgery the next day, so he really had to be there. And yet he made time to have that lunch with us. What courage love can give! Before leaving, he hugged me and told me to be brave.

"But … we talked so much about it. Yet I still wonder," I said, "How can I be brave when I'm so scared? When I'm so tired and afraid and hopeless and desperate and broken? Can I really be brave *then*?"

"Well," he replied, "That's the only time that you *can* be brave."

On March 15, my aunt visited me in Germany for a few days. I was excited to see her. She brought so much light into our everyday life. She would work on what we called "breakfast projects," where she would find creative and exciting breakfast recipes she would make for me to motivate me to eat something. Love's in the details. Just like joy.

A few days later, I was running a fever and ended up being admitted to the isolation ward to receive antibiotics and morphine. It was my first time in the isolation ward. Patients there were so immunocompromised that the slightest exposure to hospital bacteria could be deadly. I was sent there because of how low my blood counts were. What I liked the most about it was the peace—the quiet and calm atmosphere. The chemotherapy ward that I was usually admitted in was hectic, full of nurses, doctors, and countless patients; beeping sounds; and lots of crying. In isolation, however, you get to relax, and it just felt a little bit more like home. Ironic isn't it? How could an isolation ward feel like home? I didn't yet know. I hadn't yet found out.

The doctors inserted the port needle, drew blood, and started me on high-dose antibiotics and morphine for the mucositis. At this point, I had already gone about a week without being able to eat or drink, so they also started me on IV fluids and IV nutrition.

I joked about it with my mom. "Call it a cheeseburger or a donut or just a smoothie of all of the above," I told her, talking about the bag of white fluids that were entering my bloodstream.

She smiled.

Mission accomplished, I thought to myself.

This was my first time on morphine, and throughout the past few days, I'd been sleeping twenty-two hours a day. Even the doctors made a joke about the amount of sleep I was getting. For me, sleeping was the best escape plan. It was like an emergency exit from life, pain, nausea, sadness, and negative thoughts. The morphine helped a lot with that too.

Whenever I couldn't fall asleep, I closed my eyes and imagined myself going back to school and surprising everyone or imagined myself playing basketball or running again. I made up scenarios in my head, planned out trips, and made bucket lists. I imagined and planned out my wedding, dropping off my kids at school, graduating college, or getting my first car. I tried to dream about things I might not get the chance to experience. Cancer was like having a loaded gun pointed at your head and never knowing when it would shoot you. To cope with this, I needed to believe that life would continue. I felt stuck in this disease, while everybody else was moving forward. Thinking about life and making plans helped me deal with this period of "pause" in the most productive and purposeful way possible. This was also why, when not in the hospital, I started sleeping on the grey couch we'd bought, instead of my bed. It made *this*—this whole thing—feel temporary.

Sometimes, God will allow the mountain in your life to block your way, just to show you that He can carry you if you can't climb it, He can hold you if you fall. Often, the mountains in our lives are there so that we can see that God can move them—so that we can believe, trust, understand, grow, and become stronger and more empowered by trauma and adversity.

Resting is so important. Many people confuse it with giving up. However, it is far from that. Resting means surrendering to hope, while blindly placing your trust in something greater and more purposeful than you. For me, that something greater was a hope brighter than the sun, a love stronger than steel, and a grace deeper that the ocean. Even when I didn't understand, even when I hurt and broke down, even when nothing made sense and frustration overwhelmed me, God's light never dimmed. Knowing that, amid all darkness and pain, God gave me rest and peace in the chaos overwhelmed me with a "sunset feeling." Maybe this hospitalization was just that—God teaching me how to rest.

On that first night of this hospital admission, Prof. D, my oncologist, came to see me. She was an amazing doctor and an incredible human being. We talked about the infection I had and my neutropenia. She explained how strong the chemo was and a few other long-term side effects that we were expecting to soon appear.

As she was about to leave, I asked a doorknob question. A doorknob question is a question that a patient has but is afraid or embarrassed to ask, however ends up asking anyway when the doctor is about to leave. I was not embarrassed, just afraid of the answer.

"Can I ask you a last question? I've been thinking about it a lot," I said with hesitation. "Do you think it would be possible for me to go to Greece to graduate in June? We're having a big graduation ceremony at school, and I really want to be there. I have exams too because I don't want to have to repeat the school year. I'd be done with block 5 by then and with transfusions and antibiotics, I think I could go. But of course, we don't want to delay block 6 too much or risk getting infections. Do you think that something like that could happen?"

Ever since I'd come to Germany, I always looked forward to going back home. Every time somebody came to visit me, I felt trapped, because after a few days, they were always able to leave, and I was stuck here. Whenever we went for outpatient blood tests and while we sat at the waiting room, I always opened my calendar and planned out everything—who was coming when, when the chemo blocks would take place, and other appointments. It motivated me a great deal. That's why going back to Greece, even for a few days, was so important for me. Graduating was my biggest challenge, because it required being healthy enough to travel by plane *and* motivated enough to catch up on schoolwork all by myself *and* determined to put in the work despite the chemo, to make tremendous efforts, *and* to keep being hopeful despite the doubts in my mind.

"We would have to be very careful and monitor you blood values closely, but I think, with the right precautions, that *would* be possible," Prof. D said with a smile. "We can do this."

Those words were all I needed. I couldn't stop smiling. Hearing these words took a large weight of hopelessness off my heart and replaced it with unbreakable courage and hope. "Really?" I said. "Oh wow, I'm smiling so much. You can't imagine how happy I am right now," I said with the biggest smile ever.

Just that one sentence, those four words—"that *would* be possible"— were all I needed to hear. I was ecstatic to say the least. If my biggest goal was possible, then everything else was too. Beating cancer was possible, and so was even writing this book. Sure, a thousand things could go wrong, but I was somehow so hopeful, that very moment, I truly believed that, through faith, all things were possible.

Many people believe that faith is just a coping mechanism, a superficial defense system to avoid facing death and pain and accepting that life is unfair and bad things happen for no reason. That couldn't be further from the truth though. Faith is not religion. It is knowing that you are not alone. It's the choice to walk with God through life. I refuse to believe that things just happen. I really believe everything happens for a reason. And even if I can't see, understand, or even fathom what that reason could be, I choose to trust that it exists. Trusting and truly believing that everything has a certain purpose, although it doesn't make life easier, makes it more meaningful, emotions more powerful, and moments more precious.

On Sunday, March 25, my grandpa came to Essen to visit me. He brought me a box of some cookies made by my aunt that my sister and I loved to eat when we were little. Simple things like that gave me so much courage. Love's in the details. I loved it when people came to visit. Since

I couldn't go home, it was as if they were *bringing* home to me. Details of normalcy brought me comfort. They made me feel safe.

It was particularly difficult seeing people leave, not only because I'd miss them, but also because every time someone left, I was reminded that I couldn't do the same. Being in the hospital made me very vulnerable. It had become so easy for me to cry and much rarer, but special, for me to smile. Pain does that to people—it makes their smile more unique; it makes it shine brighter.

However, as the days passed, the negative voices in my head got louder. Desperation started taking over. *Constant* pain made depression stronger. But when pain gets greater, faith is planted in the soil of struggle and grows *deeper*.

My grandpa sat by my bed and held my hand. He scratched my back and told me that it was all going to be okay. "You're a fighter. Strength— you gotta hold on to strength. You'll win."

Grandpa Nick always gave me the best pep talks. Grandpa John had passed away a few years ago, and it seemed as if Grandpa Nick was giving me strength for them both. Love is so powerful. But the depth of its power is only understood through "insignificant" moments, details of daily life that we often take for granted.

On Wednesday morning, the nurses woke me up at 4:30 a.m. to prepare me for the PET scan. They gave me a pill, drew blood, and measured my blood pressure and temperature. After about half an hour, one of the nurses wheeled me out in my bed and through the underground tunnels of the hospital campus, took me to the radiology clinic of the "operation zendrum zwei," a very big and tall building where the operating rooms were. There, a team of doctors took a brief history and placed an IV line in my arm.

After about an hour, I went in for the scan. As I lay on the MRT table, I felt numb. The room was so cold. The machine made loud noises. I was scared. The radiologist placed a headset around my ears to block the noise of the machine.

As the table slid inside the magnet, I felt fear rush through my whole body. It was the first time I experienced fear like that, in a physical form. This was such a big moment. It would determine whether the chemotherapy was working. As the procedure began, the sounds of the machine got louder. And as the sounds of the machine got louder, the sound of the voices of fear in my mind grew stronger. The constant what-if haunted my heart. Everything was so loud. My mind was a war zone. I was desperate for peace. Fear is such an exhausting emotion. It rips every inch of life from you and leaves you broken and paralyzed.

At some point my thoughts were interrupted by an automated voice that played through the headset, "Please breathe in and hold your breath."

As I breathed in, I closed my eyes.

The machine started making louder sounds—more aggressive ones.

God find me here. Please. Can you hold my hand? I'm so scared. Find me here. Stay near. Meet me in the brokenness. I know you hear my cry. I know you feel my fear. You know my worries, my what-ifs. You know the demons fighting against me in my mind. I'm tired of fighting back. Can you fight them with me? Can you silence the anguish? Oh, God, make me brave.

"Please resume breathing," the voice says.

Chapter 5

A Glimpse of Joy

On Thursday, March 29, after spending ten days in the hospital and going through excruciating pain that high dose of morphine couldn't stop, I was discharged. I had four days to spend at home, and then I had to go back to the hospital for chemotherapy block 3. We were still waiting for the results of the PET scan. I was still scared. But I was trying to have faith.

On Friday morning, one of my closest friends, Mikaela, visited. She was going to spend the long weekend with me in Essen. When I saw her walk through the door, I got so emotional. For a moment, I didn't want her to see me like this—weak, pale, bald. But these thoughts disappeared as I saw the smile on her face when she saw me. We sat on the couch in the living room and started talking. I had so many questions to ask. Within a very few moments of us talking, I got very emotional. This felt like it used to when we were hanging out after school on Fridays. I needed to remember this. We then decided to play some Monopoly. I was having so much fun. We spent the day online shopping, searching for graduation dresses, and playing different board games. At night, we all sat together and had dinner. As we ate, we talked about so many things—school, teachers, inside jokes. I was laughing. I felt like me again, for a brief moment. It was a glimpse of what used to be amid what was and a glimpse of what would be as a source of strength to get through what is. A glimpse of joy.

Late at night, Mikaela and her mom left to go to the hotel they'd be staying at, and my mom picked up the table and cleaned the dishes. There was this cute cottage hotel right next door, and whoever visited me stayed there. As my mom was doing chores around the house, I walked to the bathroom quietly (as quietly as my crutches allowed). I closed the door and sat down on the bathroom floor. I grabbed a towel; put it up against my mouth, trying to not make any noise; and I burst into tears. My heart ached, and I couldn't stop crying. I lay on the floor and crawled up in a ball by the bathtub. The thoughts in my mind were breaking every piece of my heart that was desperately trying to hold on and stay strong.

Eventually, my mom realized I'd been in the bathroom for too long and came to see what was wrong. She opened the door and found me lying on the floor crying uncontrollably. She was worried. "What happened? Did you fall? Are you hurt?" she asked and knelt down. She sat on the bathroom floor next to me and held my hand.

I shook my head no.

"Then what's wrong?" she continued. "Didn't you have fun tonight with your friend? Aren't you happy she's here?"

"That's the problem," I say in a stuttering voice.

I felt my heart breaking. I didn't know if I wanted to open up to her. I didn't want her to have to fight against my thoughts *too*. But I felt like I was suffocating. Every breath was getting harder, more painful. I tried to speak, but the words didn't come out—just a loud cry. It was a cry for help. I fell in her arms. My mom was worried. She hadn't seen me so hurt before. I'd always hidden the depth of my pain—until now.

"Tonight … tonight was the first time that I … Tonight was the first time that I *laughed* in almost four months, Mom," I said.

I felt a bullet go through my chest as I saw the expression on her face.

"I had forgotten what that felt like, Mom. I had forgotten what it felt like to laugh just because you meet with friends and have a good time," I said and broke down in her arms. As I spoke, loud sobs escaped the prison of my mind. I needed help. This weight was destroying me. My hands were literally shaking, my mind was numb, and my heart was broken.

"This seems so familiar yet so distant. I can't remember the last time I was laughing with my friends over simple, normal things. I can't even remember … I have forgotten what joy *felt* like, Mom. I mean … I … What happened to *me*? Where did *I* go?"

My mom hugged me tightly. Tears filled her eyes. "You will remember again," she said and hugged me even tighter. "You'll remember again, and you'll laugh again, and you will forget the things you are going through now. You are *so* brave. You go through so much." Her voice cracked.

I hated it when my mom saw me sad or crying. I tried to keep it together and be strong—I thought I could, but I was in way over my head. I had no idea of the emotional strength that hiding pain would require. It was something I tried but always fail to do. It had become so easy for me to cry. I'd become so fragile—so broken.

As I lay in bed at night, I started thinking, trying to remember my last typical day as a healthy and normal fourteen-year-old. I tried to trace back the cancer, pinpoint the time around when it all started. But that's the thing about last times; you never know they're the last until they are. You never know that this will be the last time you see someone, until it is. You never know this will be the last morning you wake up happy, until it is, until every morning following it, you wake up in fear or hurt. You never know that these will be the last words you say to someone, until they are, until you can no longer speak to them, reach out, and connect.

And the only solution to this problem is to treat everything as if it was a last time. Go to bed tonight thankful for the little things you did today, and wake up tomorrow with the same gratitude you would if this were your last day. Tell that person you love them; tell them how much they mean to you. Connect with people, take risks, take chances, and go after what you truly love. Prioritize what truly matters, laugh more, love more, and give back more. You never know that this time you do something will be the last ... until it is.

Two days later, on April 2, Amalia and my brother, Thanos, also visited me in Essen. I'd missed them so much. Seeing my family motivated me to keep trying. Their smile gave me hope that everything would turn out OK. Seeing them helped me gather the courage I needed to stay positive and strong—*for them*. If their wings were broken, I'd give them mine—even if that meant I'd never fly again.

Shortly after Amalia and Thanos get to our apartment, we decided to play Monopoly. I was overwhelmed by this very strange feeling; my heart felt full of love, full of hope. I was feeling true joy. I wished time would just stop and this moment would never have to end.

What I find so meaningful is the fact that, amid struggle, pain and hurt, joy is born. Pure, authentic, deep joy is created *in the little moments* spent with family. When family comes together, the love that is shared is more than enough to *create* joy, hope, and happiness, no matter how dark life might look, no matter how strong the pain might be, and no matter how broken you might feel.

We all spent the next few days together, exploring Essen's countryside, taking photos and drone videos, and playing board games. My brother and I shared a passion for filmmaking, so we always bonded over that. I loved the fact that I had someone to share these interests with. I was so grateful for being able to drive around the countryside and take photos. They were small moments of joy amid great pain.

My sister, for her part, tried to help me with schoolwork. After the optimistic and hopeful response from my oncologist about us traveling home, I was filled with excitement and determination to pick up my education and continue doing schoolwork. Amalia tried to explain to me how to solve mathematical equations with variables raised to the second power. It was very confusing, if I'm being honest, but we spent multiple afternoons solving different examples. Math and I were clearly not the best of friends.

On March 28, I received another email from Mr. A. He asked me how I was doing and gave me song and movie recommendations to help take my mind off the treatment. He told me to stray strong and encouraged me to not give up. I told him the exciting news that I potentially might be able to come back home and gave him an update on the treatment.

I liked the fact that I was starting to do normal things again. I hadn't picked up a book in so long. Moments from class overwhelmed my memory and escaped my eyes, running down my face in the form of tears.

"You'll very soon be writing a test on this very material, and everything will be over, and you will be back at school," Amalia told me. "I *promise*."

I needed to hear that so much. Love is in the details. And this week I realized that joy is in the details too.

Chapter 6

Weary Shoulders and a Walk up Golgotha

It was Wednesday, April 18. I was lying in a hospital bed, staring at the ceiling.

"All right, you might feel a little dizzy, but that is normal," a doctor said as she injected an anesthetic into my IV. "Count down from ten."

I'd heard that sentence before. I remembered Dr. Vasilis and number six. I remembered hope.

"Ten," I said and started counting down. "Nine, eight, seven ..."

The anesthesia started to kick in.

As I was about to say number six, my head got dizzy, my vision blurred, and my heart rate lowered. Upon number six, memories of this past month came to mind.

So much has happened since we last left off. Let me fill you in.

About two weeks ago, I went inpatient for my third round of chemotherapy. As you recall, Amalia, Thanos, and my mom and my dad were all there. That morning, I woke up sad. I'd had such a good time with my friend Mikaela and my family that past weekend. And I knew what was about to come—feeling horrible for weeks because of yet another chemo round. I also knew I was going to be doing a stem cell collection after this round, and I was really nervous about it; I didn't know what to expect. This time, however, I was going to be getting the drugs during Easter. The days that we were supposed to all be together as a family, enjoying the moments and laughter we shared, I would be stuck in the hospital, feeling helpless, lifeless, and powerless.

Little did I know, though, that very hospitalization, during the most important days of the Easter holidays, would give me a more powerful understanding of Easter, would give meaning to suffering and hope, and would ultimately bring me much closer to God.

I was in room 112 and shared a room with another teenage girl who was going through another type of sarcoma that affects the soft tissues. I got the bed closer to the window, which was great, because the cold wind helped me with the dizziness and nausea. The crisp, winter air could somehow make me warm. It gave me peace. It gave me hope.

As the infusion started, I tried to fall asleep. My main goal was to sleep through as much of the chemo as I could to minimize the side effects it would cause me to experience. However, sleeping was impossible, since the girl next to me was crying for many hours. Her prognosis wasn't good, and she didn't have a lot of time left. She had been in the hospital fighting an infection for days, and she just wanted to be discharged so she could enjoy the time she had left. That experience was more than I could handle at the time. I wished I could do something—anything—to help her, to keep her safe, and to make her healthy. Seeing the emotional pain she was in just broke me. It also scared me more than words can capture. Her initial prognosis was good, yet now, she was at a point where she was undertaking a treatment that didn't even work, living her last days. With the stem cell collection, the uncertainty about my treatment, and that girl's story, my fear levels were through the roof. It had never hit me like that before.

I could die.

I didn't yet know whether my treatment was working, and I was crushed and torn by the thought that it might not be. That fear was so heavy—and so loud. It didn't let me sleep. I was absolutely exhausted, yet I didn't *want* to fall sleep. I was too scared to. I closed my eyes and heard the girl crying next to me. And I just couldn't help but picture myself in her shoes. My whole body was shaking every time I thought of that. I didn't want to die. I didn't want *her* to die. I didn't want *anyone* to die. The realization of how dangerous this disease truly was, hit me like a ten-foot wave. It crushed me, shredding every effort I'd made all these months to accept the situation and find the positive in it. I wanted to fight for this girl—for all the kids like her. But I couldn't. Not yet at least. First, I had to fight for me. You first have to secure your own oxygen mask before you can assist others.

Just like in every other block, I was getting four different drugs, which lasted about one to four hours, depending on how strong they were. With each drug, I'd get multiple bags of fluids to flush the chemo through my system more easily. My sister sat by my bed and lay her head on my knees. Knowing she was there made the whole process a little more bearable. After a couple of hours, the nurses woke me up to measure my blood pressure and weight. My blood pressure was super low, so much so that the nurses were worried I'd pass out every time I stood up.

I remember going to the bathroom to throw up and brush my teeth to get rid of the chemo taste, and as I lifted my head from the bathroom sink, I looked at myself in the mirror. It was heartbreaking. The person in the mirror was not *me*. That person was orange from the doxorubicin, with red puffy eyes, a dried-up mouth, no hair, no eyebrows, no eyelashes, and tears running down her face. That person was not *me*. That person was scared, exhausted, hurt, and depressed. That person was not *me*. Not really.

Every new second I spent looking in the mirror was a second of walking down the road of acceptance—a road that I hadn't dared to go down. It took all my inner strength, all the courage of my heart to come to terms with the fact that the person in the mirror *was* me. *How did I get here?* I thought to myself. Why *did I get here?*

I walked back to my room and lay down in my bed. I closed my eyes, and as I felt the drugs enter my bloodstream, I took a deep breath. I removed some of my eyelashes that had fallen out and gotten into my eye, and the same thoughts took over my mind. *When did I become so broken? When did I lose myself? How did I end up like this?*

In the blink of an eye, in the split seconds between heartbeats, my life had changed so much. Happiness had been replaced by pain, suffering, and having to endure, to hold on, even if every part of my body wanted to give up. Life used to be better. I was happy. I was healthy. I smiled without a reason and stressed over what I would wear to school and how well prepared I was for a history test. And now … Now all that innocence, happiness, and joy had been stripped away. A good day now was a day I only cried three times and not more, a day I didn't throw up, a day

I managed to sleep or eat four bites out of my lunch. That was what a good day felt like now. A good day was one when I talked to my sister on FaceTime a few minutes longer, one when I got a text from somebody at school. Life had been better before. *I* had been better before.

And then it happened. God held my hand and fought the voices in my head for me. He knew that, in that moment, I was too weak to deal with them—that I was surrendering to their lies. And that's why, suddenly, the I-was-better-before thought got replaced by the was-I question.

Was I *actually* better?

As I started thinking about it, I realized that "better" sometimes might feel backward. At school, my friends and I would often discuss which teacher was better. Someone once asked, "What do you mean better? Better as in the one we liked the most or better as in the one who actually taught us the most? There was not one, single criteria that made a teacher better. And I think this very simple question is, in fact, the answer to the even bigger questions: "Why do bad things happen?" or "Why do we feel pain?"

There will always be the teachers we like, who we have fun with, who let us rest in class, and who don't assign homework. But there will always be the ones who teach us more, who prepare us better for life, and who equip us with all the knowledge necessary to move onto the next chapter. Likewise, life will be full of fun times and happy moments, seasons of joy and health, and times when the waters are calm and peaceful; the hike of life will be a grassy field, a straight line, an easy road full of joy and good times. But there will also be storms that rock you and challenge you, mountains so high you can't even see their summit, roads that will be incredibly challenging and tough, deserts with no water to quench your thirst, and situations with no hope to give you courage.

So, when you ask the question of which is better, what is the comparison? Are you looking for the teachers you have fun with or the ones who teach you the most? In the darkness, during the seasons of difficulty, you will be equipped with patience, resilience, hope, and courage; you will understand pain; and you will experience love greater than ever before. You will explore the depths of your soul and strength. You will learn to let go and trust, to surrender, to take a step into the unknown, and to keep fighting for the deepest desires of your heart. The kind of teacher you have fun in class with is going to offer you superficial knowledge, very basic and common. But a teacher who teaches you the most is the kind of teacher who challenges you, makes you stay up late working, questions your beliefs, provokes your thinking process, and shakes up your understanding of the most fundamental things you've learned at school.

My life *before* cancer, was more fun and more joyful, full of happy moments and common struggles. But it didn't teach me anything. It didn't help me grow. It didn't make me stronger every day. It didn't make me brave. Now, every new breath required courage I'd never known I had, and every time I wiped tears off my face, I used hope I never imagined I could experience. Now, I wondered if getting out bed was worth it, but I also unlocked resilience every time I chose to do so and to persevere.

Pain changes people. It makes them cry more easily, makes them feel more deeply, and even makes them want to give up. But it also makes them grow. Pain and struggle are the very things that shape you into a better and more determined person. Many times, we are left *feeling* alone in a storm so we can learn how to swim. We are given a difficult test so we can learn the most important lessons. We are stripped of all hope, only to learn to trust. We are hurt only to feel real love. We are burned only to see that beauty rises from ashes and that flowers grow from burnt soil. Living like I used to was the kind of teacher you had fun with. But living in pain is the teacher who actually teaches you the most—and *helps* you the most.

A flower can't grow without rain. You've heard this before, right? Think about it for a moment.

Like a seed you're buried deep down. You're stuck in life, not knowing what you're here for; making bad choices; and going down the wrong paths, covered in hurt and negativity. And then it rains. And for a moment, as the soil prepares itself, as solid dirt turns to mud, you feel more stuck. When chemo first started, I felt so much worse, so much more depressed, and so helpless. Mud is worse. It suffocates you. But that can only last so long. Soon after, you begin to grow; acceptance grows, courage grows, and resilience grows. As it keeps raining, you keep growing. And oh, what a beautiful sight it is for a flower to grow *in the midst* of a storm.

So, which is better? Rain or drought? Fun teachers or strict ones? Normal life or adversity? Well, you can't really compare. You see, all these things are temporary. Clouds come and go, rain starts and stops, and storms come and pass. Even teachers change every year. Depression, sickness, disappointments, and struggle are all temporary. What is constant is *you*—the person all these temporary situations shape you into. And *that* person is better after struggles, after rain, after a really difficult test. Now you fear less, you know more, you understand better, and you feel and appreciate more deeply.

So even if it didn't feel like it, through cancer, I became better day by day—*braver* day by day. My faith found deeper roots, my hope reached out further, and my trust was placed in brighter things during darker times. Even if it didn't feel like it, through pain, I was growing. "I used to be better," was a lie. I was *now* getting better. This *was* the rain. This *was* the test. This … had a *purpose*.

As I let these thoughts take over me, I fell asleep. The night was rough, but my dad stayed over and helped me through it. He slept in a chair.

Sometimes this is how people speak their love—through actions. Through sleeping in hospital chairs, through holding you when you cry, through cleaning you after you throw up, and through being the shoulder you can lean on to relieve the dizziness, people speak love. Love is felt the deepest when pain is felt the most. I had to be so vulnerable, so hurt, and so helpless so I could truly feel the depths of the love of my family. Waking up to my sister holding my hand, bursting out in tears in my mom's arms, seeing my dad's efforts to cheer me up, and receiving daily videos with words of encouragement from my aunt—those were the things that truly enabled me to understand what unconditional love felt and looked like.

Another significant example of love emerging from pain comes in the form of hugs. During every chemo, my resilience, hope, and strength were tested greatly. Usually, I broke during the second day. That's when I would burst into tears and try to communicate how tired I was of fighting. That's when my mom or my dad would give me a hug. That hug felt like *home*. It really did.

During the chemo, I put up this armor made of all the strength and patience I had and just tried to push through every physical and emotional obstacle. But the chemo was so much stronger than that armor. It broke it just after the first day. A hug from somebody in my family was *home*. It allowed me to take off that armor and, for a moment, cry, be vulnerable, and be scared. But it also sheltered me; it gave me comfort. With that hug, my mom, my dad, my sister, or my aunt gave me *their* armor. They give me *their* strength and *their* patience. And with that new armor, I would go back into the battlefield, where I'd endure hit after hit, strike after strike, bullet after bullet, and try to hold on. I'd go back to the ocean, to the storm, where I'd hit wave after wave, lightning strike after lightning strike, wind after wind. And when that new armor broke again, I'd go back into their arms, back to my shelter, my home away from home, and they'd give me a new one.

This is why I truly believe the most authentic and deep love is created and expressed in times of pain, hurt, and vulnerability, through little details like hugs in empty hospital corridors.

The next day was even more difficult. The taste of the medicine had made the nausea ten times worse. I couldn't eat or drink anything. Being the very practical person that I am, I tried to find solutions to this problem. At first, I tried brushing my teeth every couple of hours, but after a few times, the toothbrush itself started tasting like the chemo. I then asked my mom to go out and get me peppermint gum. I started chewing a different gum every three or four minutes, but this also didn't end up working either. So, I decided to try a peppermint mouthwash, which thankfully *did* work for the next couple of days.

The third day of this treatment block was Good Friday, yet nothing seemed good about that Friday. The third day was always the most difficult during the chemo rounds. That specific "third day," however, was meaningful. I thought of Christ on the Cross as I was trying to find something to hold onto, and I realized that, on that Cross, was a God who knew pain, who knew suffering—*my* pain and *my* suffering. That was a God who knew what I was going through, who'd *seen* suffering, *endured* pain, and lost hope and found it again—a God who'd given His life for me. Christ was beaten so I could be whole, so *I* could be healed. Because *His* body was broken, *mine* could be put back together. Because *His* blood was shed, *I* could be set free from all physical and emotional chains. Because *He* went through pain, *my* hurt could be transformed. Because *He* endured suffering, *I* could be lifted over sickness, pain, and adversity. If the day that Christ died was eventually called good, then maybe *my* worst days would be called good too, maybe *my* pain would have a purpose too. In those moments of hurt and struggle, that thought gave me much comfort and courage to push through and keep on keeping on.

That night, my mom, aunt, Amalia, and Thanos all went to a church in a nearby town. My dad stayed at the hospital with me. I figured that, since I couldn't be there physically, I'd be there spiritually. So, that night, I let myself get discouraged. I let myself grieve and cry for all the things I had missed out on, the things that I *would* miss out on, and the things that I might not have time for. I didn't know what the future held, so the thought that maybe I didn't have a lot of time left crossed my mind multiple times. *Sometimes*, it moved in. It haunted me. That night, however, I let all the baggage locked in my mind out. I let all the weight I was carrying overtake me.

Pain needs to be felt. However, behind choosing to feel and express those emotions, hid the unshakable, deeply rooted faith that, just like life was restored on the Cross, light would be restored in my life. And *that* faith, enabled me to place my trust in God's promise to transform my pain into purpose and to replace those very emotions I was allowing myself to feel with newfound gratitude and unconditional joy. So, that night, I *did* grieve. But I grieved *because* I *hoped*—and because that hope was so much stronger than the pain the grief had caused. I found the courage to face Friday only because of the hope that Sunday would bring. Friday's heavy grief was Sunday's empty grave.

Looking at the Cross, I also realized that, amid hardship, love is expressed as resilience. Christ had the ability to end His pain, to save Himself, and to ease the hurt and stop the torture. Yet He didn't. He stayed. He stayed on that Cross and endured it all. He did so out of love—out of perfect, boundless, reckless love. This revelation gave me the courage to keep fighting; to keep enduring; and to keep pushing through, for my family. Out of love. Giving up was easier, but it was also selfish. I loved them too much to give up. And *they* loved *me* too much to give up on *me*. That day, I realized the profound power of the message of Easter and decided to keep walking up my Golgotha. Out of love, I would stay. I would stay in the fight, in the discomfort, and I would *stay brave*.

The next morning was Saturday, April 7—the day of the wait. Saturday was silent. It seemed to be over; there seemed to be no hope. But midnight was coming. Hope was coming. Sunday—the day of victory—was coming. Saturday, however, was the day of uncertainty. I woke up feeling just as terrible physically as I had the night before.

Right before morning rounds, when the doctors would come in to check up on me, my mom and my aunt got to the hospital. I was walking with my dad back to my room from the bathroom (special thanks to Lasix), and as we were walking, the machine attached to my medicine pole started beeping, indicating that yet another liter of saline had successfully been infused in my bloodstream. That's when I saw my mom walk in through the door of the ward. She was wearing a bright pink hoodie with matching pink sweatpants, and she had the biggest and brightest smile ever. That instantly made me feel so much better. It was like the ray of sunlight and the splash of color I needed that morning to realize that the darkness would soon be over. Sunday was coming. Hope was on the way. Hope always lasts. *Love* lasts. My mom opened her arms wide open, tilted her head to the side, and smiled brighter than ever. I rushed into her arms and hugged her tightly.

After a few hours, Dr. S walked in my room to examine me. She was an oncology resident and was part of my oncologist's team. Dr. S was Greek too. We had met her when we'd come to Germany for those two first days and had connected with her ever since. She promised she would do everything she could to help me. She really cared about me. She always motivated me, giving me courage and optimism. She had just started working there about a month before I first started treatment. That didn't feel like a coincidence to me. When she walked in, she smiled at me. Her smile was one of hope; it really was. I opened up to her about my fears. I always asked her to double-check my heart, because I was really scared the chemo would damage it. She smiled. "Don't worry. We'll take care of you. We won't let anything bad happen", she told me. She was like a best friend to me. Every time I saw her we would chat, and I'd share memories from home with her. She truly was a light of hope.

Later that day, my sister and brother came to the hospital to visit. We played a question trivia board game we'd brought from home. Spending time with them and doing something fun greatly improved my mood. And even though I couldn't speak, we always found ways to communicate. Later that day, my aunt took one of the paper boxes the nurses had given me to throw up in, flipped it around, and suggested we played hangman. I was super excited. It didn't require a lot of talking, and when it was my turn to guess, I just wrote down the letters I wanted to say. We ended up playing for almost an hour before I got too tired and nauseated and went back to sleep. My sister always said, "Keep it inside." She used to say this phrase to me over FaceTime after every chemotherapy, and it had become her catch phrase. It soon became an inside joke for the whole family.

The next day was Easter Sunday, and I was getting discharged. This whole chemotherapy block was such a symbol. Like Christ had carried His Cross up the mountain, I was carrying *my* cross, *my* suffering, and *my* pain up the mountain of cancer. What gave me hope and comfort was that I wasn't walking alone. God was right there. Every step I took, He was taking with me. Every tear I cried, His heart broke with mine. He knew my pain, my hurt. And He just wanted me to trust Him.

I believe that, when you walk with God, you never really lose a battle. Even when the outcome is not what you had wished for or expected, even then, you win. You see, what determines the winner in a battle is the *whole* fight, not just the last punch. Many times, sickness, addiction, hurt, and depression throw the last punch and change the outcome of the battle. But the last punch does not affect the winner criteria. It's the *whole* fight—the journey, the struggle, the technique, and the effort—that truly decide who won. Letting God fight your battles, choosing to hope, and placing your trust in something greater automatically places you on the winner's side. It represents a specific way of fighting, one characterized by courage, grace, perseverance, and determination. And if you fight like that, no matter who throws that last punch, *you* will be the one to win.

On the Cross, the impossible was made possible. Love was given a body. Hope was given a name. Forgiveness was bought with a sacrifice of love. Suffering was turned to strength, and pain was turned to purpose, when Love was clothed in scars. Victory was masked as defeat. And because of *that* Love, I was given courage. I was given a hand to hold, a shoulder to cry on, and a lighthouse amid the storm. Because of *that* victory, I was supplied with strength and resilience. I was filled with hope and perseverance. I was made brave.

Hope. Healing. An alliteration with deep meaning. Hope is the road to healing. Yet at the same time hope *is* the healing itself. Healing doesn't always come the way we want it to. It's not always in the form of a good medical record, a good report, or good news. Healing sometimes means the existence of hope amid heartache. I was healed that Easter. I still had cancer, and I still could die. I still cried. I still lost courage and strength. Waking up every day still hurt, and it still took everything in me to do so. Yet I was healed. How? By hope, through hope, and because of hope. Although it did not change my situation, it changed *me* and *my perspective* of that situation.

Spending the most important days of the Easter holidays in the hospital ended up helping me truly connect with Christ on the Cross. He sets an example of how I chose to fight my battles and face my adversity. He uses grace, forgiveness, hope, and trust to endure and overcome. Through opening His heart to God, He let me know that weakness is natural; fear is natural; anxiety, agony, and desperation, all these emotions are natural. But He also showed me that, if I took all these emotions—all my worries and all my fears—and placed them in God's hands, through opening up to Him and talking to Him, then these emotions could be defeated by hope, faith, and trust.

A few hours later, the results from the morning blood tests came back. My blood values were very low but, thankfully, not at a level where a transfusion would be necessary. My dad was the only one in the hospital with me at the time. Everyone else was at home preparing for our family Easter lunch. My aunt was cooking traditional Greek foods that are eaten on Easter Sunday, my sister was studying for school, and my brother was catching up on college work.

Before I was discharged, the nurses removed my port needle and unhooked me from all the machines. My dad brought the car to the Kinderklinik (children's clinic), from the hospital parking lot, and loaded all our bags in the back. I rolled myself in my wheelchair and got into the car. I was so weak I couldn't even lift my arm to press the button to call the elevator or open the car door.

When we got home, the house smelled like Easter. It was incredible but also terrible for me, considering that I had just finished five days of chemotherapy, and I was extremely sensitive to smell. My mom opened the windows and helped me get changed into fresh pajamas. We all sat around the table and celebrated Easter. I didn't eat anything. But being with my family and sharing this moment with them made every chemo side effect worth it.

We all spent the next two days together, even though I couldn't do much. I stayed on the couch all day, sleeping during most of it. Ever since the chemotherapy treatment had started, I always slept on the couch instead of my bed. It made the situation feel temporary. I didn't want to associate the warmth and cozy atmosphere of my bedroom at home with the one in Germany. Back in February, when we first came to Essen, we bought a big three-sectional couch for our apartment. Little did I know when I selected the one I liked that I'd end up sleeping there every single night.

But let's get back to the story.

This time around, after the third chemo block, they started me on GCSF injections because I was scheduled to do a stem cell collection before block 4. Those injections basically boost your white blood cells and somewhat encourage your bone marrow to produce more stem cells that will develop into white blood cells eventually. And that was your biology lesson in thirty-five seconds.

The stem cell collection was a procedure that the doctors decided I *should* do. Basically, after boosting my immune system, they would collect most of my stem cells and preserve them by freezing them. Because of how aggressive Ewing's tumors are, sometimes chemotherapy doesn't work. In that case, after surgically removing the tumor, they put you on an extremely high-dose chemo protocol, which lasts about a week. This is called a mega block, and it is so strong, toxic, and aggressive that it completely and permanently wipes out your bone marrow and causes dozens of other short- and long-term side effects. So, the doctors collect stem cells beforehand—enabling them to restart your immune system after a mega block of chemotherapy through transplantation. In the medical world this is known as an autologous bone marrow transplant.

The whole thing scared me a lot, reminding me how much was on the line. I tried to convince myself that the chemotherapy *would* work for me and that I wouldn't need to go through a mega block.

To prepare my bone marrow for the stem cell collection, I got injections daily, which also helped prevent many of the side effects of chemotherapy. And although it caused me extreme bone pain, it took away the mucositis and the mouth sores. After a few days on the injections, I could eat and speak again. My mom got me a sprinkle donut to celebrate. Joy is in the details.

My family left for Greece that week because school was about to start, and dad had to get back to work. It was me and my mom again. This time around, however, the days passed more quickly.

During the first three weeks after the chemo block, I went to the hospital daily for blood tests and transfusions. Once my blood counts reached a satisfactory level, the doctors scheduled me for the stem cell collection. The process required placing two large IV lines in both arms. Six different doctors tried finding and accessing a vein in my arm, but after poking me nine times, they gave up. The hematologist who coordinated the stem cell collection process decided it would be best to place a central line, with two catheters, in my jugular vein in my neck.

My mom was really scared and didn't want me to have to go through more invasive procedures, so when she saw me tear up, she started crying too. It was a moment of raw vulnerability—one of the most profoundly powerful moments—a doorway to experiencing a rare side of unconditional love.

The hematologist comforted us, made us smile, and gave me a hug. That afternoon, I experienced the most profound level of authentic human connection and compassion between a doctor and a family. Love emerged from adversity. I'll never forget the comfort and courage it gave me to hug my mom when we both were crying and to see my doctor smile as she told me that I was a fighter.

The next morning, my dad flew to Germany to be there with me. Early, before the sun rose, I got prepped for surgery in the PICU.

And that leads us to now. The anesthesia begins to kick in, right around number 6. Memories of this past month flash through my eyes. And I fall asleep.

When I wake up, I am hooked to a very complex, fascinating machine, which removes all my blood and, after filtering the stems cells out, returns it back into my body. My dad is holding my hand, and my hematologist is smiling at me. I feel *okay*. Not just physically, but emotionally, I briefly feel OK. It is a strange feeling of peace amid the storm—a "sunset feeling." God is in the details. In the smile of my doctor; in the warmth of my dad's hand; and in the kind words of the lady with whom I am sharing a room, who happened to be Greek as well, light is so visible in the details.

As the apheresis machine filters out my blood, I feel as if it is also removing negative thoughts, as if it is also filtering out broken pieces of my heart and clearing out all doubt. After a few hours, the procedure is finished. I receive a blood transfusion, and the doctor cuts my stiches off and removes the central line in my neck.

For a brief moment, as the doctor pull out the catheter, I feel as if I can't breathe. It hurts a lot. I remember the suffocating feeling after that surgery in my abdomen back in winter. I remember the gut-wrenching feeling of having to say goodbye to my family in the departure hall of the airport back in February. Each memory is more suffocating than the other. Yet I have come such a long way. I feel so grateful to not be in that place anymore. I feel so grateful to be getting better. I feel so grateful for the person I am becoming, the strength I am building, the trust I am learning, and the love I am feeling.

After being discharged, we go home. I am so excited today. The dress I have ordered for graduation has finally arrived. When we get home, I rush to try it on. As I put it on, I see all the scars on my body. The skin on my fingers has peeled off. The color of my skin has changed because of the drugs. I have so many scars—one my stomach, shoulder, leg, and neck. I know I still have more to get. For a moment, I feel my heart breaking. I stare at the person in the mirror and feel broken. I'm bald, have no eyebrows and no eyelashes, and I'm pale and weak. I don't want anyone to see me like that. I have changed so much.

I look at the necklace around my neck that my sister has given me. "A fighter. *That's* who you are," I tell myself. For the longest time I have been feeling as if I'm trapped in a body that has given up. But staring at myself in the mirror, I feel, for the first time, *proud*. I feel as if I'm clothed in an armor of perseverance. My brokenness is my strength, not my weakness. I know God's hope shines right through the holes of my heart. My scars are proof of courage, proof of resilience, proof that I have been broken, yet I am *still standing*. Light reflects best on scattered glass. I put on the dress and feel my heart smile.

"I feel beautiful," I tell my mom, and tears slide down my face.

"You are more beautiful than you could even imagine," she tells me with the brightest smile.

The next morning, my mom made me apple pancakes and a fresh

orange juice to celebrate the fact that we would spend the next couple of days out of the hospital without needing to worry about chemo side effects. As I picked up my fork to eat, I noticed my arm. It was purple. It started from just above my wrist and extended all the way across my elbow. Apparently, the multiple needle pricks had caused a hematoma, which was aggravated by the fact that I had a very low platelet count. My arm felt sore and was very sensitive to touch. But, if I'm being honest, I didn't really care. So long as I was out of the hospital and able to breathe without being in excruciating pain, I had plenty of things to be grateful for and get hope from.

The next few days, I was well enough to get out of the house. My mom and I decided to go to our favorite restaurant near our neighborhood. I had become friends with one of the waiters working there. He always asked about how we were doing and cared about our family a lot. Going out was very helpful emotionally. It felt good to finally be able to get some fresh air. I didn't want to be around a lot of people, however, because I didn't like being stared at, so I never really went anywhere. This time around, however, I agreed to the idea, because I knew how much my mom needed to get out of the hospital and the house.

On April 14, I woke up to a message from Elena, a girl in my year at school:

Hey Katerina,

I hope you are doing well. I was thinking last night, and I wanted to tell you that in a way you are like Jesus. You know how God sent Jesus to go through suffering in order for people to believe in the things he taught. In general, our generation and the kids in our school really need to feel what gratitude and appreciation is all about. And I think that because God knows that you are strong enough, he trusted you with this mission, and *chose you.* And also because everyone likes you because you are nice to everyone, you are most likely to have a great impact on us all. I don't know if it makes sense, I just wanted to let you know I had this thought. Everything happens for a reason, all this has a point, believe it yourself. Just go through all this knowing that in the end everything will be okay.

Getting that message felt like a tight, warm hug. It gave me hope. It brought light. Such a significant detail, the message was a star in the darkness. I didn't understand the fullness of its purpose at the moment, but I would see it come alive in my life over the next seasons that I would walk into.

What if God was speaking to me through people in my life? What if the pain did indeed have a greater purpose? There was only one way to find out; keep fighting.

Chapter 7

Questions at Life's Exit Door

On April 25, I got admitted back to the hospital for round 4. This one brought me to my knees. It was the hardest one yet. Little did I know, it would be the most challenging, cathartic, and life-changing one as well. In the hospital, I shared a room with a newborn baby, who unfortunately cried very frequently. This made it difficult for me to sleep and, as a result, made the nausea ten times worse. The doctors gave me many different meds, but on the second day, the nausea had reached an uncontrollable stage. I tried to eat something because I kept throwing up stomach acids. My taste was so severely affected that the only thing I was able to eat was half a peach, since it was cold and sour. However, it only got worse from there. I would pass out, unconscious, and then I would wake up just to throw up and then fall back down and pass back out again. It got so bad that the doctors decided to try a new, stronger medication I hadn't taken before.

As they administered the drug, I started feeling light-headed and then very dizzy very fast and very suddenly. Breathing became more difficult, and I almost lost consciousness. My brain kept screaming, *I'm not OK, I'm not OK.* But my body wasn't moving. I knew I wanted to scream out for help, but I didn't have the physical strength to move. It was such a surreal experience. Fear took over. *What's happening to me?* I thought to myself. My blood pressure dropped super low, and I felt cold sweat rush through my body. Every breath was getting harder. And then it happened. I caught a thought.

What if this is what dying feels like? I wondered.

I panicked. I tried to fight it, but I couldn't. It all happened so fast. Fear, and shock, and agony—and death and life—all overwhelmed me for a split second, and then everything went black. All faded away.

After a while, I opened my eyes and saw my mom sitting next to my bed. I didn't know what was going on. I didn't know how long it had been. I still feared I was not going to survive. I wanted to speak to her, but I was too weak. I don't know why I didn't, but I remember feeling as if I *couldn't*. And, oh, there were so many things I wanted to tell her. If you died today, what would you last say to your family? I love you?

If I love you is important enough to be the *last* thing we would say to our loved ones *then*, then why isn't it the *first* thing we say to them *now*? If it's so important, why don't we say it more often? Why do we waste time? Why do we forget? *How* can we forget how fragile and precious life is? *How* can we forget to say these words before it's too late? *How* can we not say it enough? *Why* don't we say it enough?

Those thoughts crossed my mind in a matter of a few seconds. But those few seconds were *enough*. They reminded me of my *why*—*why* it was worth it, *why* I had to keep fighting, *why* I had to gather up my strength and call for help. I moved my eyes around and then tried to speak. I still don't remember why I felt as if I couldn't, but I do remember that it took everything in me to do so. My mom realized something was wrong and went to get a nurse. At this point, breathing had become very difficult. It turns out, I was having an adverse allergic reaction to the anti-nausea medication. A doctor rushed in, quickly discontinued that drug, and gave me some other medications. I don't remember what happened next.

After some time, I opened my eyes again. I don't know how long after. I wasn't fully aware of what was happening. When I woke up, I was alone in the room. My mom had gone to the vending machine to get a cup of coffee, and the baby I was sharing a hospital room with was in the playroom area with her dad. For a moment, I was alone. It was peaceful, quiet. The only sound that could be heard came from the infusion machine delivering the chemotherapy to my bloodstream. The atmosphere felt empty. My heart did too. But it was still beating. *It was still beating.* I took a breath. And then another one. And another one. *I was still breathing.* I started crying. A rush of gratitude flooded my veins. *I was still here.* I'd literally thought I wouldn't make it. I had been so scared. All this time, I had convinced myself that it was suffering that I was scared of, not death. But just like that, I realized that death didn't only scare me, it terrified me. But why?

A few moments later, my mom came back. The smell of coffee made everything better. It brought home to me. It gave me courage. It's all in the details. I pretended to be asleep. I didn't want my mom to see me that scared. As I lay there with my eyes closed, nauseated and dizzy from the chemotherapy, getting flashes and trembling, I started sinking in my thoughts. I decided to face that fear, to dive into it. What was I actually so afraid of when it came to death?

I wasn't scared because of what came next. Neither was it the uncertainty of what came next. My faith always helped fight these doubts and worries. It wasn't so much the process of dying either. That sure was scary, but all suffering was. There was something else about death, something that terrified every part of my soul. As I thought about it more, I realized that it wasn't death itself that scared me. It was the possibility of not having lived enough. And that realization brought me to my knees. The reason death was so scary to me was because I hadn't yet lived enough. I had regrets.

As I processed these thoughts and worries, I started asking myself some big questions—questions that were formed at life's exit door. It took facing death for me to learn how to live. As I thought about that, I started reflecting on my questions.

If this is it ... did I live? I thought to myself. *If this is it, did I live the best life I could have possibly lived? Was I happy enough? Was I grateful enough? Did I cherish every single moment I got? Did I love* unconditionally, *did I love* deeply, *did I love enough? Did a* laugh *enough? Did I* forgive *enough? Did I give back enough? Did I pray enough? Did I make other people happy? Did I lift other people up?"*

You don't get to decide how much time you get, but you do get to choose how you spend it. In reality, it's not the number of days you get but, rather, what you fit into these days that truly determines the quality of your life. What you give time to, is what you give priority to. And what you give priority to is what you give value to—what matters to you. The problem is, however, that way too many people spend way too much time on way too many things that don't matter to them—because they've never had that conversation with themselves. Most people realize what matters when it's too late for it to matter. For some that's after they've lived a long life and watched their grandkids grow. For others that's after they've settled down and started a family. For me, it was before I even got to graduate high school. It was that night, during chemo 4.

That night was one of the toughest. I was mentally exhausted. Nothing could help with the side effects. My dad sat by my bed and smiled at me.

"Two more days, and this block is done," he told me and held onto my hand.

I tried to sit up to talk to him. But I couldn't. I was too weak. My lips were dry. I hadn't drunk any water in days. My face was swollen. My eyes were red and puffy. I tried to lift my head up, but I didn't have the energy to. My dad helped me sit up. I leaned my head against his shoulder.

As I stayed there, lifeless, I started thinking. Where were my feelings? I felt numb. Where was the old me? I was so tired of fighting. I didn't think I could take this any longer. This was killing me. Where had my smile gone? I hadn't smiled in so long. Where was the girl I used to know, the girl who made everyone smile, who played sports, took photos of sunsets, and helped everyone with homework? She was gone—buried under disease, under emotional exhaustion and physical pain. I wanted to feel happy again. I wanted to wake up to a day without chemo, without hurt. I felt like life was just moving on without me. I felt isolated. Waves were crushing me, but I just watched them. Underwater and suffocating, I was running out of hope and out of the will to wake up the next day. What for? More tears? More pain? More acting stronger than I felt? Living had become so difficult that sometimes I wondered if it was all worth it.

Chemo 4 was a roller coaster. I went from crying happy tears because I was still alive to crying desperate tears because I couldn't bear the weight of the pain that being alive came with. I lay in tears in bed all night. I didn't want to go through these things again. I was ready to let go.

God, I'm hurting. I'm broken. I can't grab a hold on hope. I'm tired. I stare at the walls around me, lifeless. I feel trapped. I know I promised to trust You, but God, it gets harder. Every. Single. Day. I don't know how much longer I can handle this. Take away the pain, please. It's too much. It's too heavy. I can't do this anymore. Can't you hear me? I cry out to You, but the pain only gets worse. Don't You see my tears? Don't You see my pain? Where are You? How much longer do I have to hold on for? How much more can I endure?

Just after I'd prayed these words, my mom came in the room; gave me a kiss on my hairless head; held my pale, skinny hand; and fixed my blanket so that it fully covered me and kept me warm. And then it *really* hit me. That was the proof I was looking for—the proof that I *couldn't* let go and *couldn't* give up. Not yet.

Five more minutes, I told myself. *Just get through another five minutes. You can do it. You can be brave for five more minutes.*

And so I did. I got through block 4, five minutes at a time. Five minutes of patience, endurance, and perseverance—every five minutes. Out of love.

The next morning, I woke up and felt a strange sense of peace. It was like the calm after a storm, the rainbow after rain, a "sunset feeling." As I was casually checking my phone, I stumbled upon a song I hadn't heard before. At some point, the lyrics of "Rescue" by Lauren Daigle said, "I hear you whisper you have nothing left. I will rescue you."

I teared up. Every hopeless thought dissipated, and all the broken pieces of my heart were put back together. I felt God speaking to me through that song, through those lyrics. He heard the prayers I sometimes didn't have the strength to pray—that came in the form of tears. When I was afraid, God was right there with me. And He's there with you.

Many times, circumstances don't change so that *you* can first change *in them*. Patience helps you grow amid difficulties. God is using *opposition* to make you grow. Challenges you face develop your determination, courage, and endurance. When opposition comes through the door, opportunity always comes with it.

Let's look at rubber balls. I'm sure you've all played with them as kids. Rubber balls are also called bouncy balls because they're designed to bounce back. That's their purpose—to bounce back after they've been thrown to the ground. As a believer, I think we're equipped with this ability—to be bouncy balls. We face challenges, and we bounce back; we come back stronger. The most meaningful part of the analogy is that, in order to fulfill its purpose and be used right, a bouncy ball must be thrown down at a rocky surface; it has to hit a hard surface. It's through hard surfaces, so to speak, that it bounces back higher than where it even started from. Likewise, only if the challenge is big enough, the obstacle strong enough, and the darkness dark enough can we bounce back, stronger and taller.

Light operates best in darkness. Only in the darkest skies do stars shine their brightest. And only in the most difficult times can our hope shine, reflecting our faith and revealing our light. It has to be dark enough for the stars to show. It has to be dark enough for God's light to shine through. I had to be surrounded by fear to discover true hope. I had to be surrounded by immense pain to feel unconditional love. I had to feel so helpless so I could fully and truly place my trust in God.

It *first* gets dark; *first* the sun sets, and *then* the stars appear. And those stars are the very thing that keep you company and get you through the night. Those stars are the very thing that allow you to see another dawn, another sunrise. And what's amazing is that you can only actually appreciate that sunrise after a long, dark night. God promised that the joy that's coming cannot be compared to the pain that's in the present. But you wouldn't be able to appreciate and see that joy without the pain.

It would be the very struggles, fears, and sufferings that would give purpose to my life and allow me to bounce back. The harder the floor is, the harder we're pushed down, the higher we rise, the higher we bounce back. The more difficult the challenge, the more serious the sickness, and the more hurtful the pain, the more love can be felt, the more raw and truthful hope can be discovered, the more deep and unconditional trust can be placed, and the brighter the stars can shine.

A few days later, I was discharged. I went home exhausted—and yet deeply hopeful. During my routine post-chemo follow-up with my oncologist, she said it was time to finally meet the surgeon who would do the tumor resection operation in the summer. She arranged an appointment that week.

On the day of the appointment, we arrived at the hospital very early. This is significant. Pay attention to the details of this part of the story. They seem insignificant, but they are filled with purpose that would soon be made visible.

Having arrived early, we were told to sit in the waiting room (something we'd done and would do, in both actual and metaphorical waiting rooms, many times). We were early, so we had to wait. We had to wait until it was *the right time.*

After a few hours, a nurse called us into room 2. Prof. D introduced me to my surgeon, Prof. H. The first thing I noticed about him was his smile. It was a smile of hope. Prof. H had been working in Münster for the longest time but had just transferred to Essen only a month before. That smile of hope when I first saw him was one of those details that you can find God in. We sat down and discussed the surgery options—amputation, endoprosthesis, or intensive radiation and no surgery.

Prof. D shared with me a story of a patient my age who chose the amputation because he wanted to become a professional athlete and then ended up winning in the Paralympics. Both doctors advised me, however, to go with the limb salvage surgery, remove the tumor, and replace the bone with an endoprosthesis. At the same time, Prof. D advised me against going down the route of radiation because not removing the tumor had a very high risk of relapse, especially with this type of cancer. She said that, usually, patients with Ewing sarcomas present lung metastasis as a relapse. My mom and I had already decided, way before even being presented with our options and way before the chemo even started; I was doing the limb salvage surgery. I wanted to avoid losing my leg if it were possible, and I also didn't want to leave the tumor inside.

The doctors explained that that surgery was the riskiest option, but they both agreed it was the best one for my case, considering quality of life expectations and my prognosis of course. Prof. H asked me to do a high-resolution MRI after block 5 and then explained the process of the operation. We then discussed some questions I had regarding recovery from such a surgery.

After that meeting, the doctors shook my hand, and Prof. H told me, "We got this. We'll do this."

"Yeah, of course we'll do this. She's very strong," Prof. D added and smiled.

Ah, how much courage these words gave me. They were the light of hope that I needed after that traumatizing experience during block 4. I was finally starting to see the finish line for the VIDE chemo blocks. I couldn't wait for the day I would be done with them. I often thought I would never make it to that day. But words and smiles like these gave me back the hope that suffering had stolen. All in the details.

A couple of days later, I started developing severe side effects and ended up getting admitted back to the hospital with an extremely high fever. The oncology ward was full, so I was admitted to the cardiology floor instead, before being moved to the nephrology ward that same night.

I shared a room with a one-year-old boy who was on dialysis and waiting for a kidney transplant. The room we were in was a lot nicer. It had its own bathroom and even a balcony with a view of the hospital campus. At first, I was very bitter about being back in the hospital. I didn't understand why this was happening. My birthday was coming up that week, and I had prayed and wished I'd spend it at home.

That day, one of my mom's friends came to Germany to visit. She was so nice and took care of me in the hospital while my mom drove home to take a shower. All the machines I was hooked to were transportable, so after removing them from the medicine pole, we went outside. And Georgia, my mom's friend, took me around the hospital campus for a stroll in my wheelchair. The fresh air and the sun gave me a warm hug of comfort and took away my bitterness. We sat at a bench outside the cardiology clinic and had a talk. We talked about the power of courage and what it meant to have hope. I really needed to let these thoughts out. When we got back to the room, we decided to sit outside on the balcony. As I felt the morning breeze against my face, I was thankful for the small details in my life.

I realized that, before getting sick, I was only thanking God when He gave me what I asked for. I was thanking God only for His provision, only for what I could see, for what I had. Thanking God for what He had given me was not an expression of *deep* gratitude. It was *superficial* gratitude. Battling cancer, facing death, and experiencing desperation and hopelessness, I had learned to have deep gratitude. Deep gratitude taught me to thank God "even though." Even though I felt alone, and my heart was heavy and broken by struggle and desperation, I was grateful. Even though I cried myself to sleep every night and closed my eyes scared that I wouldn't open them again, I was grateful. Even though getting out of bed required so much courage because I just couldn't take it any longer, *I was grateful.* Despite the pain, I *chose* to be thankful. I *chose* to be at peace. I *chose* gratitude.

Superficial gratitude means being thankful for what you can *see.* Authentic gratitude means being thankful and trusting God with what you *cannot.* Superficial gratitude is about thanking God when you can see evidence of His presence. Authentic gratitude, however, trusts and recognizes His presence *in the presence* of pain, hurt, and adversity. I was still grateful for the provision, for what I had, for the breath in my lungs. But as I sat at that big table that morning, I learned to sit with struggle and opposition all around me, so to speak. I had a seat at that table, but so did fear, so did insecurity, so did hopelessness, and so did depression. But *even though* they had seats too, I *chose* to sit with them. If I could be grateful for the presence of hope in the absence of my understanding and comfort, if I chose to trust amid fear and pain and be thankful for what I had faith over, I could unlock courage and resilience I didn't know was possible. I could be at peace. I could be joyful. And I could grow, evolve, and mature *using* what was meant to take me down.

The next few days, I got gradually worse, and the pain caused by the side effects could not be managed. I was on high-dose antibiotics and morphine for the mucositis. I hadn't eaten anything in more than a week, so I was given IV nutrition as well. Constipation, bone pain, numbness, and swelling of my feet were a few of the side effects I was dealing with. I couldn't even lift a bottle of water by myself. It was too heavy. I needed help to move, to get changed, and to go to the bathroom. I even needed help with brushing my teeth. My immune system was completely wiped out by the chemo, and the blood tests were more discouraging day by day. The antibiotics had helped me a lot and had reduced my fever, but my bone marrow had not produced any new cells to fight off the infection.

After a few days, the doctors decided to start me on GCSF injections again. The pain that these injections caused was terrible. But it was *through* that pain that they worked. The pain was a good sign; it meant stem cells were being produced. It was uncomfortable, but it was good. This realization got me thinking that night.

Comfort has a specific function, but sometimes it becomes dysfunctional. We are all guilty of choosing what is comfortable—comfort foods, comfort friends, comfort habits—things that are good *to* us but not good *for* us. A lot of times, however, what offers a sense of comfort and control over change becomes what prevents us from achieving our goals. Discomfort is where you learn to be brave. Just like Dr. Vasilis had told me, only in the broken can you really *choose brave.*

A few days later, another one of my mom's friends flew to Essen to visit. She was so joyful and energetic that it really helped me crack a smile or two and forget about what I was going through. We made plans for a welcome home sushi party and browsed the web for shoes for my graduation in June. My birthday was in two days. I knew my dad and my sister were visiting, and that was all I looked forward to.

That night I went to bed early. A few moments later, however, a voice woke me up. Still half-asleep, I opened my eyes. I was expecting to see my mom or a nurse who'd come to check my blood pressure or a doctor checking up on my pain levels. But that wasn't the case. I opened my eyes and saw my sister across my hospital bed with a huge smile on her face. A few seconds later, I saw my friend Aimiliana too. They both rushed and hugged me. I was shocked, in disbelief. Seeing the smiles on their faces made up for every night I had spent in the hospital that week.

"Surprise," they both said and laughed.

It was in that very moment that a strange feeling rushed through my body. It was love mixed with joy and nostalgia—a perfect mix of emotions for a birthday eve. I'd been so sad just moments before about being in the hospital, and yet in just a split second, all that had been replaced by joy and love.

If you think about it, you'll see that's a testament of a unique and special characteristic emotions possess; they are temporary. Happiness, sadness, joy, and desperation are all tidal. They come, and they go, just like waves. Sometimes the sea is calm, and there aren't any waves. We think numbing ourselves from emotions will solve our underlying problems. But here's the thing; if you don't know how to swim, you'll drown with or without waves. If we can't process and cope with our emotions, if we are numb to pain, joy, sorrow, and happiness, we will not manage to stay above water, whether life is like a calm sea or a raging storm. Emotions are tidal, temporary. But one's ability to swim is constant. What is constant amid these waves, is you—the person the waves shape you into. If you really think about it, waves can teach you how to swim. You don't know how courageous you are until holding on to courage is your only choice. In a storm like cancer, you cannot possibly be prepared enough to swim, to stay above water, to cope. But it's those waves themselves, those very storms, that teach you *how* to swim. So, if that's the case, doesn't that give a purpose to the waves?

A lot of people, me included, ask, "Why me?" "Why did this happen to me?" But that's the wrong question. Oftentimes, we cannot swim because we're too busy wondering why we fell in the water in the first place. Wrong questions push you deeper into the sea, instead of lifting you up. "Why me?" is a wrong question. "What is this trying to teach me?" is the right one. "How is this trying to change me?" is the right one. "What swimming skills does this storm offer me?" Asking the wrong questions is what often makes people lose hope, give up, and surrender to their suffering.

Surrendering itself is not a wrong thing to do. But it's what you surrender *to* that defines whether it's helping you swim. Surrendering means being brave enough to be vulnerable. It means being strong amid sorrow. Surrendering. Strength. Sorrow. What a powerful alliteration. It proves the significance of giving up control. Once you do that, you give up worrying and losing sleep over what you *cannot* control. Finding the strength and courage to let go of your need to control the outcome is an act of bravery and an example of choosing to rest.

Resting is very significant. It means recharging. Resting, however, also means risking, because once you give up control, you give up your ability, or perceived ability, to change the situation. It's the same thing with hope. Surrendering means resting, and resting means trusting. Trust is an act of bravery itself. Here's the part where people get confused. Faith is the *substance* of trust, its *foundation*. I trusted that things would be okay *because* I chose to have faith over my fears.

That night showed me firsthand how temporary emotions are—how fragile, precious, and tidal they are. They come and go, just like that. In the blink of an eye, they could disappear or overwhelm you. What matters is how you swim in them—how you cope and the attitude you maintain while swimming. An attitude of hope and trust, one of rest and risk, brings out the fight in you, the courage locked in your heart, and the strength you didn't know you had. It's an attitude that teaches you how to swim in uncharted waters, in raging storms, and in deep oceans. And it's an attitude I chose to have that night.

Hope wouldn't always come easy. Trust sometimes would be a painful process of letting go. But they would always be worth it. After the storm, oh how greatly can you swim. After the waves go and the storm passes, the swimming techniques they taught you are yours; the person they shaped you into *stays*. Because *you* are the only thing *constant* in what you go through.

The next morning was our birthday. I woke up sad that I would spend this day in the hospital but, at the same time, so incredibly grateful that I got to turn fifteen, that I was still alive, that I was getting better, and that I could spend the day with family. The nurses knew it was my birthday, and they put up balloons and birthday wishes on the door and in the room. It made me happy. I felt loved. I felt surrounded by people who cared enough to make me smile. And I was so grateful for that.

The night before, my dad stayed over at the hospital with me. I woke up to a nurse waiting to measure my blood pressure and temperature. She wished me a happy birthday and smiled at me. It was a smile of hope, I could tell. My heart felt full. My dad helped me get to the bathroom and brush my teeth. He and I cut a deal to tell my mom certain side effects had subsided, even though they hadn't, because the pain from the medications they were giving me for them was way worse. We agreed to spend my birthday without these meds and then start taking them again the day after. Small details like that made me smile.

After brushing my teeth, I looked at the mirror. I couldn't help but remember last year on my birthday doing the same thing. Every year, I take a mirror photo on my birthday and compare how much I'd grown. This year I didn't want to do that. I had changed so much in a year. I remembered doing my hair before school last year and dancing in the mirror to my favorite songs. Now, I couldn't even stand up by myself. I even needed help to sit up. I was completely reliant on other people. At some point, I couldn't even lift a fork to eat.

But relying on others is an expression of vulnerability, which reveals and projects a profoundly deep love and compassion that a family shares. Weakness is strength because it is the only thing able to unlock and reveal hidden, powerful emotions such as love and hope that are locked in people's hearts. This is why love is felt the deepest when pain gets the strongest—yet another detail that gives pain a purpose. In reality, it's like the black color that paints the canvas of the sky, revealing all the shining stars, found in the details. Love and hope and trust and compassion are the very stars that give purpose to the darkness. And they prove that dark can be beautiful or can at least reveal the beautiful. But if you think about it, you'll see that the ability of a certain thing to show what is beautiful makes the thing itself beautiful.

A couple of hours, a blood draw, and a visit from the doctors later, my sister, my mom, her friend, and Aimiliana arrived at the hospital. That day was a day of celebration, a day of joy.

At around 11:00 a.m., my friend Ourania texted me a link and told me to open it. I clicked on the link, and suddenly, a video appeared. My whole class had made a video for me, with photos and segments where each of my friends wished me a happy birthday and told me something they wanted me to know. I felt so loved. That's an understatement. It was a profound, deep love—a love not bound by pain, distance, or any other circumstance. It was a love fueled by pure compassion and human connection. It was a feeling of support, as if for a moment I wasn't carrying the burden of cancer alone. That video made me cry. I don't even know what I was crying for. It was yet another mix of emotions—nostalgia for what was, grief for what could have been, love in spite of what was, and gratitude for what would be.

Seeing these photos of me back then broke my heart in thousands of pieces. The me in those photos had something the current me didn't—an innocent joy. But the me then didn't have some really important things the me now had, including gratitude, resilience, and courage. Better might feel backward. What looks like suffering and pain can be, instead, a portal to a profound change for the better. This was me getting better. This was that change. This was that portal of growth. I just wish it *felt* more like growth sometimes.

As I was watching the video, my friends from school FaceTimed me. Everyone was there, and they were all excited to see me. This was the first time some of them were seeing me like this—bald, pale, weak, sick. I was scared to FaceTime them. But love won over that fear. As we were talking, a smile formed on my face. It was such a gift to remember what it felt like to be in class, joke with friends, see teachers, have homework, and worry about tests. On some bad days, I still feared I would never get the chance to do that again, but that day wasn't one of them. That day, my hope was greater than my doubt. That simple FaceTime call with my friends and one teacher was enough to restore my goal and to refuel my determination to get better.

After our call, I fell asleep because my body was too weak, and I'd exceeded my usual time sitting up. I hated that my body limited me even on my birthday, but I knew I needed the rest to get better. When I woke up, my mom had brought us two cakes, so colorful and nice. My sister sat next to me in my bed, and we placed the cakes in front of us. Our family, my mom's friend, Aimiliana, and some nurses all sang the happy birthday song to us, and then we blew out the candles.

Before blowing mine, I paused for a moment. I wanted to make a wish before doing so, and I wanted that wish to be meaningful. I thought of the things I was praying about. But that day, I decided to wish for something birthday related. I doubted whether I would get to celebrate another birthday, so I wanted to make that potentially last birthday wish worth it. So, as I blew out my candle, I wished to get to do that again; to have another birthday. That was my wish.

My mom and her friend took a few photos for us, so that we'd always remember this memory. For one photo, I rested my head on Ami's shoulder and held her hand. It might have been just for a photo, but in that moment as I placed my head on her shoulder, I felt as if I was placing my struggles, my pain, and my fears on her. It felt as if I was finding shelter in her shoulder, as if she was carrying my suffering with me, even for just a moment.

Moments like this is what life is all about. Moments where what cannot be seen takes over what is visible shape our lives and us. Things that are eternal and cannot be seen with our physical eyes can be found in moments when we choose to see with the eyes of our hearts and to use love and hope and kindness as a compass for our behavior and attitude amid a dark night. When we find the stars hidden in the details of darkness, we can embody and reflect their light, shining as we get through the night. All we are is light in the darkness. Think about that for a second. Then keep reading.

My sister, Aimiliana, and I spent the evening together and shared a laugh. We played cards and spent all afternoon talking and catching up.

Later that day, we ordered food and had dinner together in the hospital. My mom told me that, while I was asleep, one of my teachers had called to wish me a happy birthday. I was so thankful for little things like that.

That night as I went to bed, I reflected on the day. It had started as another day in the hospital, with very high pain levels and discouraging test results. And yet it had turned into an amazing day that I'd never forget. It had been a day full of laughter, joy, love, and a lot of hope.

Hope is not in a prescription. It's not in an IV. It's not in a number, or a report. Instead, hope shapes laughter. It sparkles in tears. To find hope, you need to dream of tomorrow, push past impossible, try a new way, question the answer, and believe in something greater. Hope is in a smile, a hug, a thought, a belief, a dream. Hope is in the details, in the insignificant. But that's the thing about insignificance; it's relative, not intrinsic. God's greatest miracles often come from what people name insignificant sources. That's why the world cannot define significance. Status and financial circumstance are assigned significance by people, but they don't intrinsically have any value. We get caught up in insignificant things and miss significant details. Hope is found in those small yet powerful details that we often deem insignificant. This is why people can't find it easily. They don't know where to look for it. It's right in front of them but not in the form they expected it to be in. This realization is profound. If you think about it, you'll see that sometimes reality and our interpretation of reality aren't in sync. This happens because we get caught up in the daily routine, and we miss the big picture. As a result, we reach a point where we call a miracle "insignificant," and we take it for granted.

After Aimiliana and my sister left, I went back to bed. It was going to be a good week.

The next day, my aunt and my friend Miltiadis arrived in Essen. My mom went to the airport to pick them up. I felt so happy when they entered the room. Milti and I had been best friends for many years, and he was always able to make me laugh with his random jokes and funny personality. We spent that day catching up. He gave me gifts and cards from many people at school. I was emotional, and my heart was teeming with love and gratitude. Love truly is the greatest force in the world. It can't be touched by pain, it can't be shaken by disease, and it certainly doesn't end in death. It's the single thing that beats time, beats sickness, and beats mortality. It's the foundation of life, of grace, and of human connection. That's also where God is the most visible—in the sole fact that the deepest, purest, most authentic and genuine expression of love exists in moments of hurt and pain, suffering, and brokenness.

This was my first time seeing Milti in five months, so, naturally, we had a lot to catch up on. He got a chair and sat by my hospital bed, and we talked for hours. Actually, *he* talked mostly; the mucositis and mouth sores made speaking extremely painful for me. So, *he* did the talking, and *I* did the listening. As he was telling me about funny incidents at school, I felt for a moment as if I were there, with all my friends.

During that period of my life, studying and doing schoolwork was clearly off the table. I had no physical strength to sit at a desk and do homework, and at the same time, I didn't have the emotional strength to do it. There were days I doubted I would ever make it back to school again, days I went to bed scared I might not wake up the next morning. On these days, catching up on school just didn't seem important. It seemed a bit pointless. Therefore, I really distanced and felt detached from this part of my life. I had forgotten what it felt like to stay up studying for an important test or to joke with your friends in class about something funny a teacher said. Now, I was staying up because the pain.

When Milti came to Germany, he managed to bring school to me. He managed to remind me what it felt like to sit in that class. And he made me feel as if I hadn't ever left.

After catching up, we decided to play cards. My aunt, Milti, and I sat there on my bed and played all kind of card games for hours. At night, my aunt and Milti went back home, and my mom stayed in the hospital with me. The next day was Saturday, May 12, Eurovision Day. Eurovision is this annual European song contest that Milti and I always get excited about. This was why he'd visited me on these days in the first place. We were planning to cook dinner together and then watch the Eurovision contest.

That Friday morning, I woke up determined to be discharged. Yet when an oncologist came to see me, she told me that, unless my white blood cells exceeded 1,000, I would not be able to be leave the hospital. I hadn't had a fever for the past five days, but the mucositis was persistent, and so were the other infections I had. To be discharged, I also needed to be weaned off the morphine and other medications completely.

At around 11:00 a.m., my aunt and Milti came to the hospital. They had huge smiles on their faces and radiated joy. Noticing these little joyful moments, observing the expression of authentic happiness amid deep pain was such a motivating force for me. It was a source of hope and a reason for perseverance.

We all sat together and talked. The little baby boy I was sharing a room with was such a funny, mighty warrior. Milti talked to him and played with him, and we both laughed at his parenting skills. After some time, we all sat outside and enjoyed the warm spring weather while plotting ways to be discharged and planning our Eurovision watch party. The love, family bond, and friendship that brought us all around that table that day was stronger than the pain, and that's why it was able to overcome the sadness the pain brought and replace it with huge smiles across all our faces and laughs that were heard by everyone in that hospital ward.

The next day was pretty much the same. Milti came over to the hospital and we spent the morning together. After a couple of hours, we decided to get some food. My mom went to the nurses' station and asked for the delivery menus. The nurses were awesome, and they gave her at least ten different restaurant menus. Luis's dad, with whom we were sharing the hospital room, suggested that we get food from an Italian place around the corner because, according to him, it had "the best pasta in Essen."

We decided to take his advice and ordered from that place. It's not that it matters what kind of lunch we had, but *having* that lunch was one of those details, those little things you can think back on, recalling the joy that was felt around that table. We went to the balcony of the hospital ward and sat at a white plastic table . As we enjoyed our lunch, talking and laughing, the warmth of the sun touched my skin. It felt like a warm hug of hope, joy, and gratitude—like a hug from God. It was a moment of peace amid chaos and pain, a detail of gratitude. For just that moment, life was good. It was simple. We were just a family enjoying lunch on a sunny day, laughing around a table, and planning our Eurovision night. The hospital setting didn't matter. The multiple IV lines and catheters didn't matter. The fear and pain didn't hold any value. In that moment, all that mattered was that moment. The love, joy, hope, comfort, and peace of that one single moment were all there was. Simplicity breathes gratitude. And it's all found in the details.

A couple of hours later, at around 6:30 p.m., the ward oncologist came to see me. She was the one who I'd talked to about being discharged. She handed us a printed copy of my test results and, with a smile on her face told me, "The blood tests are very encouraging."

I took a look at the numbers. My white blood cells were at 1.12. This means they were over a thousand, at 1,120. Just two days ago, they were struggling to stay at 400. *I* didn't even believe it at first. Milti started laughing. The doctor gave us the discharge papers and told us that, within the next two hours, I would be able to be go home. I had been completely off the morphine since that morning, but I still needed to be given one last dose of antibiotics. Once that infusion was over, my mom packed our hospital bag, and we prepared to leave.

Before we left the room, Luis's dad held my hand and said, "You are very strong—so strong. Keep going. Keep fighting. Everything will be okay."

"You too," I replied. "Luis will get through this. I wish you, from the bottom of my heart, all the best."

"All the best for you too," he replied. "All the best."

That interaction, that goodbye conversation was such a profound expression of compassion and empathy. In hospital rooms, complete strangers who will probably never even see each other again express and project deep compassion, deep love, and deep care for each other. It's incredible how tough times can bring out the best in people. Hope is in the details. *Kindness* is in the details.

Once we got home, I quickly changed into fresh clothes and switched on the TV to connect to the live broadcast of the Eurovision song contest. It started just a few minutes after we got home. Perfect timing. My mom went to that restaurant near our house and got us pizzas.

Milti and I spent the night watching the contest and rating the songs on a piece of paper with a grading layout that I had designed a few weeks ago. I love being extra and celebrating little things like that. We spent the next couple of hours laughing, eating pizzas, and signing at the top of our lungs. It was such a special night—memories I'll treasure forever.

A day later, on the thirteenth, my aunt and Milti left for Greece. I was sad about them leaving and about the fact that I had chemo in a few days, but I was also excited because I knew that, after block 5, I would finally go back home—even just for a few days. I couldn't even believe it.

On Monday, the fourteenth, I saw an email from Mr. A, my French teacher at school. He was writing to wish me a happy birthday. Being in the hospital, I hadn't gotten a chance to check my emails. I replied:

> I'm sorry for taking so much time to write back. I was in the hospital all last week. On Friday I'm going back for chemo block 5. I was supposed to have it on Wednesday, but I was too sick, and the doctors decided it would be better to wait. On the first week of June, we're flying to Greece. I can't wait. These will be the best days of all of 2018. I'm sure of it. I wish this week would never end, and I could stay in Athens forever. I'm almost at the halfway point of my treatments. There are so many times that I just can't take it any longer, but I always make it because I hold onto one thought. I think of that one day, that I'll wake up, get ready, and go to school and be healthy. When I get better, nothing will be able to make me sad. Every day will be so precious. I hope you're doing well. I am looking forward to seeing you soon.

That's what I wrote back. Little did I know how meaningful that one simple email would turn out to be.

During the days before chemo, I was able to contact a few teachers who kindly sent me some exercises I could work on to catch up with the rest of the class. The idea of going back home motivated me to want to study again.

On May 17, I sent an email to my literature teacher, Mrs. B, and submitted an assignment. The next day, she called me to tell me how impressed she was with my work and how proud she was of me. That two-minute phone call motivated me so much. I felt grateful to have people in my life who believed in me, for my family and friends and all the people who God had placed in my life during that season.

God gave me healing in so many different forms, for so many different things.

I just had to *notice.*

Chapter 8

Discouraged Determination

These past few days had filled me up with so much determination. I was ready to conquer block 5. My grandma flew to Essen to be with me during this round of chemotherapy. On Friday, May 18, I was admitted back into the hospital. Round 5 was much more tolerable than round 4. No near-death experiences this time.

I was staying in a room with another girl around my age who also had Ewing's. She was from the United Kingdom and had come to Essen just for a couple of weeks for radiation therapy. Her whole family was with her. I was happy for her, but it also made me really miss *my* family and made me think about how much easier it would have been for me, psychologically, had we stayed in Greece for treatment. This girl had already finished with her VIDE chemo blocks and was receiving the second round of chemo of the second phase of the protocol. I didn't really talk with her that much, but I did hear something her mum told mine.

"After VIDE, life gets a little better. It all gets a little better."

That sentence gave me so much hope in that moment. It filled me up with strength to endure and courage to hold on. It gave meaning and context to patience, suffering, and pain. Life would get better. It would—even if I didn't believe it and even if didn't see how. Even if it all felt permanent, it wasn't. It would get better. I found it so incredible how *her* fight gave *me* so much hope. The power of an example is greater than the power of an explanation.

That's a testament to the fact that there's a purpose behind everything.

It proves that your wounds can be somebody else's Band-Aid. Your source of pain can be someone else's source of hope. Your story can be the only thing that lifts someone up and pulls them out of the pit of their depression, hurt, and struggle. By my stripes, someone else's heart could be healed. By my tears, someone else could understand hope. By my testimony, someone else could get to know God's heart. That's the power of suffering, the power of a story.

When you are going through adversity, there's somebody who's going through something who will need what you will have after you get through what you're going through. Somebody needs *your* story. Somebody needs *your* pain, *your* hurt. If you see a flower blossom amid a storm—if you see someone find meaning in hopelessness and purpose behind pain, doing the impossible, and getting through the unbearable—that's enough for you to believe, find hope, and get strength. How what's happening to you can be used to help other people and help you unlock your purpose, reveals *its* purpose. That's why, in order to understand why certain things happen, you first have to go through them and see how you can use them and transform them.

At the end of block 5, as I was about to be discharged, a young hospital volunteer came in my room and asked me if I wanted to play some games. She and I had become great friends over the last couple of months. We would play with rackets and plastic balls all the time during the first two chemo blocks. She spoke English fluently, so I could really connect with her, open up to her, and share memories of my life with her. She knew my favorite sports, my goals, and my plans. This time around, I was feeling weak and couldn't even get up to play. On some good days, she helped me work out and do exercises for my arms and legs. This time, however, chemo had taken away that energy from me. So, I just sat in my wheelchair, and we played some volleyball. She told me she had personally asked Prof. D about skiing, and she had told her that, with the right rehabilitation, I would be able to ski again after my big surgery in the summer. I was so moved. She knew how much I worried about the things the surgery would limit me from doing, and that's why she wanted to comfort me. I felt loved and cared for. After some time, the doctors gave us the discharge papers, and we left the hospital. I was weak physically, but strong emotionally. I knew that, in three weeks, I was going home, and the mere thought of that helped me persevere.

As soon as we arrived at the apartment, my mom helped me get changed and lie on the couch. I put my headphones on and closed my eyes tightly. I started listening to exciting songs and tried to picture what it would feel like when I went back home to Greece. I made up scenarios and bucket lists in my mind. Sleeping in my own bed and going back to school were at the top of that list. A few days later, I started feeling a little bit better. I normally had zero motivation to even get out of bed that soon after chemo. This time, however, I had much to look forward to. I got up and sat in my desk. My parents had contacted the school and let them know I was coming home for the end of the year exams and the graduation. Some teachers had sent us out some instructions and helpful material to help me study for the finals.

I was ecstatic. I woke up every day with an enthusiastic and hopeful attitude. I had forgotten what it felt like to have something to wake up to. Being in so much pain both physically and mentally had stolen my day-to-day joy. I would stare at empty walls and wonder whether getting up every day was worth it. But now, just the thought of going back to school, seeing my family and friends, and waking up in my own bed made me ecstatic about life.

That morning, I printed out a calendar for the month of May. I planned out what I was going to study on which day, and I also printed out all the material my teachers had sent me. I spent a couple of hours making notes, trying to catch up, and studying. The drugs had affected my ability to concentrate and my overall energy. So as a result, I struggled to keep my focus and got very dizzy after just a short amount of time studying. I took several nap breaks, and after few studying sessions, I called it a day. I went to sleep that night in disbelief. I couldn't believe this was actually happening. I was so grateful.

The next day, I started experiencing some serious side effects from the treatment. I was weak and couldn't study that much. When we got to the hospital for my routine follow-up blood draws, the doctor noticed my white blood cells and platelets had dropped much lower than expected.

"I'll still be able to make it home right?" I asked her, full of worry.

"We don't know for sure, Katerina. I am so sorry," the clinic oncologist told me. "It's too risky. You can't travel with such low counts."

"But what if they go up?" I said, not losing hope.

"I don't think there's enough time. If you develop an infection, you'll need antibiotics for at least ten days. I'm really sorry."

My heart broke into a million pieces. My stomach dropped. The air was removed from my lungs. As soon as we left the room, I broke down crying. We stopped in the waiting room, and my mom hugged me tightly.

"We can't risk it, you know that sweetheart," my mom told me, trying to comfort me.

The doctor saw me crying and came next to me. She knelt and held my hand. "There's still a chance. If your white blood cells suddenly go up, we can discuss it again. If you don't get an infection, it *could* be possible. We just want to protect you," she told me and gave me a hug.

I knew it was better for me to not go. I knew I had to be very careful, I knew I couldn't afford to delay the treatment any longer than we would already—were I to go. I also knew that if I got an infection with this compromised of an immune system, I would not survive. But going home was all I wanted, all I'd prayed for, and all I'd hoped for. It was all I needed—the only goal that got me out of bed in the morning and the only thought that gave me courage at night. It was the only thing that made me smile these days, that was able to make me feel like me again, and that would give me back my life, even if just for a little while.

On the ride home, I leaned my head against the car window and cried. I remembered when I'd lean my head against the window on our way to school because of how tired I was from staying up all night studying. Now, I was leaning my head against the window because of how tired I was of being hurt, disappointed, and in pain and how tired I was of constantly fighting. For what? More disappointment? More pain?

I lay in the couch that night to sleep but couldn't. My heart was heavy. What would I wake up to the next day? What would I have to look forward to? My eyes were filled with tears. My mind was filled with clouds of darkness and depression. I was numb again. I had gotten so used to pain and disappointment. I closed my eyes and tried to pray. I didn't know what to say to God. I didn't know how I felt. I just knew I needed a miracle.

Oh, God, I said and broke down. I didn't even have the strength to pray. But God hears those prayers too, the ones we don't have the courage to pray, the ones that flood our eyes and stream down our face like raindrops on a cold winter night.

I need you. Now more than ever. I'm not going to make it myself. Hope is dying inside me. Can't you hear me cry, God? I feel so cold. All odds are against me, the walls are caving in, and I'm sinking. God don't let me drown. Don't let cancer win. I'm on my knees. I can't fight this alone.

I need a miracle. It's not just about going home. I'm running out of hope. I'm running out of courage, strength, and life. I feel more broken day after day. I need to remember, God. I just need to remember that life can get better—that it will get better. Because I'm running out of oxygen. I'm drowning, and I've been trying so hard to fight it and swim, but I'm so tired that I don't know if trying to stay above water is worth it any more. I need to go home to remember and to believe again.

Those few days that I was studying and preparing for my exams I felt alive again. For the past six months, I've felt dead in a breathing, working body. But for the first time these days, I felt alive again, God. I am on my knees, as vulnerable as I've ever been. Please defy the odds, surprise the doctors, and perform a miracle. But not my will but yours be done. I will try to trust you.

Tears streamed down my face uncontrollably. I'll never forget how hurt I felt during that prayer. But I'll also never ever forget how close to God I felt. I knew in that moment that I would see a miracle—through faith. Maybe it wouldn't be the one I was praying for, but healing isn't always what you picture.

But unfortunately, it only got worse from there.

About three days later, I started running a fever. There it was—infection. Late at night, I was admitted to the hospital. My white blood cells weren't even detectable anymore. I literally had zero. I was admitted to the isolation ward and immediately started on extremely high-dose antibiotics. The pain I was experiencing was so bad that even the morphine couldn't help. I fell apart that night. I believed in my heart that God would bring me through—that He would beat all odds—because He's the God of the Impossible.

But the circumstances changed for the worse.

The ward doctor told us to cancel the flight. He said I would need antibiotics for at least two weeks and that there was no way I was getting out in eight days to catch a flight. He said the situation was extremely dangerous and the infection I had seemed persistent. For the first time ever, I needed blood transfusions right from day one of the hospitalization. I received three bags of blood and two bags of platelets. The doctors also started me on GCSF injections to help my bone marrow regenerate white blood cells. As the days passed, the test results were more and more discouraging. The fever wouldn't drop, and the blood counts wouldn't rise. I was losing hope. I was hurting. I endured and waited and endured and waited but saw no change. Things just kept getting worse. I was unable to eat and too depressed to even try. I saw no point in fighting.

I hadn't given up. I was just too scared to fight. Every time I fought and endured and hoped, I just kept getting disappointed, and all that hope came crashing down and broke every part of me. Then I had to collect those broken pieces and hope again. And then they would break again and again. I was like a soldier who'd been wounded but still tried to fight. But with every new wound, I would bleed more, and I would lose more strength. And this time I was bleeding out.

In this metaphor, blood is a symbol of hope. It's what fuels me and supplies oxygen—life—to every organ and every part of me. My strength, my courage, my resilience, and my positivity were all fueled by hope. And this time, I was running out. I was bleeding.

But you see, hope is a choice. It's a choice we get to make every day. I was always willing to take the risk and hope, but I now was too exhausted, too weak, too broken to be brave. Still, as I thought about it, I remembered Dr. Vasilis's words. I realized that, even though I thought I couldn't be brave because I was broken, in reality, that was the only time I *could* be brave. That is what bravery is all about. It's perseverance amid weakness— amid darkness—and walking when your knees are giving in.

God was with me in that place—not the place everyone else saw but the one I fell into at 3:00 a.m. as I burst out crying. He was with me in the place of exhaustion, the place where I couldn't take it any longer. Faith in the absence of the miracle is what releases the miracle. Something is always happening when nothing is seen. Invisibility is the first sign of a miracle. But you have to hold on tightly and stay in faith.

One day after getting admitted to the isolation ward, Prof. D, came to see me. She walked in, and before speaking, she smiled at me. It was a smile of hope. I needed to see a smile of hope so much. As she explained to us how the chemotherapy had started to damage my bone marrow more deeply and more profoundly, she looked at me and told me, "Hey, we got this. You'll go. We'll give you lots of blood, and we'll double the dose for the GCSF, and we'll start you on oral antibiotics as well. It's like athletes with doping," she said and smiled.

I cannot find the right words to describe the hope, the comfort, and the determination her words gave me. I am brought to tears every time I think about how much these words helped me. She believed in me when *I* didn't even fully believe in myself. When everybody else around me thought the trip was a definite no, she believed in me. This felt like the miracle I was praying for without even knowing it. My oncologist's words were the rope I could hold onto to climb out of the pit of fear and disappointment. Because *she* fought for *my* dream, *I* chose to fight for it *too*. I chose to hope for it too.

The treatment for the infections, however, didn't seem to work. My bone marrow was just done. Every few days, I would get blood and platelet transfusions, and every single day, I would get two high-dose GCSF injections. I was on four different antibiotics, taking two intravenously and two orally. I would throw up ten times every night, and on good days, I'd eat three bites of an omelet my mom prepared for me. If you know me, you know I *really* don't like eggs—especially egg whites. I hate egg whites. But my mom read that it really helped my immune system, so I was trying as much as possible to just eat a bite. I was on the highest dose of morphine I had received so far, while also taking three other pain medications. On top of all that, I was on two medications for my stomach and bowel, one for my kidneys and two for the nausea. I was basically feeding on pills and drops. Because of the mucositis, I was unable to eat. And because I had been unable to eat for more than a week, I would throw up every time something entered my stomach, many times even just by taking the antibiotics.

During that hospitalization, I had to be brave enough to hope. I had to be brave enough to be *vulnerable* and brave enough to trust in what I couldn't see, despite what I couldn't understand. God and I were both looking at the same situation, but we were seeing different things. Life is lived forward but understood only in review. That's why faith is needed.

But then it all fell apart.

Two days before we were supposed to fly home, a doctor walked in and gave me the news that made all the efforts I had made to stand strong in my faith and believe that a miracle would come to defy the impossible fall apart.

"I'm really sorry. None of the treatments to fight off the infections seem to be effective. There's nothing else we can try right now. Just wait. We have to take it a day at a time. But with that kind of an immune system, you won't survive the flight."

Chapter 9

Hope in the Impossible

Yet I still had hope.

And that single thread of hope helped me find peace. The path of peace is a strange one. Peace does not come in the absence of struggle. By definition, peace exists *in* struggle. Notice how I said the path *of* peace, not the path *to* peace. It's not a destination. It's a calmness and attitude of rest, *amid* suffering. Ironically, peace is a fight. It's a constant battle between trust and doubt. Peace takes courage. It takes risk. It takes hope. It's difficult to completely surrender, to cast all your worries to something greater than you. But that's the only way to unlock authentic peace. Sometimes peace knocks on the door masked as adversity. Pain and suffering are the best teachers of peace.

Peace, however, is different than acceptance. This is a tricky subject. Acceptance hides a sense of helplessness. Peace hides a sense of confidence. It offers a sense of security—that things will be all right even if they don't turn out the way you wanted or expected. I had not accepted my situation. I didn't want to. I thought that, once I accepted it, I would lose my drive and courage to change it. Acceptance, in my eyes, was just like raising a white flag; it was a confession of an inability to change the situation, a declaration of giving up. Peace was an attitude of rest that propelled me into a state of a constant effort to change the situation, without worrying about whether that effort would be successful or not.

That day, when we got back the blood tests, there was still no increase in my counts. My dad canceled our flight. The news was devastating, but I was too weak to be sad. I knew that, if I allowed myself to feel the sadness that the situation brought me, I would never be able to bounce back. Voices in my head told me that, if I didn't get to go home now, maybe I never would. Maybe the surgery would kill me. Maybe the drugs would. Maybe the cancer would. I was scared. But I didn't allow myself to feel that fear, to let it overtake me. I locked it in a certain room in my mind. I'll tell you about it another time.

At some point, my mom left the room to get me an antiemetic. I closed my eyes and prayed. *God, I don't see a way. I don't see a light. I'm going to be honest. Make me brave enough to go through this. Give me endurance. Give me peace to be able to stand in faith and say that, even if the miracle never comes, it is well.*

The next morning, at 7:00 a.m., the nurses came in my room to draw blood again. I was half-asleep when they flushed my port and connected the tubes, but I saw them come in. I closed my eyes again. When they finished drawing the blood, I suddenly opened my eyes. Just for a split second. Just for a moment. But in that split second, I saw the nurse shake the tube with the blood and smile at me. Her smile was one of those details you can find God in. It was a smile of hope. Later that day, at around noon, the doctors of the ward came in my room for rounds.

"See for yourself," one doctor told me and handed me a folded piece of paper, with the brightest smile on his face.

I opened it up and saw the results of the blood tests. I teared up. I looked over at the table next to my bed to get a tissue and saw a note that my grandpa had given me the last time he visited. The note said, "When you least expect it, when all your hope is lost, *that's* when God will show up and something great will happen."

And God showed up. He always does—maybe not always in the way you wanted or at the time you prayed for. But He always shows up.

June 1 was the day of the miracle—the day of breakthrough. I looked at the white blood cells value—0.22. I needed at least a 1.50 to be able to fly in a plane, but this *was* the miracle. It *truly* was. I looked at the time. It was 11:11.

I felt so motivated to be healthy again that morning. I even asked my mom to make me an egg-white omelet. Imagine, haha. My dad booked a flight for June 3—two days later than we had originally planned. I found that so meaningful. The day that we were originally supposed to leave for Greece had become the day that I received the miracle of going back home. In other words, sometimes what God has in store for you is so much more meaningful than what you planned. But to see it, you first have to let go of your expectation.

You might picture things in a certain way, but God might have a different plan. I pictured that I'd be traveling home on June 1. But God's picture was different. It was better. The greatest hope I was given came through the greatest disappointment I had experienced. *After* we had made a plan, *after* we had bought the tickets, made the arrangements, and contacted the school, *then* did God interrupt my plan to fulfill a greater purpose.

It was difficult to believe that the disappointment this hospitalization had brought was a part of God's plan. It was difficult to believe the suffering I'd been experiencing was a part of God's plan. Sometimes some things, some pieces in our life just don't make any sense. How could this be a part of His plan? How could God allow this? If He loved me, how could He allow it?

It's *because* He loved me that He allowed it. It's *because* my pain had a purpose that would help me fulfill *my* purpose that He allowed it. I'm not saying God wanted me to be in pain or cry or be desperate. I'm saying He *used* that, to transform not only the pain itself but also the person I was *in* it and *after* it as well. Faith doesn't operate by sight, by visible knowledge. Everything seen is made of things not seen. This means everything has a hidden purpose. Getting worsening results is *seen*. But increasing the significance of the miracle is *not*. That's its purpose. And that's *not* seen in the original picture. It's *not* seen when you first get the news. It's *not* seen when you burst out crying late at night. Great strength is always born of great sorrow. Perhaps authentic and real strength is only ever born through deep pain. Perhaps the strongest people are the ones who've suffered the most. It's the depth of the sorrow that determines the power of the miracle. Your sorrow today can become your strength tomorrow. The tears you're crying tonight might water the seed in your heart that will rise from the ground tomorrow.

The miracle had come. The breakthrough had come. I was so happy. It couldn't fit into words. The chains of the impossible had been broken.

The uncertainty, the prison of pain, and the cage of disappointment had all been destroyed. Light had come. Hope had come. Provision had come. And that provision revealed the purpose of the pain. Provision is understood in the pieces. It's when you put all the pieces together that you can see the provision. When you put the pieces that didn't make sense, the pieces of darkness, the pieces of depression and hopelessness together with the pieces of grace, the pieces of love and life, you are able to finally see the big picture. And the big picture reveals the purpose of the pieces. But here's the catch. Provision isn't always what you pictured. It's not always in the form of a good report, good news, or physical change. Sometimes provision is found in your heart. The greatest provision is peace. Peace in the face of a provision that doesn't look like what you pictured is, in fact, the greatest form of provision.

Later that day, my oncologist stopped by my hospital room to see me. She was so happy to see me smile. "You look happy," she said with the brightest and biggest smile ever.

"I've never been happier," I told her and teared up.

She gave us some instructions and advice about flying home. She agreed to take the risk and let me travel with lower blood counts. However, she told us that I would need multiple blood transfusions the next two days and one or two bags of platelets just an hour before the flight. She also told me to keep doing double injections of high-dose GCSF and to go to the hospital in Athens to monitor my counts closely. She gave us a specific mask that was great for traveling and instructed me to wear it, both in the airport and on the plane.

That night, my mom made me a second egg-white omelet. But I couldn't eat it. The nausea was intense—more than any other day during this hospitalization, maybe even worse than that of block 4. It was pure torture. My mom tried to give me my antibiotics. I needed to take them. It was the only way I could travel. I gathered all my leftover courage, suppressed the discomfort, and took the first one. Right then, I went into a "throw-up shock." I started throwing up uncontrollably and just couldn't stop. It got so bad I couldn't even take a moment to catch my breath. My oxygen saturation levels decreased, and the nurses rushed into my room to help me. After throwing up about forty times, it stopped. I started crying. I was terrified. Imagine not being able to breathe because of how aggressive that passive movement of throwing up is. I looked over at my mom. She was upset and worried.

"Mom I can't do this anymore. I just can't take it," I told her. "It hurts so much, I am so scared, and I feel horrible. I really don't feel OK."

"I know but, you haven't eaten anything; how will your white blood cells be produced? You need these antibiotics. What if you travel and get sick in Athens? We can't risk it."

My mind was a mess. That happiness I'd felt a few hours ago had now been replaced by agonizing pain.

During this hospitalization, there were many days that even breathing was difficult, many days that I just couldn't take it and wished I wouldn't have to. But I always kept fighting. And I was fighting not just for me but also for my family. I needed to be here for them. Staying alive while suffering didn't offer me anything. I didn't want to die. I just wanted the pain to *stop*. I wanted the suffering to *stop*. I wanted *peace*. But I couldn't leave them. I *had* to fight. This hospitalization literally brought me to my knees. I felt guilty that I was not getting any better.

Later that night, I gathered up some courage and tried to eat again. It wasn't that I wanted to. I just didn't want to let my mom down. I wanted to fight as much as I physically could. That incident that night opened the doors of my mind to a thought that got comfortable and stayed there. That thought told me that going back home wasn't worth it. It tried to convince me that the discomfort of the pain, the nausea, and the medications would destroy the trip and would make going home a very bad experience. It told me I was a burden to my family and that I caused them pain. It tried to convince me to give up, to let go, and to stop fighting.

But it *had to* happen. The enemy will always attack you when God is doing something big in your life behind the scenes. The enemy could be anything. *You* could be your worst enemy—your doubt, fear, worry, trust issues, insecurity, you name it. The enemy that was attacking me that night was that thought that had entered my mind. When great purpose and blessings are about to enter your life, that's when you face the most opposition. And that's so significant. Adversity doesn't only prepare your heart to receive the true nature and value of the blessing; it also amplifies the importance and greatness of that value and the grace and love it projects. I was about to receive the greatest blessing of going back home.

And that's why that thought was attacking my heart that night. I was trying to escape desperation and move toward discovering true resilience and hope; that's why the enemy was trying to stop me with these thoughts. I knew, however, that these feelings lied, these voices lied, and this guilt lied.

As I cried myself to sleep that night, I realized I could not let these lies get to me and change my purpose. My purpose that week was to go home. That was my dream, my goal, and my desire. I had promised myself I would do anything physically possible to accomplish it. So, that night, I closed my eyes and made a declaration to myself. I would not be shaken. My determination would only grow stronger in the face of opposition and disappointment. And I would never give up until I was up on the stage of the school theater receiving my junior high school diploma. Despite all odds, all thoughts, and all opposition, I would choose to be brave, to hope, and to stay determined in faith. It would be hard and painful, but it would be worth it.

The next day was so much better. My dad flew early in the morning to Germany to help us with the bags. Before leaving the hospital, I was given red blood cells and platelets. I always got allergic reactions to the blood, ever since my second transfusion in February. That's why they also gave me an antihistamine to prevent anaphylaxis. That injection, however, made me so sleepy. I could literally sleep for the rest of the day. But I knew I had a flight to catch.

After the transfusion, I saw Prof. D, smiled at me and said: "We did it. Now go have fun. And eat a lot. Good luck with your exams too. It's going to be great."

I'll never forget that. My oncologist was the only one who truly believed in me and fought for me. All the other doctors in the isolation ward just told us to cancel the flight, yet she believed it would be possible. And here we were now. What *could be* had been transformed into what *was*. Even when *I* gave up on myself, *she* didn't.

"I promise I'll eat more," I said and laughed. "Thank you for everything from the bottom of my heart. I'm so, so grateful."

She smiled. I did too. They were smiles of hope.

The ward doctors gave us the discharge papers and those special masks I told you about. They wanted to make sure I was safe. One nurse came in my room and gave us a box that had some anti-nausea pills inside. This nurse was there last night when I was crying and helped a lot. She saw the pain and discomfort I was in and wanted to give us these pills just to help us out. The pills couldn't be found in Athens, and they were very expensive in Germany. That's why she told us she would give us the leftover pills in that box. I truly appreciated her action. It meant a great deal to me. It was an action of humanity, love, compassion, and empathy. Compassion is the greatest compass. It's the greatest expression of selfless love and the core foundation of human connection. This was an action of pure compassion. Empathy is the best road to the human heart. It's what ties compassion and love together. It's a byproduct of love and a source of compassion. And it's in the details.

Chapter 10

Miracles in the Making

As soon as I was discharged, my mom moved all our things downstairs and loaded them in the car. It was raining outside. June 3 and there was a thunderstorm. *Interesting*, I thought to myself. We went back to the apartment, unpacked the hospital bags, and packed our suitcases for the trip back home. I packed my photography bag and my schoolbooks. I went in the bedroom for the first time in months. Usually, I spent all my time in the living room, and I only slept on the couch. Sleeping on the couch always made the situation feel temporary. And I needed to feel that it was temporary. When I went in the room, I felt a strange emotion—a feeling of nostalgia and pain. I was hurting for what I had been through and feeling nostalgic for what I could have lived, were I to have been home and not sick.

After we packed our bags and everything was ready, my mom made me a sandwich and gave me my medications. My dad also gave me the two injections of GCSF. We always joked with my parents about how Dad was the only one who actually knew how to give me the injection without hurting me or causing a hematoma.

When we got to the airport, I put on my mask and walked in with my crutches. This was my first time in a public place in almost half a year. I had forgotten what it felt like. I had forgotten how to go to a store and get a coffee, how to be social, how it felt to be in public. That's when it really hit me; I had been living in complete isolation. For a moment, I got

115

scared. *What if, when I go back to school, I don't remember how to be around my friends?* I wondered.

As we walked to the luggage drop-off, I could feel people stare at me. It made me feel horrible. I wondered how the people at school would react. For a moment, I almost didn't want to board that flight. That, however, was the enemy controlling my mind. And I couldn't let these thoughts win.

After we dropped off our bags, a person who worked at the airport brought us a wheelchair and helped me get to the gate. Being in a wheelchair attracted even more stares, but it also skipped lines and made us get through airport security faster than ever, so I'm not complaining.

When we got to the gate, boarding hadn't started yet, so we stopped at a café to grab a bite to eat. I had promised my oncologist and myself that I'd eat as much as possible during this trip. I was at an incredibly low weight during that time. It scared me a little bit. My fingers and arms were like sticks. I had absolutely no muscle mass in my body. You could even see some ribs in my stomach area and in my chest.

I had accepted the challenge and was ready to enjoy as much food as possible during this trip, without worrying about the chemo or the nausea. After that snack, we boarded the plane. The flight attendants were Greek, and I truly cannot describe the feeling of hearing someone speak in Greek again. It finally felt like home. It gave me so much comfort and courage. I was finally going home. I couldn't believe it. Because of my leg, my mom and I had business-class tickets and sat in the first row. I, of course, took the window seat. As the plane started moving to get to the takeoff lane, I closed my eyes and prayed.

Oh, God ... I have no words right now. I honestly don't know how to describe what's on my heart. I wish I could just squeeze all the gratitude I feel and give it to you. I am so thankful, God. Thank you. From the deepest bottom of my heart, thank you that I'm here. God, this was impossible. You know it was. But you are the God of the impossible, of the hopeless, of the desperate. You make everything worth it. You make every tear, every stabbing sharp pain, every hopeless thought, every sleepless night, worth it. God this is a miracle. Thank you so much. I'll make the most out of it.

Just after I prayed, the plane took off. In that moment, a flight attendant approached me and gave me some oil. She said it was from

Jerusalem and that she, herself, always carried it with her. She said it could give me strength. I felt my heart filling with gratitude.

"I don't know why, but I have this strange feeling that I need to tell you that everything will turn out fine. Everything will turn out better than you think," she told me and teared up.

I felt God speaking to me through her. It was as if He'd placed her on that plane for a reason—to meet me and give me hope. She anointed me with oil and then smiled. It was yet another one of these smiles—a smile of hope. You can tell a smile of hope by the person's eyes, only by their eyes. Remember that as the story unfolds. I could tell this was a smile of hope by how it made me feel. God's in the details. I would see that flight attendant again—when I needed to the most. But little did I know that then.

The flight was, overall, enjoyable. I didn't sleep. I was too excited. It was my first time traveling business class in a trip from another country, so I was really excited about the menu and the three courses that were served. I hadn't told my friends I was flying back to Greece that day, but a lot of them knew. Staring out the window, I noticed the clouds. They gave me peace. As I sank in my thoughts, I realized that's what my life really was—a flight.

I was sick, and I was traveling to healing. That flight was bumpy and tiring. It was painful and emotionally drenching. But throughout all the turbulence, I was still in flight; I was still in the plane getting to "Athens." Athens was a symbol of healing, a source of resilience, and a purpose for patience and determination. The treatment, the nausea, the pain, the low counts, and the surgeries were all part of the flight. They were all clouds the plane was passing through. But the destination made them worth it. That's when I realized I had already found Athens during the flight itself—before actually getting to Athens. I had found what I was looking for, *while* looking for what I was looking for, *before* actually getting to where I thought I would find it.

On my quest for hope, determination, and purpose, I was on a journey to Athens because that's where I thought I would find what it was all about. However, what I realized was that I'd already found these things, *on* the flight, so to speak—*in* the treatment, *in* the pain, and *in* the suffering. *During* my journey to the destination, I had discovered what the destination was all about. I thought I would find hope only when I got a good medical report. I thought I would find joy only when life want back to normal. However, *during* my flight, *during* the pain, *during* the challenge, I had discovered my destination before getting to it. I realized that true hope was not found in the absence of pain but, instead, emerges in the *midst* of the storm and rises from the pit of depression and suffering. Bravery, courage, and resilience were all stars with a very unique light. However, for these stars to shine, darkness needed to take over; the night needed to come. I thought I could find strength and gratitude only when I got to my destination, to healing. But the flight, the journey, made me realize that these stars *were* the destination.

During the flight, I wondered what the first day back in school would feel like. I tried to picture and imagine people's reactions. I started putting an outfit together in my mind and tried to imagine what going up on that stage during the graduation ceremony would feel like. I was so excited. Ecstatic is an understatement. After a couple of hours, the pilot announced that the landing process had begun. Just by the sound of that, I felt butterflies in my stomach. I counted down the minutes until I would finally get home. As I saw the land come closer and closer, a feeling of disbelief overtook me. I had dreamed about going back home many times, and this truly felt like one of those dreams. But it wasn't. It was real. This was what I'd prayed for since day one. This was what I'd hoped for and looked forward to. This was what I'd doubted would ever come. And yet it was here. It was real. It was now.

After the plane landed, we waited for all passengers to get out. An airport employee was waiting for me right outside the plane with a wheelchair. As we were leaving, I said goodbye to that flight attendant who had given me the oil and gave her a hug. I sat in the wheelchair, and we started walking to go pick up our luggage. As we were moving, I could hear the people around me speaking in Greek. That alone brought me much joy. I was home. I was finally home. I didn't mind people staring any more. It didn't matter. I was home. We picked up our bags and then moved to the exit.

As the doors opened, I saw my family and friends waiting for me outside. I teared up. I can't put into words that feeling. It was as if, in just a moment, I was feeling all the joy that cancer had stolen during the past few months. I rushed to hug them. Amalia was there, along with my aunt;

my grandparents; and Ageliki, my older sister. So too were Thanos, my friend Mikaela, my friend Ourania, my mom's friend Georgia who had visited me in Essen and her family, and another friend of my mom's. All these people had come there for me. My heart was full of love. I felt so motivated. I was seeing my "why" come alive every time someone hugged me. It reminded me why I kept fighting, why I had to keep going. They gave me flowers, and we spent some time together in that arrivals' hall in the airport. After a while, we went home.

As I walked in, I felt my whole body collapse under gratitude. Every negative thought, every thought that had told me I would never make it home, every thought that had told me I would never get to sleep in my own bed again was destroyed and burned as I walked from the elevator to my room.

Later that night, I noticed signs of bleeding and, as a result, found myself in the emergency room at 2:00 a.m. I met with a team of oncologists there, and they drew some blood to check my platelet levels. The doctors were all incredible. I connected with them right away. Little did I know how much they would help me in the future. After about an hour or so, the results were in. My platelets were normal, so the doctors concluded that the light bleeding stemmed from the sores all over my GI tract, caused by the chemotherapy drugs. They told me to monitor it and come back in two days for another blood draw. I went home happier than ever. I was finally going to sleep in my own bed for the first time in six months, and the next day, I would get to go back to school. I couldn't believe this was real. I put on my favorite pj's and lay in my bed.

Lying there, I closed my eyes. I breathed in and held my breath. I tried to take in the moment. I tried to feel my body lying in my bed. I tried to lock that feeling in my heart. I knew I would need to remember what lying in my bed felt like in a few months, as I would lie on the surgical table. I opened my eyes and breathed out. It seemed surreal. I looked around. I was really home.

That night, I tried to sleep, but the pain was just too much. I would get horrible side effects from both the chemo and the medication I was on for the side effects of the chemo. It was exhausting. But I didn't care. It didn't matter. I knew in just a few hours, I would be back at school. I would see my friends again. I would get to sit in those desks again and take a test

119

again. And oh how excited I was. I truly didn't believe it was real. I had doubted that day would ever come so many times—more than I admit.

As I tried to fall asleep, a specific Bible verse came to my mind that reminded me that the sorrow of the present times cannot be compared to the joy the future will bring. This verse got me through the night and helped me push through the pain. I knew the pain that was keeping me up could not be compared to the smile the next day would put on my face. It could not compare to the gratitude and the happiness I would feel in my heart in just a few hours.

The next morning, I woke up after only getting about four hours of sleep. I was exhausted, but the excess adrenaline gave me more energy than I'd had on any other day. I felt full of life. I hadn't felt like this in months. I hadn't experienced such excitement or energy since getting sick. It broke my heart to realize, yet again, just how much this disease had deprived me of, but it made me grateful to know that there was still a breath in my lungs. I was still here, and that was all that mattered.

I moved toward my closet and picked out what I would wear. I'd already thought about it like three weeks ago, and I was finally going to try that outfit on. I wore black leggings, a pink T-shirt, my new converse shoes, and a black chemo cap on my head. This was especially important because, for about eight months, ever since my leg had started hurting, I hadn't been able to put on leggings or jeans. The pain, swelling, and soreness I'd been experiencing all these months made sweatpants my only clothing option. Being able to finally wear leggings brought me back to the mornings I would get ready for school and made me feel healthy again. It's all in the details.

After I got dressed, I moved over to my desk and packed my pencil case. I took two pens with me, one my grandpa had given me before he'd passed away and one I always used in the hospital. They were both important to me. I'd written all my important exams with the pencil from my grandpa. It made me feel like I was not taking the test alone, and I always had him with me. The other one was just a random supermarket pen, and yet it was so significant. I used this pen every time I was in the hospital to communicate with my mom and the doctors, since the mucositis made speaking impossible. This was the pen I'd used, to write, "I can't do this anymore," on that paper box. This is the pen I'd used to write, "I don't want to have to fight anymore," in my diary. This was the pen I'd used to write, "I am tired of waking up to more pain every day," on a random piece of paper at the hospital. And now, I would be using the same pen to write the exam I'd worked toward all these months. I would be using this pen to write the very test I'd doubted I would ever get the chance to take. I would be using this pen to do something that embodied faith and projected determination—something that proved all things are possible.

In that pencil case, I also put the printed image Grandpa Nick brought to me in Germany that said, "When you least expect it, when all your hope is lost, that's when God will show up and something great will happen." This day was exactly proof of that.

Once ready, Amalia, Ageliki, my mom, and I left for school. On the drive, Amalia and I were going over the main chapters and the most important parts of the test material to get ready for our history exam. She helped me memorize some important dates and told me about some events I hadn't really understood. Ageliki was in the car with us, encouraging me and hyping me up. As we got closer to school, I asked them not to talk to me for a few minutes. I wanted to take in the moment, to remember it, to appreciate it, and to believe it was real. I was nervous and excited; I felt butterflies in my stomach.

"Hey, Ami," I said at some point, "can I ask you something? Can you tell me some phrases or cool words that kids use at school? I think I have forgotten how to talk to people and be social."

"Kate, don't even think about that," she replied. "You are amazing, and you got this. Everything's gonna be all right. Just be you. That's more than enough. Be you."

Love is in the details—in short conversations, in a smile, in a car ride. Love is in the details.

As we pulled up to the gate, the song "What If" by Johnny Orlando was playing on the radio. I got emotional. As I listened, I thought of all my what-ifs, all the things I thought I would never get to do, all the dreams I thought I would never accomplish, and all the nights that worry and fear had consumed me. What if I never make it home? What if the chemo damages my heart? What if the treatment doesn't work? What if I never see my friends again? What if the pain doesn't get better? The list goes on.

I was crushing all these what-ifs today. Every step I'd take when I got to school, every person I'd hug, every word I'd write on that exam paper would be punching these what-ifs in the face and destroying them. I was ready to get better.

When we got to school, my mom dove onto the campus so that I didn't have to walk a long distance. There were already a lot of kids outside our building, so they all gathered around the car. Before stepping out, I took a deep breath. This was it.

"Hey, you got this!" Ageliki told me upon seeing me breathe more deeply and frequently.

I smiled. Grabbing one of my two crutches, I opened the door and stepped out of the car. In a split second, some of my friends rushed to hug me.

I was nervous to see everyone at school. Yet everyone was so kind and welcoming. One teacher came up to me and gave me a hug. There were smiles on everyone's faces. I was overwhelmed with gratitude. I remembered seeing people's eyes on my last day at school, back in January. They'd been red and watery, and they had hidden sadness and uncertainty and fear. Now, as I observed people's eyes again, they were full of love and joy and compassion. The uncertainty and the fear still existed, and some pity was present too. But love was the strongest among them. This moment gave me so much hope. It embodied the transformative power hidden behind every adversity.

After the first bell rang, we went in our classrooms to take our tests. Let me break down the exam process for you. Normally, grade nine students had finals on four classes—math, language, physics, and history. However, since I'd missed out on most of the school year, I had to take a final exam on all fourteen classes. When that bell rang, I went to a different room with two teachers; I was so immunocompromised, I couldn't be around many kids. As I walked into the classroom I was directed to, I realized it was the same classroom where that physics class incident had taken place back in January. For a moment, I stopped walking and just paused. I was emotional, but I didn't want to show it. I knew this was a form of healing.

Back in January, when that incident had happened, I'd been desperately crying and having a panic attack over how aggressive this cancer seemed to be. And now, six months later, after five VIDE chemotherapy blocks, three surgeries, and countless sleepless nights, after battling thoughts and fears of death and pain and enduring trials, and after countless prayers, I was there, in that same room, taking an exam. The exam itself wasn't important. But what it symbolized was significant. Taking a simple history exam that day was a miracle, a testament to the fact that everything is possible. Just a few days ago, doctors had been telling us there was absolutely no way I would be able to travel back home and that my bone marrow was more than "too weak" and I wouldn't survive the flight. And yet there I was, in that classroom, in the core of a traumatic memory—redefining it, recreating it. In the same classroom where I'd broken down, crying in fear, I was writing an exam that symbolized a miracle and proved the power of hope. This is what transformation power is all about.

That day became a source of closure and healing. Taking that exam symbolized the victory of faith over fear; it emphasized the power of hope and determination. Purpose is in the details.

As I walked in the room, I saw my history teacher and my language teacher, Mrs. B, with whom I was really close. They were both excited and happy to see me. I noticed their smiles—smiles of hope.

That night, two of my friends came over for dinner. My aunt cooked some pasta with a very interesting almond sauce, and we all gathered around the table and enjoyed each other's company. We talked about the exam, laughed, shared memories, and made plans for the future. It was amazing. Memories I'd treasure forever were made. Love is in the details.

The next day, we had another exam. I did well in all of them, mostly thanks to my sister, who told me all the important things to study and explained to me everything that I hadn't understood. I loved being at school, being around my friends and my teachers. It gave me so much hope. On some days, I'd give exams on two or three different subjects. In between the tests, my mom and I would go to the bathroom, and she would give me my medications. No matter how normal life seemed while I was at school taking an exam, cancer always found a way to disrupt that and remind me of reality. But I couldn't let that fear and sadness destroy the incredible gift I'd been given, to spend these ten days home.

I tried to fill that time with fun memories. I believe that we have the power to make today happy. All it takes is living in the moment. How? By appreciating each moment, by noticing the details of joy, by feeling grateful for the little things that make each moment special. And that was my biggest goal; living in the moment. That was why I did all I did. Each small mountaintop I climbed, each small battle I won, was a source of strength for future me and a thank you to old me for helping the present me get there.

On June 7, after my exams, my mom drove my sister and me home. Before we got home, however, we made a pit stop at a camera store. It was my big day. I was finally getting my own first camera. I'd spent hours and days and weeks doing research, learning all about every camera I was interested in, understanding the specs of each model, and comparing them all. It had been a hard decision to come to, but I'd finally found the one I wanted. Since I was too immunocompromised to go into the store, my mom went in for me. My sister and I stayed in the car. We listened to throwback songs and sang at the top of our lungs in that parking lot. It's all in the little things.

When we got home, I unboxed my camera. I was excited. It wasn't the material object that mattered but, rather, the happiness in my heart from getting it after months of dreaming about it, saving up, and waiting for it. Joy is not born out of material objects but, rather, out of what these objects symbolize and mean to someone. For instance, it wasn't the camera itself that made me happy. Rather, it was the fact that that camera would allow me to pursue my passion; I could keep seeing the world through a different perspective, painting with color all the grainy, black-and-white images that my reality consisted of. That camera was something that could make me excited to get out of the house, to get better so that I could be strong enough to use it and to hold it. It still reminded me of all the sleepless nights, the desperate prayers, and the times that the fear of suffering woke me up drenched in sweat. In a way, that camera symbolized that I'd been through these things, I'd fought these battles, and I'd come out a winner. The next day, a couple of my friends came over, and we took photos together.

On Tuesday, the twelfth, my mom, Amalia, and I decided to watch the sunset together. It was one of the best, most colorful, and most magical sunsets I'd ever witnessed. Hundreds of shades of pastel orange, pink, yellow, and red mixed together, painting the canvas of the sky with the most beautiful sunset. As I stared at the sky, sinking deep in my thoughts, the sound around me faded out. I remembered sitting on the exam bed in that hospital room after the oncologist gave me the diagnosis. I remembered looking to my left, outside the window, and seeing the most incredible sunset I had seen. The sunset after the biopsy results was just as beautiful as the sunset before the graduation ceremony. How meaningful is that. But how could they be tied together?

As I was thinking, a strange sense of peace rushed through my body. For a moment, the pain didn't matter, the tumor stopped hurting, and the fear and worry and uncertainty faded. I was calm. I was at peace. A sunset feeling overtook me. And that's when I realized that's what ties everything together. This sunset feeling—this strange peace that stemmed from placing my trust in something greater than me and stronger than my pain. The sunset after the diagnosis could be just as beautiful as the sunset before the graduation because it stemmed from faith and was born out of hope. The unexplainable peace I felt after we got the results could be just as strong as the peace I felt before getting up on that stage and receiving my junior high diploma because they both stemmed from an unconditional hope born of bold and brave faith. That's what made them so beautiful, so colorful.

That's the power of a sunset.

Chapter 11

A Walk across a Stage

Today was the day. It was June 13. Graduation Day. This was also my last day home, and it needed to be the best one yet. I woke up excited, and my mom made me a fruit plate for breakfast. It reminded me of the summer before I was sick. I missed these times, but that nostalgia was quickly replaced by excitement and gratitude for the day that would follow.

Since that day was my last at home, my sisters and I decided to make the most of it. As a result, we figured it would be a great idea to try and make our own sushi rolls from scratch. Let me set the scene. Ever since I first tried sushi, I fell in love with it, and it quickly became one of my favorite foods. Unfortunately, being on chemo, I wasn't allowed to eat sushi or anything similar. My immune system was extremely suppressed, so I had to be very careful with what I ate. But that Wednesday was graduation day—a day of victory. That was the day on which my biggest goal for the past months would come true. Therefore, we *had* to celebrate. So we decided to make chemo-friendly sushi.

Before we started making the rolls, however, I noticed symptoms of bleeding, my feet got swollen, and I developed a strange rash. My mom and I quickly went to the hospital. I did many tests, but all my counts were relatively normal, all things considered. I was given a medication, and then we went home. As I'm looking back to that memory, I now realize that going to the hospital, which I then thought was just wasting my precious time home, actually hid a deeper purpose for the development of my life's plot.

At the hospital, we met two families, one of whom was going to go to Essen for treatment as well. That hospital visit made me realize the significance of compassion; it gave me the chance to meet other kids my age who were battling cancer, and it showed me how love can shine right through pain. But that's not all. That simple hospital visit lit a flame in my heart that started as a small spark but would later evolve to be a raging fire. That flame was my desire to become a doctor myself and help other people who were going through similar conditions.

There was a family who'd just gotten very bad news about the prognosis of their child, who was bravely fighting a very aggressive form of cancer. As they were sitting in that waiting room, grief overtook them. I saw their eyes. I saw the pain in them. Something in me that day changed. All I wanted in that moment was to do anything it took to help that family. It was deeper than surface-level empathy; it was stronger than regular human compassion and more powerful than just feeling sorry for them. It was a profound form of determination to give all I could to help, not just them but all families in such situations.

Everything happens for a reason; I believe that. That day, all I wanted was to spend my last few hours at home doing fun things with my family. And yet it almost seemed as if I *had* to go to the hospital, as if I *had* to sit in that same waiting room with that family, so that spark could be ignited. It almost seemed as if everything was happening according to a plan, for a specific reason. The flame would not turn into a fire any time soon. I first had to deal with the fire around me. I first had to go through my *own* pain and my *own* journey with cancer. But once that simple spark became a fire, nothing would ever be able to put it out. As a result, that day was much more that a fun day. It was much more than my last day home. It was even much more than the big moment of the graduation. That day was the start of a path of purpose.

No sooner had we arrived home than I was up in the kitchen with Amalia and Ageliki making sushi. I find it fascinating how small moments of sheer happiness can exist in a season of incredible pain. I find it significantly beautiful how, amid times of great suffering, there can be many small individual moments where a carefree version of happiness abounds and somehow makes you, just for a split second, forget about all the pain. Somehow, these moments of pure innocent happiness, help you escape the dark reality of sorrow and enter a world where you feel at peace, which, even though lasts for a split of a second, feels like a lifetime.

As soon as we finished making sushi, my friend Mikaela arrived. We all enjoyed the rolls we made for lunch and talked about tonight's graduation ceremony. Time went by so quickly—nothing like it used to during chemo. My sister and Mikaela headed to Amalia's room to get dressed. It was time to get ready.

I go downstairs to my room, take my dress from the closet, and put it on. After getting dressed, I lift my head up and stare at myself in the mirror. A strange numbness rushes through my body. I have to fight yet another battle before the big moment, the one in the prison of my mind.

As I stare at the mirror, all I see is brokenness. I see a bald, sick girl. I see her eyes. They hide pain deeper than the ocean and mask grief, for who she once was and for who she could have been. I stare at her body. It is discolored from the chemo, full of scars from needles and surgeries. It is beaten down. Frail. Weary. I look at her hands. I see how the drugs have affected them. It hurts so much to stare at this girl in the mirror. I look back at her eyes and see tears stream down her face. I touch my face and wipe them away. That brave heart of hers, how much it has endured.

I close my eyes and take a deep breath. Every part of me is wishing that, when I open them again, I will see a different girl in that mirror, a girl who has just come back from the hairdresser, whose body and soul isn't scarred and scattered. I take another deep breath. I feel it reach my lungs. As I exhale, I open my eyes again. Suddenly, my knees collapse. I kneel. Tears fill my eyes. This time, however, these tears aren't tears of grief and hurt. They are tears of love and overwhelming gratitude. It's as if these tears washed my vision clean and helped me truly *see.*

This time, as I stare at the mirror, I don't see a weak, sick, and helpless girl. I see a fierce, brave, and courageous warrior. I see an overcomer, a girl who has suffered and fought, has lost hope and cried, has screamed and given up and hurt and yet *still* stands here, bravely staring in the mirror. How beautiful she is—not because of what she is wearing, not because her hair is nice, but because of the bravery and boldness of her heart. She is beautifully broken. She has cried more tears than the winter rain, and yet she is *still* standing. She is *here.* She *keeps* trying; she *keeps* going. She chooses to hope, to stand, and to persevere. She is broken. Yet she chooses to be brave—*even* in the broken.

Staring at my reflection in the mirror, I see a small girl with a big God by her side. I picture His hand on my shoulder. I smile and place my hand on my shoulder as well. The girl in the mirror does too. I smile. She does too. She knows how proud I am of her, just for finding the courage to stare at the mirror.

That was one of the most pure, vulnerable, and important moments of my life, because I realized that my deepest weakness was my greatest source of strength, that beauty was so much more than hair and clothes, and that flowers can grow from broken soil. In that moment, a sunset feeling overwhelmed me. In that moment, I chose to be brave enough to love myself.

That white graduation dress symbolized my weapon. It was a testament of the fact that anything was possible. I'd started searching for it back in March when my oncologist had told me that flying back home for the graduation ceremony would be possible. Even when the chemo's side effects got worse and all the odds were against me going home, I kept searching for that dress; I kept looking for the one. It gave me hope, since it represented hope itself. It was only after a very challenging time—the difficult chemo block on Easter when I gained a deeper understanding of hope—that I found the dress. So I ordered it. But when it arrived and I put it on, at first, I didn't like what I saw. Thus, I embarked on a journey to feeling confident and beautiful in the same dress that I'd felt insecure and damaged in. The dress itself was a symbol of hope.

That Sunday morning when we'd flown home, I'd packed the dress in my suitcase, and it had traveled with me. That same dress was with me in my worst moments, in the desperation and the worry, and it was with me throughout the journey, as I tried to get from insecurity to self-love; from worry to trust; from doubt to determination; from pain to purpose; and, ultimately, from Germany to Greece. The dress was there through the hurt and the challenge, waiting to be used. That same dress was with me when I put it on and felt a gut-wrenching feeling of brokenness, and it was also with me as I looked in the mirror with a brave smile on my face, seeing only the beauty and strength the dress itself showed out in me.

When Prof. D had told me that going home "would be possible," that was enough for me to go look for the dress, to go look for hope. I didn't find hope right then and there, but I did start looking for it. I went on so many websites trying to find the right dress. Family and friends showed me suggestions. Yet I knew I had to find the one by myself. I looked for hope in so many places, and people tried to give it to me, but I had to find it myself. I had to find a dress that would fit *me*. People's input on dresses really did help me; it showed me my taste, my needs, and my preferences. It showed me what kind of dress *I* was looking for. But I had to pick out the final dress at the end. It's the same thing with hope. People's actions and support intended to give me hope helped me immensely because it showed me the kind of unconditional hope *I* was looking for. I was not looking for a when-then type of hope or for a circumstantial hope, a conditional hope. I was not looking for a hope that depended on what I was going through but, rather, for a hope that disregarded what I was going through, a hope that sustained me in my pain and delivered me from it.

As I saw the chemo making me worse, as I saw the effect it had on my body and how aggressive and difficult it was, that goal of flying home to graduate seemed more and more impossible. That phrase, "it would be possible," felt like something from the distant past. Despite the uncertainty, however, I kept looking for the dress, *even* when I thought the reason I needed it in the first place no longer existed. I kept looking for the right dress, *even* when I thought I would never attend the event I needed it for. I was still looking for hope *even* when I didn't know what I hoped for.

But even when the dress arrived, and I put it on, I couldn't see its beauty and significance. Even when I'd found and accessed hope, I couldn't appreciate it and fully experience its transformative power. When I first tried the dress on, I stared at myself in the mirror and didn't like what I saw. It wasn't that the dress wasn't pretty; I hadn't learnt how to appreciate it and understand true beauty, beauty that stemmed from within. Even after I accessed hope, I felt too broken to use it, to fight with it. Just like a weapon, hope is a means that helps you fight. However, you *still* have to fight and try and keep on keeping on. But I was tired. When I looked in the mirror, I didn't see the dress; I saw my scars. But what I didn't realize, until graduation day, was that my scars didn't ruin the dress; they *complimented* it. My brokenness didn't cover and shadow hope; it enabled it to *shine*.

It was *through* my scars that the beauty of the dress was revealed. It was *through* my hurt that the power of hope was experienced.

That afternoon as I was getting ready for the graduation ceremony, I realized something that changed everything. I realized that the most beautiful thing about the way I looked was not the dress itself but how the dress showed my *scars*, my story. The purpose of the dress was not to hide my scars but to embrace them and use them as a testament of how much I had overcome. The purpose of hope was not to mask my pain and hide my brokenness but to shine right through it. Hope was meant to transform suffering, to be a soil in which the flower of unconditional love and faith could grow. That realization was a revelation of what true beauty is all about. It's so much more than hair, eyebrows, bodies, or even dresses. Beauty is about embracing your scars—loving and appreciating your bravery in battle. And so, that afternoon, I felt more beautiful than ever.

Before I got cancer, being a teen girl, I always struggled with trying to be beautiful. I always took care of my hair and cared about the type of clothes I wore. And yet, despite all that work and all that effort, I never truly felt beautiful; I never truly loved myself. I believed my hair was beautiful or my clothes were beautiful, but I didn't believe *I* was beautiful. It was only after I had been stripped of all these external characteristics, which I thought were making me beautiful, that I truly discovered what real beauty is all about. God showed me that it wasn't my hair that made me beautiful. It wasn't my face. Nor was it my body. It was *my scars*. What a powerful revelation that was. He helped me see that I was beautiful because I was brave, because I held on to courage, and because I kept being thrown in deep waters and kept swimming. And when I couldn't swim any longer, when I got tired of fighting, I dared to be bold enough to be vulnerable and surrender to hope, to give my struggles to God, and to trust Him to bring me out of the storm. And that was what made me beautiful.

Before cancer, the nice clothes I wore couldn't change the fact that I was actually clothed in insecurity. Through cancer, however, no matter what type of clothes I wore, I was always clothed in hope, faith, and courage. Before cancer, I thought my hair made me beautiful, but through adversity, I realized that what made me beautiful was how I stayed brave when I watched my hair fall out. Beauty flows out of things so much deeper that what is seen on the outside.

After we all got ready, we drove to school for the ceremony. We were too many to fit in one car, so we split in two. Mikaela and I went with my dad, and Amalia and Ageliki went with my mom. When we got to school, it was still early, and the campus was almost empty. I thought we were the first students to arrive.

As we were about to get out of the car, fear paralyzed me. I didn't know if I could do this. This day meant so much to me. I had dreamt and expected it for so long, and yet the fact that it was finally here somehow scared me. I knew that what I was living was a once-in-a-lifetime experience. And that scared me. I didn't want to let even a second slip through my fingers and go by unappreciated. I wanted to make the most out of it.

I knew that this time tomorrow I would be back in Essen. And this time in two days, I'd be on chemo, unable to even lift my head up or turn to the side to throw up. And that scared me too. I knew that this night could give me so much courage for what was to come, and the pressure was on. I couldn't let this slip away. I had to make the most out of what I was about to experience. This was what it had all been about. I closed my eyes, tightened my fists, and gathered up courage. *God, help me be brave,* I asked.

"Hey, Katerina, are you okay? Why aren't you getting out of the car?" my dad asked.

"I'm okay," I said. I really meant it.

God helped me be okay, be courageous. He helped me be brave.

I stepped out of the car, and we all walked toward the theatre. There were people still setting up everything. Just a few minutes later, Amalia and Ageliki arrived too. We gathered outside the theater entrance and took a bunch of pictures. Only a few moments had gone by before my friends Aimiliana and Ivy arrived. They were from another school, so they wouldn't be receiving their diplomas tonight, and yet they came to support us. I felt so grateful for friendship. We all took photos together. A couple of minutes later, some teachers arrived. Everyone was really happy to see me.

Soon the theater doors opened, and we went inside. There were over nine hundred seats, all still empty, soon to be filled with parents, relatives, friends, teachers, and students. My family chose a row, and they all took a seat. My grandparents; my aunt; my dad; and his girlfriend, Demy, soon arrived. I was so grateful for my family. I couldn't imagine this moment without all of them here. I reserved the third seat of the first row at the left section of the theater. It was next to the three stairs that led up to the stage. I didn't have the crutches with me, so I tried to sit as close to the stage as I could, in order to minimize the distance I'd have to walk. I was worried about walking, if I'm being honest. I hadn't walked without crutches in over six months. But I trusted God. I knew He'd carry me if I lost my balance.

Within the next half an hour, the theater was almost completely full. Many of my classmates approach me and greeted me with a hug before taking their seats. They were all excited to see me there. I took in every single hug. I tried to remember all of them, to capture the feeling of courage and comfort that each hug gave me, just like I had before I'd left for Germany. Back then, I'd been worried that would be the last time I hugged my friends. But every hug tonight destroyed worries and doubts like this. It smashed them. It made the impossible possible. And that was why, this time, I didn't feel scared. This time, a strange calmness and certainty overwhelmed me, and I was sure that I'd see and hug all my friends again, some day. That confidence that stems from hope gave me peace. It was a strange kind of peace, deeper than any understanding—a sunset feeling.

Many teachers greeted me and hugged me as well. I felt so loved. I looked at my family. They were all so happy and emotional to see me standing there, knowing that I'd made it to the ceremony. There were people who needed me to be here, who needed me to survive. It was difficult a lot of times, and it was scary, and it hurt—a lot. But I couldn't give up—ever. I just couldn't. It wasn't an option. I had to endure and fight. I had so much more to do—more love, hope, and hugs to give and receive.

At some point, the school principal greeted me with a firm handshake and a smile. It was a smile of hope—undoubtedly. He and his secretary, Mr. V, told me how proud and excited they both were for me. Mr. V has been a source of strength for me. When my knee first started hurting, and the chapter of cancer first began, I would stay in my classroom during PE, and Mr. V would always check on me and ask me if I needed anything on his way to his office. The Monday of that physics class incident, just two days before my diagnosis, Mr. V had passed by like he usually did.

"Hey Katerina, do you need anything?" I remember him asking.

"No. Thank you so much. I'm all good," I'd replied.

Mr. V tended to leave, but something stopped him, and he turned back. "Ithikon Akmaiotaton," he told me.

I didn't know what he meant at first. I later found out. In a free translation of the essence of that Greek phrase, it means to have a good morale, to be determined, *to be brave*. Little did I know at the time how important that phrase would be for me. From that day on, he always told me the same phrase every time he saw me. I'd thought about that phrase many times during treatment when I wanted to give up. What a significant little moment that was, full of meaning, hope, and God's presence. It's all in the details.

So, today, after speaking to the principal and Mr. V, I turned to him as he started walking towards the stage and told him, "Ithikon Akmaiotaton."

Suddenly, a huge smile formed on his face. His eyes became red and watery. He was really moved; I could tell. It was my way of thanking him for giving me so much strength back in January. After these special little moments of hope and love with my friends and teachers, we all took our seats. The theater was already full. There were way more people than there were seats. Many were sitting in the aisles. The lights dimmed. The ceremony was about to begin.

The vice principal of the school kicked off the night by welcoming everyone and congratulating all the students. She then introduced the principal and handed off the stage to him. He was the next to give a speech, congratulating students and talking about the importance of this day. He then invited my friend Dimitris to the stage. The president of the student council, Dimitris was to give a speech to all the students. After his speech, the class presidents took turns, each giving a short speech about the significance of these three years of junior high school and the fun memories shared. I used to be my class president, but obviously, I couldn't give a speech. I had no memories of that year to share, and for a moment, that made me sad. For a moment, I felt a sense of heaviness and grief for all the things I could have experienced but didn't, for all the laughs I could have had, for all the tears and fears that replaced the innocence of these teenage years.

My sister Ageliki, who was sitting next to me, saw that I was feeling a little sad. She held my hand tightly and said, "Hey, don't be sad. Think about it this way—you'll be the only one who will be able to fully appreciate the next and better memories that you'll create over the next few years. You missed a few class jokes. Who cares? You gained so much wisdom and strength."

These simple words took away all sadness and gave me much courage. And I took heart. Just like that, I was reminded of all the miracles that had led me to here. Just like that, I was reminded of all the mountaintops I'd conquered, all the things God had brought me through. As students gave their speeches, I was at peace. I felt grateful, not only for being here in this room but also for the fact that, to be able to sit here, I'd had to overcome the impossible, the scary, and the painful.

After these quick speeches, the vice principal took the stand again, briefly explaining the procedure. Basically, she'd call the students of each class to the stage, alphabetically, and they would, one by one, go up and receive their diploma for grades 7 through 9. I was in C3, which meant that there were three classes, or about sixty kids before me. The wait made everything even more nerve-racking.

And with that, the ceremony begins.

At some point, I take a moment to pause. I look around me. I try to freeze this moment, capture it in my heart, and lock it in my mind. I try to grasp the fact that what I am now experiencing has been deemed impossible. I look around once again. The atmosphere is full of emotions. There is a slight breeze in the room. I get goose bumps all over my body. This is surreal. This can't be actually happening. I get so emotional.

I look around again. I see lights and people holding up phones and cameras, others clapping for their kids, and still others just staring at the stage. I look at the ceiling. It's so high up. I try to look all around me and remember the room, the scene, the atmosphere, the moment. I don't want to miss it. I don't want it to be submerged, over time, under pain and suffering. I don't want to ever let go of the gratitude that overwhelms my heart this very moment. I don't want to ever lose this incredible sense of awe at how meaningful and full of hope this very moment is. I can't neither understand nor fathom it. I can only experience it and capture it and carve it on my heart and keep it with me—forever.

As my turn approaches, I stare at the ceiling once again. I hold my hands together tightly. They are sweaty and moving spastically because of how nervous I am. And yet when I hold them together to pray, they remain still, steady, and strongly tied together. Looking toward the ceiling, for, a moment I close my eyes.

God, I prayed with tears filling my eyes, *thank you. You never gave up on me. Some doctors gave up on me, the odds gave up on me, my body gave up on me, and my mind gave up on me. But you never did. You fought for me. You brought me through. This is a miracle, God. Help me make the most of out if. Help me walk across that stage. I'm scared to do so. I'm scared my knees aren't going to be strong enough. Please hold me up. Keep me steady. Help me treasure every second. But above all … help me be brave.*

The vice principal starts calling out names of kids from my class. I am at the edge of my seat—even more nervous than I'd been in the hospital waiting room before we got the biopsy results. My pulse is strong, my heart rate high, and my adrenaline through the roof. As the vice principal calls out Vasiliki, a classmate of mine three names before me on the list, I stand up and get in the line that has been formed. My knees are trembling. My hands are sweating. My mouth is dry. This is the moment. This is now. This is happening. This is what I'd been waiting for. This is it.

When the vice principal calls my name, everyone starts clapping. The sound radiates and reverberates across the whole room. It's so loud. Usually as students go up, about ten to twenty people clapped. But when I make my way up the three steps to get to the stage, every single person in the room is clapping. The sound echoes and crosses the walls of my heart. I feel strength and motivation enter my soul. I can't fit into words the significance of this sound, how much it means to me. It overwhelms my heart with a profound courage, comfort, and love. It motivates me not only to walk across this stage but also to learn to walk again—across the hospital hallways after my surgery and across the hallways of fear, doubt, peace, trust, and surrender. The incredible loudness of the sound is a part of what makes it so influential. It is louder than the voices of fear, louder than the voices that told me I would not make it, louder than the demons of my mind that told me I couldn't escape pain and experience hope. It is so incredibly louder than all that. What a hope!

As I made my way up to the stage, I was still clothed in that dress, characterized by the same hope I'd searched for so long—the hope I'd doubted I would ever find. On the second stair, I felt the tumor aggressively press against my knee, causing it to suddenly collapse. It literally just gave in. For a split second, fear took over. But somehow, through a small miracle that only *I* noticed and felt, I managed to stay steady, to keep walking. I almost fell, but God was right there. He held me and carried me. He didn't let me fall. My knee gave up on me, but God didn't. He never did. And the fact that God was there to hold me gave a purpose to the fall. It had to happen. My knee had to give in. It had to collapse. Only through that did I truly and profoundly experience God holding me, carrying me, and helping me get up on that stage. That moment was scary and yet meaningful and purposeful. It showed that meaning and purpose flowed out of fear and pain.

As I found the strength to continue walking up the stairs toward that stage, the roar of people clapping grew louder and louder and then suddenly stopped, becoming distant—an echo. It was like I was underwater, hearing someone call out my name from the surface. I stopped listening. I spaced out. Memories took over.

As I walked toward the principal, memories of the last six months flashed in front of my eyes. They were strong, as if they were actually happening. I literally felt the very pain and hurt, the discomfort and nausea of the memories that flooded my mind. Voices told me, "You can't get on a plane with such a suppressed immune system." "You can't fight off this infection." "You won't make it out." "You can't do it." I was overwhelmed.

I thought of my questions—the questions I'd asked myself on the second day of block 4. The sound of pain and hurt got loud. But the sound of people clapping, the sound of hope, and the sound of love was louder. It's always louder. I felt as if God was in the crowd too—clapping and rooting for me, smiling, and holding up a thumbs-up to give me courage. And yet at the exact same time, I felt Him right next to me, holding my hand, helping me walk, and *making me brave.* The memories disappeared as I walked to the principal, who, while holding back a few tears, handed me my diploma and shook my hand, holding it tightly and transfusing me strength. He spoke to me, but I was too overwhelmed to understand what he was saying. Memories were spinning in my mind. Voices of doubt, fear, and worry were being crushed one by one.

At some point, I snapped out of it and listened to what he was saying. "You are an example of strength for all of us. *You are so brave.* And that's why you will win."

I was filled with gratitude. I shook the principal's hand tightly, and with the most genuine smile and watery eyes, I thanked him from the bottom of my heart. What a hope.

As I walked to the stairs on the other side of the stage, tears flooded my eyes. *I did it*, I thought. It felt surreal. For the first time in my life, I felt stronger than cancer. I knew how scary it was and how aggressive, but when I heard this sound that echoed through the whole campus, when I thought of my family sitting among the crowd, when I felt God holding my hand, cancer seemed like nothing. Cancer looked small. For the first time ever, *I felt stronger.*

I felt as if all my suffering, my pain, and my tears; all the times I'd screamed out that I couldn't take this any longer; all the doubts; and all the times I'd woken in a puddle of sweat from nightmares of dying without saying goodbye or collapsed on the bathroom floor and burst out crying or thrown up till I couldn't even breathe—all that pain—was leading up to this moment. It was all leading up to these steps, that handshake, that sound of people clapping, these words from my principal, and these tears of joy streaming down my face. It was all leading to this walk across that stage.

After I got off the stage, Ageliki was there to help me. My legs were tired. The tumor pressed against my knee, threatening me, trying to stop me from walking, from taking any more steps. Cancer knew that every step I took was an attack against it. It knew that every clap I heard made me stronger. For the first time ever, it wasn't me who was scared of cancer. For the first time ever, it was cancer who was scared of me. It knew the depth of the love of my family, it knew the strength of the support from my friends, and it knew power of my faith. And for the first time ever, I didn't fear cancer. *Cancer feared me.*

As the night ended, the dress had fulfilled its purpose; and it remains a symbol of that night and that journey and a testament of how powerful hope is, how beautiful scars are, and how anything is possible. If I had to describe that whole trip home by one thing, it would be that dress. It wouldn't be the tears or the medicine; it would be that dress. If there was one thing that could characterize this whole season of my life, it would be hope. It wouldn't be the uncertainty, the doubt, or the fear. I might not always have had hope or known where to find it, but its power was projected through everyday details, smiles, conversations, sunsets, 3:00 a.m. cool limes, and 5:00 a.m. prayers. It could be projected through insignificant things like cereal for dinner and long FaceTime calls with Ami. The power of hope was all around; that night helped me see where it could be found. That night showed me that difficulties, pain, and scars can be beautiful and purposeful if you just clothe them in a white dress, if you surround them and view them through the lens of hope.

Tonight, hope was revealed through hugs, smiles, and firm handshakes; through words of encouragement; through steps on a stage; and through tears that ran down my face. Hope came to life through the roar of applause, the sound of love, the power of human connection, and the transformation of vulnerability and weakness to courage and strength. Tonight, hope became a dress that clothed me and hugged my scarred body as I nervously sat and prayed, waiting my turn; as I courageously walked across the stage; and as I tightly hugged my friends and family. Hope hugged my scattered soul, my broken parts, and clothed them in white, in peace, in courage. Hope showed me the depth of God's love. It showed me that nothing, even what is deemed impossible, is impossible. Hope revealed my scars, my brokenness and yet shined right through them, redefined them, and grew into the most beautiful flower, whose color touched everybody's heart. What a hope.

Some kids had organized an after-party to celebrate the graduation. At first, I didn't want to go. I couldn't dance since the tumor caused a lot of pain and since there was a very high risk for my bones to break. But I decided to go with Ami and Mikaela; I wanted to spend more time with them.

As we were driving we stopped at a restaurant, bought a souvlaki, and we parked on the side to eat. In that moment, I realized something about joy. It's in the details. It's in the spontaneous adventures, the random souvlaki pit stops, and the careless dance parties less than forty-eight hours before the most aggressive chemo. That's where joy is found.

I remembered the time I thought I was dying from that adverse effect. I remembered the questions I asked myself after the promise I made myself, when I realized I was still here. I had to make the most of every moment. I had to squeeze every inch of hope and joy that every little detail of life could give. How? By embracing it, acknowledging its significance, and being grateful for it. So that night I decided to go to the after-party after all. There were some risks, but life without risk is meaningless. Even hope itself is a risk. And both were risks I was willing to take.

The after-party turned out to be fun. As my friends and I were dancing, the DJ suddenly put a song on that directly spoke to my heart. I had been listening to that very song during every chemo block and thinking of what life would be like after cancer. That song had been with me through the hardest days of chemo, and now I was singing its lyrics at the top of my lungs, I was dancing to it with my friends, and I was showing to myself during chemo that anything was possible. Happiness is simple.

At around 4:00 a.m., we got home, and I had to pack. I didn't want to take anything with me, as I wanted to convince myself we'd be back soon. I thought that, if I packed lightly, then I would believe we would be back soon. However, the truth was, I didn't believe that; I was afraid of the suffering that the future held. But despite the natural fear, this time I knew it would all lead to hope, purpose, and growth. All that was to come would teach me how to walk across the path of doubt, worry, uncertainty, faith, forgiveness, love, and trust. It would all ultimately teach me how to be brave. And it would all lead to a walk across a stage.

Chapter 12

An Infusion of Memories

We got back from Athens on Thursday, June 14. As we walked in the apartment, a sense of numbness took over me. For a moment, I felt empty. I felt stuck again. I lay on the couch and opened my phone. I watched the video of me getting up on that stage and graduating and saw the photos of me and my friends. Instantly, I was given strength. I was reminded of why I was here, why I was back. I needed to fight. I needed to win. I needed to beat this. For my family. For my friends. For me. For whom God wanted me to become. For whom I needed me to be. For whom I dreamed to evolve into. I needed to go on. I needed to endure. I needed to keep fighting.

My mom prepared me a sandwich, and I lay down to get some rest. She went to do some chores around the house, and I was left thinking. As I reflected on the past week and what was coming, going through fear and what-ifs and doubts, I felt a strange feeling—a sense of peace. It was a sunset feeling—peace amid storms.

What's interesting about the sunset, though, is that it exists for a quick moment before day turns to night, and light turns to darkness. It's like a testament of the fact that this transition can be beautiful. It's proof of the fact that, though it's painful, it can be graceful. Darkness itself has a great purpose. It's preparation for the sunrise. The sun always rises, but what makes the sunrise significant is the darkness that it's born out of. Darkness is exactly what makes the sun able to rise again, and it's the very thing that makes the sunrise beautiful. You see, everything in life is relative.

Intrinsically nothing is beautiful or messy, good or bad. In reality, we're the ones who give things and situations these characterizations because we have other things and situations to compare them to. Light is not light if darkness does not exist. Happiness cannot be happiness without sadness. It's arbitrary. Therefore, even though darkness is scary, and sadness is painful, both have a profound purpose—to intensify light, happiness, and hope. Even though it hurts, this very pain is what gives waking up with no pain its value and significance.

As I thought about that, I fell asleep in peace, knowing what I was going through was shaping what I would find once I'd made it to the other side. Knowing that the suffering and pain of that present time would be the very thing that would make the future beautiful and meaningful was the most comforting thought.

The next morning, my mom woke me up super early. It was chemo day. It wasn't just any chemo day though. This was my last VIDE chemotherapy ever. I got up dreading having to go to the hospital, but I instantly remembered the words of the mom of that girl with whom I'd shared a room back during chemo 5. "Once VIDEs are over, life gets a little easier. It all gets a little better."

I had been waiting for things to get better ever since my diagnosis. Yet time always moved slowly. I always felt stuck, powerless. As a matter of fact, I'd felt *so* powerless at times that I doubted things would *ever* get better. I remember moments from the first couple of chemotherapies, especially blocks 1 and 2, where I truly didn't think I would ever be done with these treatments—or the pain and discomfort they caused. Yet there I was. I was getting ready for my last VIDE block—ever. I couldn't believe it.

After I got ready, my mom handed me a small teal tablet. It made me nervous. I knew what it was. It was the pill you take before a PET scan. That day, before starting block 6, I had to have a PET scan to see whether the treatment had continued to work and evaluate if the tumor had responded. That car ride to the hospital was one I'd never forget. So many thoughts, fears, and what-ifs clouded my mind.

When we got to the hospital, we went to the operation center where the radiology clinic was. The doctor operating the PET scan and I had met before, during my first scan in March. He remembered me instantly. He was one of the few people who spoke fluent English, so he was always able to make jokes and comfort me before a scan. Such people and situations prove how meaning and light are found in the details of darkness.

Here's the thing about darkness. It affects the sky, but it can't affect the stars. It affects the big things in life, but it can't affect the details. Lucky for me, hope, love, and purpose are all found in the details. That's why cancer can't hurt love, can't hide purpose, and can't beat faith. It can challenge them, shake them up a little, weaken them. But it can never beat them. Isn't it significant and incredible how you can see stars *better* when the darkness gets *stronger*? Life is so beautifully ironic. Pain only brings out hope and love. It can never beat them. When the big things fade under adversity, the details emerge and shine through.

As I lay on that PET scan table, a big what-if paralyzed me. What if the answer wasn't what I expected? Instead of trying to convince myself it would be, I convinced myself that, whatever the answer was, I would get through it. I had no way of knowing whether or not the treatment had continued to work, but I had a profoundly deep confidence that God would give me the strength and peace to get through it, whatever "it" was. Healing does not come in one form, and it's not always what you expected. That's where faith comes in.

After the scan was over, I was admitted into K3, the chemotherapy ward, and began treatment. This time around, I was in a room with two other kids and their families. We were six people sleeping in the same room, one of whom was just a couple of months old and cried most hours of the day. I had shared a room once before with that baby, and to be honest, it was no joke. Sleeping despite a constant crying sound was difficult.

My other roommate this time around was a girl around my age, who had something wrong with her heart. I instantly connected with her. She seemed so nice. She would smile at me once in a while—a smile of hope. At some point, her mom introduced herself to my parents, and they started talking. Well, actually, my dad mostly did the talking, since he was the only one who spoke German. The girl's mom shared some information about their story and my dad about ours. I didn't understand their conversation, but the empathy and compassion that was shared was not bound or limited by language. Instead, it radiated and was felt greatly even by me, a half-conscious, mostly asleep fifteen-year-old with absolutely no knowledge of the German language aside from the words "ya," "nein," and "danke."

Block 6 was relatively easier than the rest. I can even go as far as to say that it was the easiest of the six, probably because I'd been taking double-dose GCSF injections for two weeks, I'd been eating, and I'd given my immune system time to heal—a little bit at least. But still, it wasn't fun. That's one way to put it. Right from day one, I was experiencing most of the side effects. As I closed my eyes and breathed in, enduring the pain and nausea, I started thinking.

Only a day ago, I'd been dancing with joy at the graduation after-party, enjoying time with friends, eating a souvlaki, and wearing a smile on my face. Now, just hours later, I was bed bound, in a cold hospital room, nauseated, in pain, unable to even lift my head up by myself, and too weak to even hold my phone. Just a sunset later, I was attached to three different machines. That joyful smile had been replaced by tired tears, and I even needed help to get a tissue and wipe them away. It was as if the me a day ago and the me a day later were two completely different people.

While I was home in Athens, I'd made a summer playlist to listen to during chemo. Blasting the songs that I'd listen to during that week home gave me a lot of strength and motivation. Sound is a very strong memory trigger. And during this block, I was really triggered—in a good way. Hearing the leaves rattling as the summer breeze passed through them, I recalled memories from years ago. My room was directly above the hospital's playground, and the creaking noise the swing set made took me back to the times my grandpa would take my sister and me to the playground and help us collect blueberries as we cycled along the park. That memory was so strong that it calmed all fear and gave me peace. The dizziness from the chemo, for the first time ever, actually helped, as it intensified the experience of the memory, creating the feeling of being on that swing set with my grandpa. I felt as if he was fighting this round with me. It was the first time in years that I felt so connected to him after he passed away. It felt like, from heaven, he was protecting me here.

That same day, another small detail of hope was revealed to me. My parents received an email from Prof. D, who had just seen my graduation photos. "You have a really wonderful and tough daughter," the message said, "the only one I know who graduated during VIDE courses."

My heart was filled with determination and courage once I read it. It felt as if I was back in that auditorium, walking across that stage. Her words felt like a whole school auditorium clapping. It felt like the tightest hug and the most beautiful and gorgeous sunrise. Just like a sunrise symbolizes a new day, my oncologist's words symbolized a new seed of determination that had started growing in my heart.

On the second day, the girl I was sharing a room with was discharged. As she was leaving, she waved at me, and I waved back and smiled. She did too. Oh, how present is hope in such details. How many words and emotions do such little things hide. How much meaning do such small things store…

After a while, my dad got back from the cafeteria, where he'd gone to get lunch. I saw he was emotional, and I used my little pen and paper box to ask him what was wrong. He told me that, as he was coming back to the room, he'd come across the mother of my current roommate, the girl with the heart condition, and she'd so generously offered to help financially with my treatment. She told him that, when her daughter had gotten sick, she'd realized the importance of giving back and of kindness, and after hearing we were from Greece and didn't have German health insurance, she wanted to do something for us. My dad thanked her and told her how appreciative he was but that there was no need for her to do that, since we had it all covered. I saw how thankful he was and admired him for kindly refusing. But I mostly admired that woman for her selfless act of kindness. I wanted to be like her, offer hope like she did. This treatment block was already teaching me so much.

On the third day, the room, thankfully, did not have any new members. The baby was discharged too, so for just a few hours, I was alone and managed to fully rest and sleep all the drugs off. However, that night I woke up loopy, half-conscious, dizzy, nauseated, and with a new roommate. During the doxorubicin infusion, my mom placed her hand on my knee—just like she had back during the first chemo. Strength transfusions.

The next day, some medical students came in to practice taking a family history and a history of present illness. It was fun talking to them, if you put the talking part aside. That wasn't fun, since the taste from the chemo made it super uncomfortable. Interacting with the medical students infused me with hope, as it allowed me to picture myself doing the same thing in a couple of years. I pictured myself wearing the same white coat. I was given hope amid great fear as we were waiting for the PET scan results any day that week.

That evening, the doctors gave us some difficult news. They realized the polyneuropathy one chemo drug had caused had led to a leg infection. With my immune system destroyed and a huge operation in line, this was very bad news. The doctors told us not to worry and started me on an antibiotic and chamomile bath to treat and prevent the infection from spreading.

This whole round brought home back. It was as if God knew I would be nostalgic and I'd miss being home, so He took care of that and brought home to me, in the most unexpected ways—through the tiniest of details. Here's a cool thing about the details. They hide so much but can be easily missed. It's so important to pay attention to the little things, to those so-called insignificant things. Meaning, purpose, and hope are found in these details and in the stars of sorrow.

Monday, June 18, was the fourth day of block 6. And it was a day of miracles. Shortly after some recovery meds started, Dr. S came in and told us she had the PET scan results. A huge bright smile on her face gave away the news. The tumor was responding exactly the way the doctors wanted it to and showed significant necrosis. I was so emotional when I found out. This day was hope embodied. I was filled with gratitude. Hearing these words felt like being "dumped in really, really cold water to the point you can't even breathe—but in a really, really good way," as Zach, a friend of mine, once put it. I was so excited. For the first time ever, I felt life getting better. For the first time ever, a weight was lifted off my shoulders.

Tuesday was the fifth and final day of VIDE chemotherapies. I woke up ecstatic. You couldn't really tell, though, since I was very weak. It seemed unreal. This was it. VIDE would be out of the way. Forever. Something was finally changing. Things were finally getting better. I couldn't believe it. It was better than all my imaginary scenarios had painted it. It was a day of hope.

I remembered that first conversation with Dr. Thanos in our hotel room, back in January after I'd met my oncologist for the first time. I had asked him what this day would feel like. I also remembered the conversation I had with my mom on the bathroom floor, after crying in her arms. I was asking her when the suffering would end. I remembered begging my dad to take the nausea away. That was when I hit rock bottom. My body was shredded to pieces. My soul was ripped apart. Yet now, it was finally time to heal. For the first time ever, I could heal. The thought that I would never go through VIDE chemotherapies again brought me more gratitude and joy than words can possibly describe. No more unbearable pain from the tumor, no more horrifying side effects, no more red tears from the doxo. The day had finally come. VIDE was over—done.

The following days, post chemo, were extremely difficult. We'd expected them to be, however, which made dealing with them easier. On June 22, I received two bags of red blood cells. And then again five days later. This time, a bag of platelets was added. I didn't mind. After each blood transfusion, my appetite improved over the days that followed, which was helpful, since I was trying to get stronger for my surgery.

Since my diagnosis, I'd received over fifty transfusions. The first two had gone fine. However, starting with the third transfusion, I'd had an allergic reaction every single time I received either platelets or red blood cells. The doctors had no clue why this was happening every single time. The first allergic reaction followed a platelet transfusion. I'd developed rashes all over my hands, face, and stomach. A few seconds later, breathing had become difficult, and my throat had started closing up. It was extremely scary. I was trying to breathe as deeply as I could, but all my efforts were in vain. It felt as if I was suffocating. My mom rushed to get a nurse or a doctor. When they realized what was going on, a nurse ran to the supplies cabinet, retrieved a big syringe, and raced back to me, quickly injecting epinephrine in my arm. It hurt a lot as it flooded my bloodstream. Ever since that incident, I always received a high dose of an antihistamine before each transfusion, which made me sleepy and loopy. My body felt heavy, and I couldn't stay awake. I guess that could be a good thing, however, since it helped me sleep through the whole four hours each transfusion usually took.

On June 28' my mom flew back to Greece to spend a few days with my sister before she left for a summer camp in the States. My dad and Demy came to Essen to stay with me, while my mom was back home in Athens. That day, we decided to go on a road trip to a village outside

Düsseldorf. We first got the essentials for the trip—my meds; my camera; and, last but not least, a cool lime from Starbucks. We then drove around the countryside for a couple of hours. I took so many photos. There was something about road trips that just made my mood a million times better. My kind of road trips didn't need to be across countries or over mountains. They didn't need to involve nine-hour drives. Going to school, for me, was a road trip. The way I saw it, every car ride with music on max volume, windows down, and a cool lime or a coffee in my hand was considered a road trip.

After our spontaneous adventure, we stopped at a restaurant and enjoyed pizzas and steak. When we got home, we all watched a movie together. Demy gave me my night meds, but they made me nauseated and dizzy. I threw up a few times and then passed out on the couch. That was the harsh reality of cancer. During the day, I didn't feel sick. I was taking photos, singing songs in the car, laughing at jokes, and enjoying a slice of pizza. Yet just a few hours later, I was feeling horrible, throwing up, struggling to breathe, in pain, and exhausted. It was a heartbreaking realization I had to come to terms with, but I knew I could use gratitude to face it. I was hurt by the discomfort cancer caused, but I was also grateful for it, because it was that very discomfort that made the rest of the day so incredibly fun and precious. Experiencing pain again and again made joyful moments shine a thousand times brighter. So that night, as I fell asleep next to my dad on the couch, with the TV playing in the back, my headphones on, and listening to music, my heart teemed with gratitude. And, oh, how much stronger and more powerful than pain gratitude was.

My mom flew back on the thirtieth, and a few days later, we were back in the hospital for more tests. That Monday, I had my regular cardiac evaluation. One of the drugs I was on during VIDE blocks, could cause cardiotoxicity, so once a month, before every treatment block, I always had a full cardiac evaluation. My cardiologist was a rock star. She was a kind person and an amazing doctor, dedicated and determined. I admired her and looked up to her a lot.

Every evaluation so far had been normal. This one, however, was not. The doctors found that my left ventricle, the part of the heart that pumps out blood to the rest of the body, was dilated. I'd had a feeling there would be something wrong this time. I'd been getting tachycardias and shortness of breath often. I had thought it was due to the chemotherapy-induced anemia, but I was wrong.

"The good news is that we found it early, and we can monitor it closely. So that's what we'll do for now. It's also really good that you're finished with the VIDEs because you're not going to take doxo in the next treatment phase," she told me in a peaceful tone.

I stayed silent. I had always worried about my heart. It had always been one of my biggest fears. During every chemo, I would ask Dr. S to double-check my heart and to examine me twice with the stethoscope just to be sure. Now, that fear was becoming a reality.

After the appointment with my cardiologist, we went upstairs to the Ambulanz (the outpatient oncology clinic). We sat in the waiting room and waited to be called in. For the first time ever, the waiting room was empty. It had to be. Little did I know what that waiting room would soon symbolize. As I was sitting there, processing, I started crying. I was terrified and exhausted. I didn't think I had the strength to fight yet another problem. The clinic doctor saw me and knelt next to me. It was the same doctor I'd seen before going to Athens, the one who had told me I would probably have to be admitted in case of an infection, the one who'd held my hand as I cried. She was now holding my hand yet again, sitting by my side, fighting with me. That moment embodies the fullness of the powerful impact a doctor can have.

"What's wrong?" she asked me in a quiet, soft voice.

I told her about the results of the cardiac tests. I told her about my fears. I told her I was tired of dealing with problems. "Every time I get out of one problem and escape some suffering, more just keeps on coming. It never ends," I told her with tears in my eyes.

"I know it can feel that way. And I know you're tired. But you can't give up. It's good that we found the problem. It's good that, whatever is going on, we can find it. That means we can fight it and deal with it. We will monitor your heart, and we will fight it with you. Let's take it step by step," she told me.

That moment was so significant. Her words felt like a hug for my broken heart, restoring the courage I'd lost. And just like that, fear was replaced by gratitude. I felt protected, and that gave me peace—a sunset feeling. I smiled. In that waiting room, I experienced great fear, yet through the details, through that simple conversation, I was overwhelmed with gratitude, comfort, and *light*—all in the same room, in the room of uncertainty.

Light is abundant in the darkness of the waiting room. But it's hidden. Where? It's in the love shared between people; the compassion, kindness, and smiles; the conversations and hugs and post-hospital cool limes from Starbucks; the calls from friends and the FaceTimes with Amalia; the mango mint drinks and jokes my waiter friend made; the 3:00 a.m. prayers; and the daily videos my aunt would send me to give me strength. That's where light is found. In the details.

On July 5, I had a high-resolution MRI of my leg, as it was needed to prepare for the surgery. Before being called in, they told me, yet again, to sit in the waiting room. Foreshadowing.

Chapter 13

The Waiting Room

Two weeks after block 6 was over, I started recovering and gaining back lost energy. Summer plans, bucket lists, sunsets, and cool limes from Starbucks were the only things that got me through these past weeks. The pain was much more manageable, since, this time, I was started on GCSF injections right from day five of cycle 6, which meant right when I got discharged. The doctors were really concerned with how much time it had taken for my body to recover after block 5, and now with an infection in my leg, they didn't want to take any changes. These injections had long-term side effects, but they were crucial at the time.

In a conversation I had with my oncologist, we planned the surgery to happen four weeks after the chemo was over. During that third week, we visited the hospital to meet with my surgeon and the anesthesiologist. Knowing that my big surgery was coming up, I decided to finally name my tumor. I don't know why, but it was a detail that made me and my friends and family smile. I named the tumor Felicia. There was a funny meme a few years ago that said, "Bye, Felicia," which, in a weird way, had become my family's inside joke.

When we got to the hospital, we went to the operation center in A1, where the orthopedic clinic was. We gave our names and sat in the waiting room until it was our turn to see the surgeon, Prof. H. Sitting there, in the second chair across the hallway, my heart was filled with hope and joy. It was a certain joy that coexists with pain and shines right through the darkness—a joy that isn't circumstantial and isn't affected by emotions or situations. This joy is fueled by the deep gratitude for the presence of unconditional hope in the absence of my understanding. That kind of joy overwhelmed me in that waiting room. That moment was so significant, but little did I know.

After some time, the physician's assistant called us into room 4. The surgeon came in, greeted us, and shook my hand tightly. "OK, are you ready? This is it," he said with a smile on his face—a smile of hope.

"Okay," I replied and smiled back.

He went on explaining the risks of the surgery. They were many. I didn't expect all of them. Severe blood loss, loss of function, infection, blood clots, chronic pain, amputation … and cardiac arrest. The risks went on and on and on. I was so scared.

"Okay," I said at some point, "one question. How high is the risk of infection?"

"We don't know unfortunately," Prof. H said. "We do everything we can to prevent it, everything. But we just don't know."

The uncertainty killed me.

"It's the only way," he said at some point, "the only way."

That phrase got me through. "Yeah," I said with courage.

"Other questions?" he asked.

I paused for a moment. I needed time to process—time to reflect, to understand, to worry, to trust, and to hope. I needed time to take it in.

"Well," he said, "think about it and write the questions down, and you tell me when we see each other again."

"OK great," I said.

He shook my hand tightly and said with a smile, "We're doing this. We *got* this."

His words were engrafted in my heart in that moment. "We got this," I kept repeating to myself.

On the ride back home, we stopped at Starbucks for yet another cool lime. There was a Starbucks in Essen's Banhof, the train station. I never went in, as I couldn't walk. While waiting for my mom to get back, I looked out the window to the sky.

"God, I need you with me. We only got this together. I can't do it on my own. Prof. H said it. "We got this." I need you with me. I can't get through this alone.

Later that day, we went to Zwofl Apostles, a restaurant near our house. It was magical in the summer. They had set up the tables outside by the river, surrounded by trees and valleys. We got our classic pizza, and I got my classic German "Ramsteak". That waiter was there too, the one we were friends with. He was very happy to see me walk with crutches and not in the wheelchair. To celebrate, he brought me a "mango mint," which consisted of sparkling water, mango syrup, and mint leaves. Little did I know how important that single drink, that single detail, would become. Purpose and meaning are found in such details, in things that often go by unnoticed and unappreciated. But if you just pause and look, their significance and light is revealed.

A couple of days later, we went back to the ortho clinic for a follow-up with Prof. H to go over the surgery one more time. Upon arriving, we sat in the waiting room again. There was hidden significance that would soon be revealed—hidden light that would soon shine through the darkness. But for light to shine, it first needs to get dark. For stars to be revealed, there must first be a sunset, a moment where light fades, seeming to dim. In reality, however, light doesn't disappear with the sunset; it just changes forms, so it can shine through stars amid darkness. Therefore, for the purpose of these details to be revealed, there first needed to be a sunset, a moment that looked like defeat but, in reality, prepared the ground for the greatest and most glorious victory.

During our appointment with the surgeon, he explained that the surgery unfortunately had to be postponed due to an ongoing nurses' strike. I couldn't believe it. A strike would delay the operation for God knew how many weeks, which would risk tumor regrowth. It didn't make sense to me. Why was this happening? I was frustrated. If I'm being honest, though, I was also a little relieved. The surgery had created a great deal of fear, doubt, agony, and worry that my faith was not yet strong enough to fight against. Maybe that's why these obstacles were on the horizon. Maybe my faith was being strengthened to pull me through the traumatizing darkness of the surgery. Maybe the waiting room was just a preparation room for faith to mature and grow stronger.

I spent the next couple of days at home chilling. My older sister, Ageliki, visited at some point. We spent much-needed time together. I was so thankful for little moments with her. Just sitting on the couch together

155

and planning future trips or talking about clothes brought me so much comfort and joy amid the chaos.

Opportunities for love and hope to be shared justified the opposition that came before them. When opposition knocks on the door, opportunity always comes with it. But it hides in the details. It's not accessible unless you acknowledge its presence. The meaning that hides in such details and moments answers, little by little, the why questions. There's a reason for everything; every puzzle piece has a place—not to your picture but to God's. And His picture is better. Maybe I didn't see how a picture filled with pieces of my heart that were scattered as it broke from pain and crashed from suffering was better. Maybe you don't see it either. But that's what trust is all about. That's what faith really means.

A couple of days later, we got another email from Prof. H, telling us he'd squeezed me in among the few surgeries that were happening while the strike was still ongoing. He told us he needed me to do a CRP check and then meet him to sign the consent forms. A quick biology lesson is necessary for this to make sense. C-reactive protein is a specific protein marker that indicates the level of inflammation in the body. If there's an infection, the CRP would be higher. A high CRP count is a risk factor that increases the chance of periprosthesis infection, which lead to things going really badly really quickly and, possibly, to amputation. That's why it was crucial to check that protein marker before proceeding with the surgery.

On Thursday, July 5, we had a meeting with my anesthesiologist, Dr. M. Dr. M was Italian and very funny—not that there's any correlation between the two; they're just notable facts. I liked him a lot; he made me laugh and was able to take away some of my fear. After the operation I had in January, when I'd been given too much anesthesia, I was terrified of going through the same thing again. Dr. M understood, validated my fear, and assured me he would not let that happen again.

He went on to explain pain management after the operation. He told me I would be given very high doses of morphine and multiple other medications. He also said that, normally, patients were given epidurals; however, that was not possible for me. Due to my low platelet count, I would be given two nerve blocks instead. The nerve blocks involved placing two catheters directly next to certain main nerves in my leg and continually administering a paralytic and an anesthetic. This would help with the pain, which was why we agreed to go with it, despite the fact that it was riskier and more dangerous, with permanent damage to the nerves possible. The anesthesiologist tried to prepare me for the fact that the pain would be very strong, but little did I know at the time just how strong it would be.

The next day, we went to the Ambulanz for blood draws to check for that CRP, and a consult. We met with Prof. D and went over the surgery and its risks. She noticed that the infection in my leg hadn't subsided even thought I'd been taking antibiotics for over two weeks. She told us she would consult Prof. H and let us know. After that, we went back to the waiting room, both literally and metaphorically. You'll see what I mean.

Later that day, my mom got an email from Prof. H. My CRP levels were way too high for us to proceed with the surgery. With the infection in my leg persisting and my CRP levels high, Prof. H gave us two options. Along with putting me on antibiotics again, he explained we'd either proceed with the surgery on Tuesday, after seeing a normal CRP level on Monday, or we'd postpone it for a month and instead do another operation to clean out the infection.

That Monday, my mom received yet another email from Prof. H. The CRP counts were within normal range, and the antibiotics had worked. I was so relieved. Yet I was scared. This was great news, as we could finally proceed with the surgery. And yet it was frightening news as well, for that same exact reason.

We scheduled the operation for Friday, July 13. I know what you're thinking, but I'm not superstitious.

On Wednesday, July 11, just two days before the surgery, my mom got a third email from Prof. H, asking to see me in the ortho clinic that same day. He said it was urgent. We quickly left for the hospital and went straight to that waiting room on A1 to meet him.

After a couple of minutes of waiting, he called us into room 4 again. "I'm sorry, but we cannot do the surgery," he said as soon as we walked in.

"What happened now? Is it the infection?" my mom asked.

"Yes. I'm sorry, but it's too risky. It's almost certain you'll get a periprosthesis infection."

"I've been taking antibiotics for it for two weeks and stopped taking them just few days ago because a doctor on the chemo ward said I should take them just for two weeks," I explained.

"But see, I didn't know that. I didn't know about the infection persisting. I thought it was cleared out with the antibiotics. But it hasn't. And nobody wrote it on the file."

Doctors write everything in the file. They had a huge folder for each patient that was more organized than my mom's office cabinet (my mom is obsessed with organization). There was no way they just hadn't written it. And yet there was. And yet they didn't. No reference of the infection was in the file. At first, I was upset; my mom was too. But it was all part of a higher plan. It was a puzzle piece that didn't make sense then but would turn out to be one of the most important pieces for the final picture. You'll see.

I wanted to have the surgery that Tuesday, but God had other plans. I love the significance behind that sentence. Yes, it was frustrating, *but God* had purpose in store. I was in pain, *but God* was there. I was desperate and scared to fall asleep at night, *but God* would transform all that pain into purpose. So many times, we just read the first part of the sentence. So many times, we just focus on the fact that it hurt, that fear was strong, and that anxiety overwhelmed us. So many times, we stop at the coma. But comas are not the end. Comas signify that there's more to the story, more than we can imagine, more than we can see.

And here's what I've found out as I got to know God better; He loves using comas. That's because it is in the very nature and foundation of faith to be intertwined with comas. There's so much we can't see, so much we can't know. That's where trust comes in. The question wasn't why the infection happened, why it was not in the file, or even why I'd gotten cancer in the first place. The question was whether I was brave enough to have faith, whether I was courageous enough to trust God even when it hurt and when I didn't understand. Finding the inner resilience, the courageous boldness, and the raging trust to read past the coma is the most powerful, most profound expression of faith, and the bravest thing somebody could do. When you know who the author is, you don't worry about what's coming after the coma. When you know who's surrounding what's surrounding you, you're not scared to read past the coma. And when we're bold enough and brave enough to get past the coma, the greatest "but

Gods" are revealed. There's always a "but God." It hurts, *but God* ... I am scared, *but God* ... I feel alone, *but God* ... Read past the coma. It's not the end; it's just the sentence's waiting room.

My doctors ended up canceling the surgery yet again and scheduled another surgery for that coming Monday to clear out the infection. We asked Dr. M to be my anesthesiologist in that operation too, and he gladly agreed. I went home that day confused. I was in a season of waiting, and I didn't understand why. I had suffered so much and for so long; I just expected things to be better, for once. I'd had the expectation that, from then on, life would get easier. What I didn't understand at the time, however, was that God was waiting *past* my expectation to reveal what was hidden after the coma. What if that expectation was keeping me from allowing the change God wanted to do *in* me, to prepare me for what He had prepared *for* me?

I spent the next two days at home, drinking cool limes from Starbucks and watching the World Football Cup. I'd supported France ever since the games started, and I was very excited to see them win. Maybe, just like my team was winning, I would win too. I'm not a soccer fan, but this year I didn't miss a game—in which France played. The final was on July 15. Notice that date. Notice the details. Only a month later, I would see another victory—just like France did on that game.

That Sunday, my dad flew to Germany and got me breakfast on his way home from the airport. Looking back, I don't know if he got enough breakfast for me or for the full soccer team of France. He got two *huge* boxes of donuts, a cool lime drink from Starbucks, a cinnamon roll, and coffee. We could literally live off the donuts for the rest of the week. I enjoyed breakfast over a game of soccer and then took a nap. I was so grateful for such details. They gave me a great deal of comfort and hope. Life was painful, and yet little moments like these made it extremely, undeniably beautiful. I was in a lot of pain from the infection in my leg, the tumor, and the GCSF injections. I spent the day watching movies with my dad and driving around Essen. Hope hides in the details. It was in that box of breakfast donuts and in my dad's smile when he saw me finally eating and in car rides chasing the sunset in Essen's countryside, while listening to my favorite songs as loud as it gets and taking photos of beautiful landscapes. Moments like these made it all worth it. Every stabbing sharp pain, every tear, and every suffocating fear were all worth it because of such small details of hope and joy.

The next morning, we woke up at around 4:30 a.m. to go to the hospital. I changed into fresh clothes and, with my slippers still on, left for the hospital. Since I didn't walk, there was no need for shoes. To be honest, I didn't really sleep that night; I was too nervous. On the car ride there, I put on certain songs that really hyped me up. For this surgery, the song "Unstoppable" by Sia pulled me through. As soon as we arrived, we were admitted onto the surgical floor, and I was given a room.

I shared the room with an older lady who was struggling with pain after an operation she'd had a while ago. It was a foreshadowing, but little did I know that. I changed into a hospital gown and wore an anticoagulatory sock on my other leg, to prevent clots from forming. A doctor came in and marked my right leg with a cross. For the doctors, it was a reminder of the leg they had to operate on. But for me, it was a reminder of the victory, the hope, the comfort, and the purpose of the cross of Christ. It was a subtle detail that reminded me that I was not alone.

They moved me down to the OR floor, and I said goodbye to my parents. Two nurses wheeled me in the operating theater and confirmed my history, procedure, and information. In the pre-OR room, two other nurses inserted an IV line and put me on oxygen. Finding a vein to place the catheter in was impossible, so they had to try a lot of times. One of the nurses was holding my hand as they poked and prodded my arms and hands. She was Greek too, so she tried to take my mind off the pain by starting a conversation about home. God's in the details. Dr. M came in after a while and placed the IV line himself. He got it on the first try. I was impressed. He then inserted the anesthesia and started talking to me. He asked me which season I preferred and whether I liked the mountains more than the sea. I was grateful for that conversation.

The next thing I remember is waking up in the recovery room next to my parents. This time, there were no breathing problems. I was in a great deal of pain, but it didn't even matter. I could breathe. That's all that did matter. I don't really remember much of what happened after. I just vividly recall thanking Dr. M every time he came to check up on me because of how grateful I was that I could breathe.

After about twenty thank-yous, he smiled and told me, "Hey, it's just my job."

I smiled too and then fell back asleep.

I woke up again in my room on the surgical floor. I was in pain, sore, unable to speak from the intubation, and really loopy and nauseated from the anesthesia. I opened my phone up and wrote this down on my notes: "Words can't describe the pain, but they can't describe the gratitude either. My leg hurts unbearably, but my lungs are full of air. And that makes it all OK. This breath reminds me that everything is going to be OK—even if I'm not. The important thing is that finally the infection is gone! No more delays."

But, yet again, little did I know.

After a couple of hours, I was finally discharged. The new cast on my leg looked like a very weird shoe. I went home and slept the rest of the day. I spent the next couple of days pretty much just sleeping and feeding on pain meds. On Tuesday, July 19, as I was scrolling on social media, a very significant photo suddenly popped up. Here's what it said:

July 19, 2018. Day 200 of 365.

God is saying to you today:

For every tear you've shed, and

for every sleepless night,

I have a blessing for you. *Don't give up.*

Seeing that post gave me so much courage. Little renders like that kept me going. Later that day, my grandma came to Essen to visit me. She was going to stay with me for about a month, and I was really grateful for that.

On the same day, I received another what felt like a confirmation that things would get better. Mrs. V, my French teacher at school this year, sent me an email to motivate me to keep fighting. At some point in that email, she wrote, "I believe that, in life, when a lot of problems hit us all together, that then there's something really, really good that's waiting for us in the future."

Her words gave me so much hope.

I spent the next couple of days at home recovering. One day, we decided to go to Düsseldorf because my grandma had never been there before. After driving around Düsseldorf, we went to a football arena, where Ed Sheeran was preforming. The tickets were sold out, but we parked right outside and listened to him perform for a while. My grandma got me one of the sweatshirts they were selling and a T-shirt with the concert date on it. After a few songs, we drove back to the apartment. Concerts—that small detail would turn out to be one of the strongest sources of courage for me. You'll see how.

The next day, it was chemo day. This chemo would be different, and I didn't know what to expect. Once we got to the hospital, I went to the lab on the UG floor. The ladies there knew me really well. They understood English but only spoke German; therefore, communication had always been difficult. Yet love and compassion are not bound by language, or any other barrier as a matter of fact. I had connected with these two ladies from the first time I met them, back in February. Before starting chemo or before seeing an oncologist for a follow-up checkup, I would always go to the lab for "finger pricks"; this was what they called the blood test, as they collected blood just from a finger prick. After the blood test, one of the two ladies, whose name was also Katerina, would write down the cell counts on a paper that I would then take up to the Ambulanz, for the doctor to see. Since I'd started treatment, I'd had thousands of these "finger picks." The two ladies in the lab used plasters with drawings and shapes for the little kids, and they always let me pick out the plaster I wanted. However, there was a specific one, a green one with a red ladybug on it, that they would always give me. They told me it was for good luck. Love's in the details. This, time was no different. After the finger prick blood test, they wrapped that same plaster around my finger, and I went up to get admitted to K3, the chemo ward.

During the chemo prep with the clinic oncologist, she noticed that my white blood cells were extremely low for me to have the treatment. She called Prof. D, and they decided it would be best if I just received 80 percent of the chemo dosage. They also decided that, because of the extensive damage to my peripheral nervous system caused by vincristine, one of the chemo drugs, it was better if I didn't receive it at all during this phase. This news was frightening. On the one hand, I was scared to receive chemo when my immune system was so compromised. However, not receiving chemo was even scarier because I'd been off treatment for almost two months now, and the risk of tumor regrowth was really high. Receiving only 80 percent of the dosage and taking out one of the drugs, which I knew was very aggressive yet effective, really added to my fear. Despite that fear, however, I chose to trust there was a reason these things were happening, even if I couldn't understand or imagine what that reason could be. I knew the why isn't understood in during the hardship but in the after.

This chemo flew by. The side effects were manageable, and I even felt well enough to eat a grilled cheese sandwich my mom made. The regimen I was on during these blocks was called VAC. Normally, patients on VAC take vincristine, actinomycin, and cyclophosphamide; good luck pronouncing these. Chemo drug names are super long, I know. As I told you before, however, due to the severe neuropathy the vincristine had caused, I was not going to take it. According to the treatment protocol I was on, I had to do eight blocks of these phase two chemotherapies. And I had just completed the first one of them.

After being discharged, we went home. I went straight to the couch to sleep. I was exhausted from the treatment. Ever since my surgery the week before, I'd been on anticoagulation meds, so I had to have a Clexane injection every night to prevent clots from forming. Purple and green dots soon covered my legs—hematomas from the injections. I didn't really mind though. I would use the bruises as eyes and draw smiley faces around them. Joy's in the details. Don't take life too seriously.

The night was peaceful, and I managed to get some rest. The next morning, on Wednesday, the twenty-fifth, I woke up excited. I was ready to do my best and recover speedily from this chemo so that I could get back to photography and road trips. Soon after breakfast, however, my left foot started hurting. We noticed the presence of redness and swelling, so my mom emailed my surgeon. He was worried and told us to come in so that he could examine my leg.

At the hospital, we sat in the waiting room yet again. This season was full of uncertainty, doubt, and worry. It was a season of waiting rooms. But it is those very waiting rooms that release the most significant miracles. Every season of darkness is a waiting room. It's an anticipation of the sunrise. We patiently wait through the night because we hope for the day that follows. We wait through the pain because we hope for the purpose that is hidden. Hope is based on things still unseen. This is what faith is all about. And it's that very faith that enables us to hope in the waiting.

After a while, we got called in, and Prof. H examined my leg.

"Oh no," he said at some point.

"What is it?" my mom asked, worried.

"This is another infection. We can't do the surgery," he said and exhaled deeply.

"Another one? You gotta be kidding me. How? Why?" I asked, worried.

I couldn't understand why this was happening. I'd been struggling to stay above water, and every time I tried to catch a breath and got a hold on the pieces of the broken boat of hope, ten-foot waves pushed me back down.

"I'm sorry, but we need to do another surgery. We have to clean this infection too before it spreads."

"Why do these infections keep happening?" my mom asked, upset.

"I don't know. I really don't know. I'm sorry. I've never seen the same infection on both legs in sarcoma patients. Maybe three out of every hundred patients get one such infection. But twice? On different legs? I've never seen that before in my whole career," the surgeon replied.

"Why does it keep coming back?" I asked with desperation in my voice, trying to understand the situation.

"It's resistant to antibiotics it seems. And also, you're really, really immunocompromised, so I'm not that surprised. But with the surgery, we cleared out the infection site completely. I don't know why it's back," Prof. H. said, vexed. "I'll schedule an emergency surgery for tomorrow; we have to fight this as soon as possible. It's a good thing we caught this one early."

I was crushed. I'd been punched to the ground by so many disappointments and difficulties, and I just couldn't catch a break.

"Will I need to do more chemo? More antibiotics?" I asked.

"We can't know. We take it day by day from now on, OK? First, we need to completely get rid of the infection. Then we can take out the tumor," Prof. H replied.

These words broke me. The uncertainty beneath them were prelude to the sleepless night to come. Prof. H saw that I was really discouraged by the news. Before we left, he squeezed my hand and, with a smile of hope on his face, told me once more, "Hey, we got this. We will do it. *We will get it.*"

His words were like a rope I could hold onto. God's in the details. I didn't feel Him near me at the time because my faith was being tested; the mountains were too high and didn't seem to move. Many times in my life though, God didn't move a mountain just to show me that He could carry me over it and to teach me how to trust Him. I was expecting to feel God's presence and hear Him in the form of good news, comfort, a scheduled surgery date. However, the proof of the presence of God was not in the presence of comfort but in my ability to endure and withstand discomfort.

I was so focused on the presence of darkness that I missed its purpose. I was so focused on the absence of the sun in my life that I completely dismissed the presence of stars. Discouraging news, heartache, hurt, fear, worry, and doubt were all making the night darker and darker. But details like the courage I was given by these words my surgeon told me were redefining darkness.

That night, I lay in bed full of fear.

God, I don't understand. I prayed about the infection, but it came back. I trusted you, but it didn't work out. If you had been here, it wouldn't have happened. I don't know why you would allow all these obstacles. I'm tired of constantly fighting. But I will. I will wait. The breath in my lungs, I don't take it for granted. There's a sunrise every day, a new day. These things remind me, God. I am reminded of how much you've gotten me through. But now … I feel alone. I'm so weak. I don't think I have the strength to keep trusting you. Please, God, stay close. Make me brave. I'm broken. But, I need to be brave. Please make me brave.

We all have things we hoped would happen but didn't and things we hoped wouldn't happen but did. Sometimes, the exact opposite of what we wanted ended up happening. We all have hopes that are crushed, moments that are stolen by fear, doors that closed just as we tried to walk through them, and dreams we aborted because they seemed impossible. The discouraging news from the doctor caused a lot of such buried disappointments to resurface. Sometimes, these disappointments are big events. For example, I prayed with everything in me for negative biopsy results, but it still was cancer.

Other times, however, these disappointments are insignificant, so much so, that they might barely affect you when they happen. But imagine holding a glass of water in your hand for a really long time. The water inside the glass might not be heavy at first, but the longer that you hold up the glass, the heavier it will start to feel.

But I want to remind you, it's okay to let go. It's okay to let it out once in a while. It's okay to get discouraged, to cry, to feel the hurt. It's okay to let the water fall, because as it falls it will wipe clean the pain. It's okay to let go. Let the heaviness be heavy until it isn't any more. What's not okay is staying there; staying desperate, staying hopeless. Because even the darkest night can only last for so long. Light will shine again. And it will best reflect on scattered glass.

The sun had set in this season of my life, and I was forced to be here—in the waiting room. What made the waiting room so uncomfortable and painful was that I wasn't alone in it. Doubts sat next to me. Uncertainty sat across from me. Fear, discouragement, anger, bitterness, and hopelessness were all siting in the waiting room with me.

I imagined a place on the other side of what I was going through, at the end of the pain. I called that place "there." I believed that, *there*, things would be back to normal. *There*, I would be happy. *There*, I would find peace. *There*, I would rejoice. *There*, I would let go of fear. *There*, I would find hope. But hope was not *there*. Hope was *here*. Peace was not *there*. Peace was *here*. It was here—in the darkness, the pain, and the dirt, buried, surrounded, and overwhelmed. Here—*in the midst*, not at the end.

A lot of people think pain is a path to peace, to purpose, to progress. But that means that peace and purpose and progress are out there, in the after, on the other side of the problem. Pain, however, is not a path to; it's a path of. It's the path of peace, of purpose, of progress. For peace, purpose, and progress are found in the *here*, in the *now*, in the waiting and the uncertainty.

The waiting room showed me something about the nature of hope that I couldn't see in seasons of comfort and normalcy. It showed me that hope had the power to give me comfort in my pain and deliver me from it. But I wouldn't have been able to know that unless I first sat in the waiting room. The night taught me something about the nature of light that I couldn't learn during the daytime. It taught me that light has the power to overcome darkness. But I wouldn't have been able to know that unless darkness first overwhelmed me.

The light that overcomes darkness is not the one that shines in the sunrise when the night is over, when I am "there." The light that overcomes darkness is the one that is born in it, the one that emerges from it. Hope is not found in the happiness, comfort, and normalcy restored after a difficulty. Hope is found in the love, compassion, kindness, faith, trust, vulnerability, surrender, resilience, and the details that are revealed during the difficulty.

When a seed is planted, the first signs of growth come long after the growing process has begun. The first part of that process happens underground. The deeper the seed is buried, the longer the waiting period between the beginning of growth and the visible signs of growth. However, growth still happens even when we can't see it, proving that something is always happening when nothing is seen. It can be painful and still help us grow. It can feel overwhelming, uncertain, and unpredictable and still be fruitful. There's growth in the waiting room. It proves that opposition becomes an opportunity for the seed of hope to grow into a tree of purpose. And as it grows, it'll break—again and again. And it will be painful. Yet it will manage to emerge through the dirt, through the very thing that trapped and surrounded it. And there it will be standing, bearing fruit, and giving back hope.

One day, as I was in life's waiting room, I got a call from Make-A-Wish. We scheduled a Skype call and talked about hope, wishes, and courage. That small detail of light filled me with hope.

If you think about it, the only place where hope can truly and fully be experienced is *in the waiting room*.

Chapter 14

The Month of Tides

The next morning, July 26, my mom took me to the hospital for the second surgery. My grandma came with. I didn't want her to see me in pain, but the deepest form of human connection comes from moments of vulnerability. The procedure was the same: I was admitted to the surgical floor, got changed into a hospital gown and was taken down to the OR. In the prep room, I saw Dr. M, who smiled and asked me, "Back so soon?"

I smiled. This time around, placing an IV was much faster and less painful.

"Ready?" Dr. M asked me and placed the oxygen mask around my face.

"Yes," I replied confidently.

On Monday, July 30, we went to the hospital to meet with Prof. D for a chemo follow-up checkup. She walked us through the potential treatment routes we would follow after the tumor removal surgery, explaining that, based on the pathology report, treatment would be different. If the tumor had a necrosis rate of over 90 percent, then we would normally proceed with the eight blocks of VAC chemo, one of which I'd already completed. However, if the necrosis rate of the tumor was below 90 percent, then I would need to do a mega block. I'd known this was a possibility, but I hadn't expected the necrosis rate to need to be so high.

A few days ago, I had just heard about the case of a young boy (the one from that physics class announcement back in January, who received treatment in the States) who'd had a 75 percent necrosis rate and yet proceeded with the first treatment protocol. Prof. D explained, however, that, in Germany, they believed in high-dose chemo, which was why they proceeded with the mega block in such cases. I was extremely scared. That's when it all hit me a little too hard. I was expecting the necrosis rate, in my case, to be at around 80 to 85 percent and still thought that was too high. It turns out, however, that it wasn't. My mom didn't expect it either.

Fear took over.

Prof. D walked us through the mega block and the stem cell transplant that followed. The idea was that they would blast you with so much chemo that it permanently shut down and wiped out your bone marrow, which was why they then gave you the stem cells they had collected after block 3, to restart your immune system. I was terrified. I needed a sign. And there it was. In the details. In the next room. In the next conversation. In a sentence. In a maybe.

After that appointment, we went to the orthopedic outpatient clinic to meet with Prof. H and discuss the surgery. While in the waiting room, I tried to process what we'd just discussed with my oncologist. Fear and worry overwhelmed me, chaining me to doubt and locking me in the cell of despair. I closed my eyes and took a deep breath. I felt my lungs expand as air flowed into them. And just like that, I was reminded of how far God had brought me through. I'd been so caught up in fear and anxiety and constant worry that I'd forgotten to pause and truly appreciate the waiting room I was sitting in.

As I closed my eyes, I remembered sitting in the waiting room in the hospital in Greece, waiting for the biopsy results. I remembered sitting in the hospital waiting room before receiving my first chemo. I remembered sitting in that front line in the auditorium, waiting to be called onto the stage to receive my diploma. And now, after all the suffering, the uncertainty, the agony, the fear, the trust, and the hope, I was still sitting in a waiting room. This time, however, the *way* I waited was different. I decided right then and there that I would choose to hope for a miracle—in that waiting room, on that day, after that discussion with my oncologist. The when of the wait is significant if we're to understand the why of the wait. I was about to be given a confirmation—a sign that God would protect me. It was there—in the next room, in the next conversation, in a sentence, in a maybe.

"I'm thinking maybe we can do the surgery on Wednesday, August 15," Prof. H told me when we went in.

August 15—Dekapentavgoustos—is one of the most important days for the Greek Orthodox Church. It's all in the details.

A few days later, Amalia flew to Essen and spent the rest of the week with me. Getting to spend time with her was my greatest source of hope and strongest motivation to keep going.

The first morning of August was full of smiles, since my mom and I went to the airport to pick up my friend Milti, who was visiting for a few days. On the drive home, we made a plan. We decided to go on a three-day summer road trip and explore three different cities, one each day. We both were excited. August 1 was day one of our summer adventure. Since it was already pretty late in the morning, we decided to explore Essen and most of its suburbs. We started off by going to Starbucks for a quick cool lime and then began our trip.

Milti and I were in the back seat, with all the windows down, singing songs loudly and laughing. It was pure happiness. It's all about the little things in life. Every now and then, we stopped at the side of the road, and I took photos of the landscapes. We drove across the scenic routes of Kettwig, a suburb next to Werden. We raced the river, speeding against the wind. As the summer breeze hit my face, I smiled. For a moment, I felt free—free from the chains of pain, sickness, and depression. I felt happy. I was simply enjoying a car ride with one of my best friends, singing, taking photos, and sipping on a cool lime. I was *happy*. I still had cancer. I still was in pain. And yet, in that moment, none of that mattered. All that mattered was the moment itself. Singing. Chewing on ice cubes and laughing. Nailing that photo. That very moment was all that mattered. Pain didn't matter. Cancer, fear, and worry—none of that mattered. The pure joy that stemmed from the simplicity of the moment could not be overcome. Life was good.

At night, Milti and I had cereal for dinner and then watched a movie. For the past week, I'd been basically feeding on milk with cereal for all my daily meals. It made me happy. Such a small insignificant thing was big enough to make me smile.

The next day we took a break from our road trip. We had another activity planned. When Milti came to Essen, he brought me a cookbook.

It was an inside joke. As a result, we soon turned that day into a cooking challenge. We picked out some recipes from the cookbook, came up with some of our own, and compiled a six-course menu that we prepared for my mom and ourselves. I tried to help as much as I could, but I often took breaks to catch my breath. Standing for over five minutes made my heart race. I was also very anemic, so my energy levels were in the tank. It didn't matter, however. I chose to see all the beauty and joy of each moment, to focus on all that I *could* do, instead of dwelling on what I couldn't. After multiple hours of preparation, the challenge was complete, and our dining table was full of homemade food.

Happiness is homemade.

As we were enjoying lunch together, we shared many stories and smiles. That's what life is all about—sharing smiles.

The next day was day two of our road trip. Day two would be spent exploring Düsseldorf. After enjoying breakfast, we started our adventure. At some point, we passed through a tunnel that was long and dark. But streetlights guided us toward the light, toward the exit. As we approached its end, the sunlight shined brighter and brighter. It was blinding.

That simple moment got me thinking. Life is the same. It's like a long road trip. In order to get to your destination, you inevitably have to go through the tunnel. It's the only way out. In the tunnel, it gets so dark you forget it's still bright outside. Likewise, in the tunnel of cancer, it often got so dark I forgot what the light of laughter or safety or carelessness felt like. But no matter how dark the tunnel got or how long and endless it seemed, there were always streetlights, guiding me toward its end. Throughout my battle with this disease, with despair and fear, there were always small moments of hope or joy that, just like streetlights, guided me toward the sun and reminded me of what it looked like. These moments were oftentimes small and went by unnoticed. As I was fighting cancer, trying to make it to the end of the tunnel, I oftentimes doubted it even had an end to begin with. I feared darkness would always overwhelm me and things would never get better. But here's the thing about the end of the tunnel. You only ever get there if you keep moving. The only way out is through. The only way to rediscover light is to keep looking for it, keep believing and trusting that it exists.

That afternoon, we went to our favorite restaurant, Zwolf Apostles.

There we saw our waiter friend, and I got to share my love for that mango mint drink with Milti. Sharing something that brings you joy with someone you love is one of the purest forms of human connection.

The next day was the last of our road trip. So we had to make it count. We had to make it the best. We woke up early in the morning, had breakfast, made coffee for the road, packed a camera bag, and left for Amsterdam. I'd always dreamed of visiting Amsterdam but had never had the chance. Yet, to my surprise, it was in a time of sickness that I crossed things off my bucket list. How meaningful is that.

Why does it take facing death to truly start living life?

The next morning, Milti left for Athens. I was sad that he was leaving, but I had an exciting project to jump into that took away all my negative thoughts. I spent the entire day on my computer editing the video footage we'd taken and making it into a short film about our little road trip. I also went through the photos I'd taken. I was grateful that I could still pursue something I was passionate about, something that brought me much joy, despite going through cancer. Photography and filmmaking were always the tools I used to take any situation and show what I saw in it, what was hidden within it. Especially during treatment, I challenged myself to try and portray the beauty of Essen through photographs, even though I associated it with being sick. I remembered my camera theory. I'd been applying it a lot lately. It allowed me to view difficult situations from a perspective of joy and somehow extract hope in the process. I was so thankful for Dr. Vasilis's lenses. I hadn't bought my own collection yet, so I was using his. I felt as if he was taking these photographs with me, in a way giving me the right perspective and helping me see the potential of hope amid pain and uncertainty.

A day later, on August 6, my friend Mikaela flew to Essen. Ever since we were really young, we would always spend a week or two together during summer holidays. This year, even though life was different, we decided to keep the custom going. I was very excited to see her. I felt blessed to be surrounded by family and friends who made me feel loved in times when pain was making me feel lonely. I was thankful for the healing God gave me daily in different forms. Sometimes healing looked like a conversation, a joke, a family dinner, a smile, a sunset, a car ride, or even a refreshing cool lime from Starbucks. The details of hope were also details of healing. Hope is a path of healing. Yet, at the same time, hope is the healing itself. It doesn't always come in the way we want it to. Healing sometimes means the mere existence of hope amid great suffering.

Mika and I spent her first days in Essen, enjoying the coziness of home, drawing for hours, driving at sunset viewpoints, taking photos, and watching TV shows. We were doing exactly what we'd be doing if we were back in Greece and I were healthy. It seemed as if nothing had changed. I loved how familiar every day suddenly looked. I was excited to wake up in the morning. I knew every new day wasn't filled with the uncertainty of my reality but, rather, with the comfort and nostalgia of a past memory that, despite having faded in time, remained extremely powerful and influential. It was a glimpse of what had been amid what was. And that momentary glimpse was strong enough to give me hope for what would be.

August 10, 2018

Five days until the big operation. I am scared. But fear is tidal. And even though the waves have been high this week, there are moments when the sea is calm, and a strange peace overwhelms me. A sunset feeling.

August 11, 2018

4 days until the big operation. Today was fun. We explored some suburbs close to Werden with Mikaela and my aunt. We all took some photos together. Details that give me comfort. Life is scary. But I lay my hope in something greater than me.

August 12, 2018

Three days until the big operation. Today was really special. We woke up early and prepped a picnic. We drove around for over an hour, but we didn't find a good picnic spot. We took some amazing photos and explored some remote roads *through the forest though. We ended up having the picnic in our backyard. At first, I was disappointed. But then I realized how incredibly more special it was this way. Happiness is homemade. It's not the place that makes a successful picnic. It's the food, the laughs, the jokes, the conversation, and the joy that is shared. I'm scared about the surgery. But days like today help a lot. Ami is coming tomorrow. I'm excited. If happiness is in the details, maybe home is too.*

August 13, 2018

Two days until the big operation. My dad and Ami flew to Essen this morning. Amalia got a temporary tattoo to symbolize that 90 percent necrosis rate that we are all praying for. I was so emotional when I saw it. Love is in the details. She gives me courage to fight. Today, we went to this sunflower field in Werden. It was surrounded by the most beautiful grass fields. It has become my favorite sunset spot. You can see the whole sunset from there. I've been to that place so many times, yet today, I witnessed something I never had before. I witnessed a sunset that surpassed the meaning of the term beautiful. Just like that first one, that day in the hospital, after the biopsy results, the one that started it all. A sunset feeling. A profound peace that took over my heart just as the colors of the sunset took over the sky.

As soon as we came home, it started raining. That sunset was the calm before the storm. Peace before the pain. But a sunset is what gives you strength to get through the storm. I've experienced the peace. I will get through the pain. I am scared. So scared. But I choose to trust. To be patient. To be brave.

Part II

Chapter 15

"Be Brave"

Tuesday, August 14, 2018

One day until the big operation. Let's do this.

That Tuesday, August 14, I was admitted to the hospital. We had another appointment with Prof. H in the morning. As we sat in the waiting room, my friend Mikaela and I enjoyed some Greek gyros that my family had brought from Athens. Enjoying Greek food with my best friend a day before my surgery was a reminder of why I had to fight through this season of difficulties. It reminded me of the normalcy I was battling to gain back. It was a glimpse of what could be if I kept fighting in what was. Later during the day, I did some pre-op tests and spent the afternoon with Mikaela and Amalia, playing cards, talking, and connecting.

At night, we all gathered in my hospital room. My mom, my aunt, my dad, Amalia, and Mikaela were all there. We spent a few hours hanging out and discussing school, the surgery, and me walking again.

At some point later that night, I received a text from my good friend Bill. He told me he'd organized a surprise for me and that he hoped it would make me smile. No sooner had I read that text than my phone was flooded by people posting on their stories, sending me thoughts, love, and prayers:

These days are really crucial for a good friend. Pray this night, and always have her in your mind. Pray for her to return to her good old life and be the amazing person that she is. Stay strong, Kat.

My heart felt full of love. I felt as if I wasn't fighting alone. I felt like I had an army of friends and family fighting with me, being by my side. Distance means nothing when someone means so much. I felt close to my loved ones and friends. Love heals. What a powerful revelation that is. I was able to see God's love through the love of the people around me. It felt like a confirmation that I would not fight alone and that, even though it would get lonely in my mind, I would always have an army of love, a tight hug, a safe place to fall back on and land and hold onto. That surprise was a source of determination that gave me the courage to take the risk of hope, to dare to be brave.

That night was one of the most stressful, restless, exhausting nights of my life. And yet it was the night I felt and experienced the most profound, incredible sense of peace. Every anxious thought stole my breath, and yet every breath I boldly chose to take filled my lungs with trust, courage, and comfort. Before going to bed, I asked my parents to give me some time alone. As they went outside, I switched off all the lights and sat in my bed. I took a very deep breath. I allowed myself to feel all the emotions of that moment. I can't explain how profound this moment was. I'd never experienced anything like that—pure vulnerability. I chose to be as brave as I could and allow myself to feel, process, cry, expose all my fears, and surrender. Just after that deep breath, I started crying. I couldn't stop. Fear had taken over my body. It paralyzed me. I pictured God sitting by my bed, keeping me company. I pictured Him smile at me and tell me, "Breathe, release it all. I'll keep you safe. Give it all to me. I'm here."

I closed my eyes as tightly as I could. As I opened my heart, all the worry, the fear, and the anxiety haunting and torturing it was released.

God, I need you tonight. Please, find me here. I'm desperate for hope. I'm desperate for peace. Tonight. In this dark, cold hospital room. This fear is so cold. These anxious thoughts, they steal my breath. I can't do this on my own. I'm so scared. Oh, God, fear has made these holes in my chest. As vulnerable as I've ever been, I lay it all to you. As brave as I've ever been, I trust you. Help me wake up from the surgery tomorrow. Guide the surgeons to take out the full tumor. Make it so that the tumor has full necrosis. These what-ifs—they're tearing me apart. They're breaking me and crushing down every part of me. Give me peace. Be with me in that OR tomorrow. I need you there with me. I'm scared of the pain. I'm scared of the risks. Hold me in Your arms tonight. As I lay awake and wonder, as the what-ifs get louder in my mind, as fear paralyzes me, God be with me. Get me through tomorrow. I don't want to suffer any more. I don't want to have to go through this. But, God, not my will but yours be done. Find me here. Don't forsake me. I don't want to leave, I don't want to die God. Help me. Please help me.

That was the rawest, most emotional, and bravest prayer I'd ever prayed. I don't quite know how to describe that moment. It was sudden, but a strange feeling rushed through my body and overwhelmed me. For only a moment. It was thousand sunset feelings—all at once.

After a while, my mom and dad walked in the room.

"Everything all right?" my dad asked.

"Yeah," I said confidently.

I truly meant it. Everything was going to be all right.

That night, I tried to sleep but couldn't. I was too nervous and uptight. I twisted and turned in my bed. I was restless. At some point, I looked outside the window. A subtle ambient light flooded the room. It was the moonlight. It was a full moon that night. I put on some music on my headphones and, staring at that light, tried to rest. All my efforts were in vain. The worry and fear were heavy weights on my chest. I was terrified of the suffering I would have to go through and of the results of the pathology report. I was even scared of the possibility of not waking up from the surgery. I tried to block every negative thought. I locked them all in a closet in my mind and trapped them there. If my mind was a house, there was a specific room that all my fears and doubts were locked in. I wished I could light it on fire and just burn that whole room to the ground. What I escaped from had started becoming what trapped me. I blocked pain and acted stronger than I felt, but depression and fear leaked under the locked door at 4:00 a.m. at night. Nobody's ever been in that room. I don't let people in. If I do, I'm scared the demons of fear might hurt them too. So I lock the door. I lock it to protect the people around me from the fire inside. But protecting others from the fire sometimes means burning alone. It keeps people from getting in, but it also keeps me from getting out. Choosing to not talk about my fears sometimes makes the chains holding me to them stronger. So I'm barricaded inside my own mind, trapped by my own fear.

As I lay there in silence, I realized the only way to break the chains of anxiety and fear was to process the pain they caused. I needed to grieve for all the suffering I'd endured these months, for the things I feared, and for my what-ifs. Pain has to be felt. It has to be processed. I closed my eyes and started crying. I needed to let it all out. My mom was sleeping in the bed next to me, and my dad had fallen asleep on the chair, and I didn't want to wake them up. They needed to rest. They needed to gain strength for the next day. So, I cried silently.

That's the worst type of crying—the silent tears; the weeping at 2:00 a.m. when everyone is asleep; the cry where you feel a lump in your throat and your eyes are flooded with tears, red, blurry, and puffy. You have to hold your breath, cover your mouth with a pillow, and grab your stomach to stay quiet. And you release it all—all the pain that's haunting you, the grief for something that isn't gone yet, and all the hidden hurt. After crying for some time, I had no more tears left. I'd felt so much, all at once, that now I no longer felt anything. Lying there, staring at the ceiling, I wondered how emptiness could feel so heavy.

I didn't know this at the time, but there was much purpose behind the pain I was feeling. There was much meaning beneath it. I couldn't see it at the time, but later on, when all the puzzle pieces were placed, the big picture would be revealed, and it would all make sense.

I knew that healing is not always what you picture, and I trusted that God's picture was greater and more purposeful than mine. So, that night I decided to write goodbye letters to my family. It wasn't only the surgery I feared, but if the pathology didn't show good results, then I just wanted to be prepared. I knew I wouldn't find the strength to write letters if we got dim news, as the overwhelming pain would paralyze me, just like it had after I got diagnosed. So, I decided to write them that night. I opened the notes on my phone and started typing. As I wrote, tears flooded my eyes. I had to stop many times. I just couldn't find the right words. That was probably one of the most difficult things I'd ever done.

After a few hours, I texted my friend Bill again. We talked for a while.

It helped me escape the anxiety and fear. After about half an hour, I went to bed.

"Stay determined tomorrow OK?" Bill said. "And *be brave*."

That phrase. Little did I know how significant it would turn out to be, how much it would end up symbolizing. As I've thought about it in review, I've realized that God was using people—my friends, family, and doctors—and even situations, phrases, and small details to show me He was there next to me, to give me comfort and strength and to encourage me to keep fighting. These details helped me take heart and know I would overcome this.

The next morning, I awoke at 7:30 a.m. The nurses came in and measured my blood pressure. They also gave me a muscle relaxant to take half an hour before the surgery. Soon after, a doctor came in and marked an "X" on my leg where the tumor was. I opened my phone and randomly stumbled on a photo with the caption, "Trust God with all your heart."

I do, I told myself. *I do*, I screamed at the voices of fear and anxiety in my mind.

After a little while, everyone arrived at the hospital. At 9:00 a.m., a nurse walked in and told me to change into my surgical gown. I went to the bathroom to put it on. As I tightened it around my back, I looked up and stared at the girl in the mirror.

"OK listen," I told myself, pointing at my reflection. "You have to be brave. This is it, OK? This is the day you've been thinking of and worrying and praying about. This is it. You have to stay strong. OK? You're going to wake up." I spoke fiercely, and my voice cracked. "You're going to wake up."

My eyes filled with tears. But this was not a time to cry. This was a time to have faith, a time to fight, a time to be brave.

"You are going to wake up. This isn't the end. Today the tumor loses. This is the day. You have to fight. OK? Stay strong, all right?" I begged myself. "Be brave. You *have* to be brave, OK? Let's do this. Let's go. Let's beat this cancer. Listen up, heart, you're going to *be brave*. And I'm going to wake up. I *need* to wake up. I can't die today. I'm going to wake up."

After whispering these things to myself in the mirror, I walked out of the bathroom and lay back in bed, waiting to be taken to the OR. Before being wheeled to the surgical floor, I hear my phone ringing. It was Dr. Vasilis. I'd tried calling him last night, but the call hadn't gone through.

Maybe that was because God knew I would most need the hope that Dr. Vasilis could give me this morning and not last night. The timing was perfect.

Dr. Vasilis told me everything was going to work out perfectly and that he would pray for me. He encouraged me by reminding me that this day was all that we'd been expecting for the longest time. Before we hung up, he told me to be brave—as if he'd heard what I'd told myself in the mirror, as if he knew what my heart needed to hear. It's all in the details. True hope is hidden in the meaningful details of our situation, not in the situation itself. Meaning is found in the stars of the night sky, not in the sun of the daytime.

Lying there in my bed, I saw the "X" on my leg. I felt grateful for the fourteen years I'd had with my knee. I was grateful for the adventures I'd taken, the runs I'd gone on, the hikes, the silly races at school, and the soccer games I'd won because of that knee. And just like that, anxiety transformed into gratitude—just by staring at that "X."

The clock was ticking down to the big moment. As the nurses wheeled me toward the elevator, I took the pill they'd given me. On the outside, it really helped, since it relaxed my muscles and helped me with the trembling and high heart rate. However, deep in my heart, I was overwhelmed by a strange peace—deeper and more profound than that of a simple sunset feeling. This felt more like a very distant and bright star, one that sparkled and reflected its light across the dark sky. It was a peace that surpassed all understanding. It stemmed from the choice I made to use my fear as a foundation for faith to grow deeper. It was the result of my choice to trust, to hope, and to be brave. Was I still scared? Absolutely. Did I still have doubts? Absolutely. But amid that fear and the doubts, I chose to be brave.

Before entering the OR corridor, we stopped at the "goodbye door." It's exactly what it sounds like. Visitors and family members aren't allowed past that door. It's something like the "goodbye corner" at the airport. My family hugged me tightly. I smiled at them. My mom took my hand and squeezed it tightly. She was crying. One tear streamed down her face and fell on my hand.

"It's all going to be okay, Mom. I promise," I told her and squeezed her hand back tighter, with a subtle smile on my face, trying to hold back my tears.

I hugged my sister. What if this was the last hug I ever gave her? I didn't want to let go. But I had to. I had to be brave. I then hugged everyone else. I notice their eyes. They were red. Some filled with tears, some would soon be. It was overwhelming, but again, I had to be brave.

As the nurses wheeled me past the door, I held up a peace sign at my family to say goodbye. The peace sign is kind of my thing. It's something silly I always do. Today it was a way to tell my family not to worry, trying to show them that it was all going to be OK and to give them comfort.

As the door closed behind me, the whole thing became real. I was transferred to the surgical gurney and then wheeled into a prep room. There, Dr. M came in and placed my IV line. He told me he would place all the other lines once I was under anesthesia, asleep. Dr. M then started the process of placing the nerve blocks, the two catheters that would paralyze my leg. He was teaching some medical students how to do this procedure, which made the waiting longer. The insertion of the catheters was quite painful, but thankfully it was quick.

Dr. M then placed the oxygen mask on my face and said, "Are you ready? We're about to start."

I took a deep breath. What if this was the last one I ever took? I wasn't ready. Not nearly ready. But I had to be brave. "Okay," I said boldly.

That simple word hid so many thoughts and sentences. It hid prayers, tears, conversations, dreams, goals, fears, and promises. It hid pain, doubt, and uncertainty, and yet it also hid undeniable faith, trust, and courage. It was like my faith had been tested all these months, my trust had been challenged, and my determination had matured through what I'd gone through, all leading to this moment, this choice, this one single word—*okay*. It felt like all the preparation of the waiting room and all the perseverance through suffering had been teaching me to say that one word, *okay*.

Similar to the "okay" I had said after getting my diagnosis, only this time... much braver.

As Dr. M injected the anesthesia, he asked me to count down from ten. When I reach number eight, I start getting dizzy. My body felt paralyzed, and a sense of heaviness overwhelmed me.

This is on you, God, I thought and closed my eyes. *I leave this on you …*
And I… I'll be brave.

It seems only a split second later that I wake up in the operating room. In reality, it is about six hours and a long surgery later. Anesthesia is really fascinating if you think about it. I am wheeled to the recovery room. Though I am not fully conscious yet, I am in pain—more pain than I've ever experienced in my life. It is unbearable. Every second is worse than the last. Being able to be in pain, however, means that I've survived the operation. It means that there no longer is a tumor in my body. I thank the doctors again and again. I am not really aware of what I'm saying, but I'll later learn I am speaking half in English and half in Greek. The doctors can't really understand what I am saying either.

I keep falling asleep and waking up shortly after because of the pain. I am on very high-dose morphine and nerve blocks. It still isn't enough. The pain is unbearable. I feel like somebody has cut off my bone, which is exactly what has happened. The pain overwhelms me. I cry loudly—desperately. Screaming. Sobbing. The few moments of peace as I fall back asleep feel like eternity and like a mere heartbeat at the same time.

"It hurts so very much," I scream out, crying.

The next thing I remember is waking up in the elevator going down. I see a person next to me. I can't see their face, just their arm. I hold their hand and tell them, "Thank you so much, so very much"

I hear a woman speaking. I can't understand what she is saying. I fall back asleep. I later find out that that woman thanked wasn't a doctor but was responsible for transport to the ward. It didn't matter, however. She was still part of my care, and I needed her to know I was grateful for her.

As I sleep, under the influence of the anesthesia still, I feel the pain intensify. I open my eyes and find myself in the underground tunnels of the hospital. I look around, surprised. I don't understand what was going on. The transportation makes the pain so much worse. The bumps of the road feel like a mountain being crushed on my leg. Every time they stop and start rolling the bed again rips strength from me. It is the most traumatizing experience of my life. I close my eyes again.

The next time I open them, I am in the children's ICU in the "Kinderklinik," the pediatric hospital.

"Mom," I say in agony. "It hurts so much."

I am sobbing. Loud screams and shouts precede a moment of silence as the remaining anesthesia makes me fall back asleep. It's like the moon eclipses the night every time I wake up. All light is gone. Reality is dark, full of pain, and I am lying there helpless, screaming out, and trying to fight the pain. And then as the eclipse passes, light shines again. I am at peace. I am asleep. Reality is still dark, but I'm at rest. When I open my eyes, I am overwhelmed with pain, and when I close them, I am overwhelmed with peace. How meaningful is that?

When I choose to see—to look around, to live by what is seen, by the odds, the facts, and the reports—then pain enters my heart and tears it brutally, ripping it apart. But when I choose to close my eyes—to rest, to surrender, to give up control, and to trust and place my hope in what is not seen, in faith—then peace enters my heart and fuels me with strength. Resting, both physically and emotionally, means giving my pain and suffering to God, finding refuge in hope, and letting it guide me through the path of hurt. Resting means suffering patiently and gracefully. I know, in this moment, I have to rest. I have to win this battle. I have to defeat pain. But I am sinking in its ocean. I am drowning in its waves. In these split seconds of peace, in these quick moments of rest, my heart is sheltered, and I am given more strength to keep enduring. During this time, however, I do not understand all this. In this time, I am just in pain. I am amid the battle, in the center of the storm.

I am in the ICU. At this point, I have no sense of time. Every moment escapes the borders of time, both in my mind and in its significance because of its profound but hidden purpose. At some point, an ICU doctor comes to check up on me. I tell her I am in pain, but I think she can already hear that, as I am crying loudly. I tell her I feel an electric shock in my leg every few minutes. Little do I know what this pain is and where it will take me. I don't understand what the doctor is saying. I can't hear her. I fall back asleep. When I open my eyes again, I see her standing next to me, giving me medication.

As she turns to leave, I hold her hand with both of mine and squeeze it tightly. "Thank you so much," I say, crying. "Thank you for saving me. Thank you for what you're doing for me. Thank you."

I see her smile, and before she has the chance to reply, I fall back asleep. The pain in my leg only gets worse as the anesthesia wears off. As the night falls, I find myself waking up frequently. I don't know how long I've been asleep. It feels like forever. Every time I open my eyes, I see my mom sitting by my bed holding my hand—every time. I can't imagine how she must be feeling—how scared and tired she must be, how much it must hurt her to see me cry and shout in pain.

At some point, I wake up and call out for her. "Mom," I say, crying.

I see her jump off her chair. She was asleep, and I've woken her up. She sees me crying, then calls the doctor and asks her if they can give me more pain meds. But I am already maxed out.

My mom sits back down and holds my hand. "Go back to sleep," she tells me. "And when you wake up, you'll see, it will all be better."

"What time is it?" I ask her.

My mom tells me the time, but I can't understand her. I can't focus or remember. As my eyes start closing, I catch a glimpse of hers. Her eyes are so tired, so hurt. All I want in that moment is to hug her, comfort her, and tell her I'll be okay. But the pain us too strong. The anesthesia still makes me sleepy. So I give in. I let go. I stop trying to fight myself. Instead, I fall asleep in peace, leaning toward God, trusting He will get me through the night, that He'll hold my mom as her heart breaks, and that He'll comfort her and give her strength.

This moment of peace, however, is only that—a moment. And it slips through my fingers every time I try to find comfort in it. Just as I fall asleep, I am woken up by the pain. I feel restless and exhausted.

"What time is it?" I ask my mom again at some point.

She tells me the time, but I still can't understand her. I think probably a few hours have gone by since I last asked her.

"Tell them to give me something for the pain," I whisper in agony.

"They can't, sweetheart. I'm so sorry. They've already given you something; you can't have any more pain meds."

"How much time has it been since then?" I ask, confused.

"Ten minutes," she replies.

This is when I realize I have no sense of time whatsoever. I thought hours had gone by, but in reality, it has been only ten minutes. This realization makes me desperate. I don't know how I'll get through the night. I am in agony. Pain wins. On this night, pain wins.

But purpose hid behind it. The suffering was a setup. The pain that trapped me was trapped itself; the suffering that surrounded me was surrounded itself. When pain wins, purpose wins. In order for purpose to be revealed, pain had to overtake me. It had to happen. It was part of a plan, part of a trap. The very pain meant to take me out and hurt me would be used as a source of purpose. The night that was meant to hide the light of the sun would be used as a canvas for the light of the stars to be painted on. The difficulty itself would be used to develop me, and the development it would lead to would deliver me from that same difficulty. I had to be in pain. I had to go through these things to grow in ways I could not imagine, to know God deeper, and to experience a peace, protection and provision in a form that surpassed all understanding. The night had to come for the stars to shine. And though it seemed as if darkness had won, in reality, it was trapped. Light used the strength of darkness to triumph over it. Darkness had to win for one night, for light to win for forever.

The next morning was pretty much the same pain-wise. At some point, a doctor removed my arterial line. I still had a central and two IV lines in. Prof. H visited me during the day. He said the surgery had gone great but that there had been a complication and a nerve had been damaged. We couldn't know the extent of the damage yet. I was too exhausted to feel the hurt, too weak to process the fear.

Late in the afternoon, two ladies from the physiotherapy and rehabilitation department visited me. They tried to help me sit up. They put their hands on my back and pushed me to sit up. But all our efforts were in vain. I was in wracking pain, aggravated with the slightest movement.

After a few tries, the physiotherapists told me to get some rest and try again tomorrow after first taking some pain meds. After they left, I fell back asleep. I was a wreck. Broken and shattered, I'd been shredded to pieces. Physically, I was in unbearable pain. But mentally, the exhaustion of holding on, the fear and the disappointment, and the uncertainty and the doubt tore me apart. Not being able to even sit up by myself, four days after surgery, seemed like a very bad sign. Terrible scenarios broke into my mind and got a hold of my thoughts. The whispers of worry and anxiety grew thunderous. I couldn't find rest. I couldn't find peace. I needed to fight. I was giving in. I had surrendered to pain.

I had to be brave. That's what I kept telling myself. *Be brave.*

So, that night, at around midnight, I asked my mom to help me sit up.

"Let's wait for the physiotherapists, sweetie," my mom told me. "They know how to hold you up and help you. I don't really know how to do this, and I don't want you to be in pain."

"No, Mom," I replied, determined. "I want to do this now. I want to sit up."

My mom smiled. I knew her heart was breaking, but she held on and stayed strong. I knew that sitting up would be a much-needed source of strength for both of us.

So, I held on to her hand, and she placed her other hand on my back. I tried to sit up again, but I still failed.

"Let's do this tomorrow. It's better if we do this tomorrow," my mom told me as she saw me crumble in pain.

I saw her eyes. I saw the pain they hid. I felt it in mine too. But I couldn't give up.

"No," I replied in a fervent tone. "I can do this. I got this."

In that moment, a fire was set in my heart—a fire of determination, a fire that enabled me to fight. It lifted me up from my weakness, my sickness, and my desperation. It helped me be brave enough to face the risk of disappointment, to look it in the eyes, and to crush it; I would overcome it. I closed my eyes.

Do it brave, I told myself then sat up. As I was moving, the pain grew strong, but my determination was stronger. I pushed through and managed to sit up. Immediately, I felt dizzy, and my blood pressure plummeted. But I didn't care. I did it. I made it. I overcame the first obstacle.

With cancer, it's so important to celebrate the small victories, the small battles that are won. Back in February, the school's guidance counselor had come to see me, telling me to celebrate the small mountaintops I conquered until I got to the highest one. I always remembered that phrase and tried to live by it. It was impactful and significant. Small victories are so powerful. They hide hope that fuels perseverance and strengthens resilience.

The next morning, the physiotherapists came again. With a huge smile on my face, I told them I'd managed to sit up the night before. They were excited and, I think, impressed. They suggested trying to sit on the edge of the bed and maybe even trying to stand up. I was scared for a moment. I knew I'd be in pain. I knew there was a chance it would all fail. But I had to be brave.

"Sounds great!" I told them, smiling.

After a few tries, a lot of tears, and many silent *be braves* of self-encouragement, I managed to sit on the edge of the bed. After staying there for a few minutes, I felt dizzy and passed out. I fell back on the bed, unable to understand what was happening. The physiotherapists told me to relax for now and suggested having some juice with me tomorrow so we could try to get up and stand up, without worrying about the low blood pressure. I wished I could have stood up that day but remembered to celebrate the small mountaintops.

The next day, we woke up super early for rounds. The doctors came in and changed my bandages. That was such a painful procedure, as it involved a lot of moving my leg around. After the bandage change, I was in incredible pain. I took some morphine and some other pain meds to calm down. My mom tried to encourage me by telling me that today would be the day I stood up. I tried to focus on that goal, but the pain got in the way.

A couple hours later, Amalia and Mikaela visited me in the hospital with my dad. Seeing them there meant so much to me, even though I couldn't really interact with them. My parents often had to take Ami and Mikaela into the waiting room so they wouldn't have to hear me scream in pain and cry desperately. It was emotionally draining. I didn't even recognize myself.

When the physiotherapists came, they helped me sit up and put my shoes on. They tied my foot upright to help me keep my balance despite the paralysis. After multiple efforts, I managed to sit on the side of the bed. I then pressed my feet to the ground and stood up. This was my first time I'd stood in a week, yet it seemed as if it were the first time ever. I had forgotten what it was like to feel gravity in my legs. The feeling of standing there, touching my two feet to the ground, keeping by body upward was so surreal, so strange, and so new. But it felt right. It gave me strength. I was standing—still standing. After everything I'd gone through—the suffering of the chemotherapies, the trials and tribulations, the many tests on my faith, the countless sleepless nights and tear-drenched prayers, fearing I wouldn't recover from the surgery, the incredibly painful night in the ICU, the discouraging news of the paralysis—I was still standing. This simple, normal thing I used to do every morning when I woke up and got ready for school now had gained a whole new and profound meaning. The simple act of standing up would, from that moment on, never go by unappreciated.

Despite that small mountaintop that was conquered that afternoon, the night that followed was very difficult. The pain was not manageable at all. My mom tried putting towels, pillows, and gauzes against my leg to hold it steady and elevated. It was hugely swollen and felt like it was burning up.

"Mom, I can't do this anymore," I told her at some point, in tears. "I'm sorry. I can't. I just can't take this any longer."

As my mom heard me cry out these words, I felt her heart break. I knew it ripped her apart to see me like this. I knew she would take my place if she could. I wanted to stay strong for her. But I just couldn't endure that much pain anymore. I wasn't prepared for this. It was so much harder than I thought it would have been. The nerve damage, that complication from the surgery, was what was creating the unbearable pain. It wasn't something that patients in my situation typically went through. I didn't understand why it had to happen to me. I had gone through enough already. But at the time, I couldn't see the purpose that pain masked. It was hidden; it was a work in progress. It would turn out to be the most perfect soil from which the most beautiful flower would grow. I had to trust, be patient, and be brave.

"Hold on just a little longer," my mom told me and held me in her arms. "I know you're tired. I know you feel weak. But I promise it will get better. You don't believe it now, but it will all get better. Hold on to this thought. It will all be all right soon. I promise."

"I just don't know if I can wait until then, if I can hold on for so long," I replied. "Every few minutes I feel shocks run through my leg. I can't take it, Mom."

"I know, sweetheart, I know. Please, have some patience. You are already making so much progress. You stood up again for the first time today. Look at you! It's all getting better—little by little. Tomorrow, you'll try to walk, and slowly, slowly, it will get better. C'mon. Have a little bit of patience. You're a fighter."

Her words gave me so much courage. I noticed her eyes. They were full of pain and exhaustion, and yet they were also teeming with love and resilience. My mom was such a rock star. Her words that night were a rope I could hold onto, so I could crawl out of the hole of despair. It felt as if God had given me my mom as a gift, as His ambassador, as someone who could give me comfort, love, and a warm hug. I felt grateful for family—my dad, my sister, my aunt, my grandparents. Knowing I had people like that in my life was all the proof of God I needed. Knowing I was not alone, knowing I was loved, was a reminder that God had not abandoned me; He was right there with me.

I was incredibly grateful for my doctors too, for conversations with nurses, the waiter at the restaurant next to our apartment, the woman at the lab where I went for blood checks, the woman who visited me during chemo to play racquetball, and even the woman who cleaned my hospital room, who happened to be Greek too. God is in these details. These people all were in my life, momentarily or for a while, for a specific reason, a specific purpose. That gratitude filled me with strength, as it showed me God had a profound plan, proving that pain was an opportunity for purpose and human connection.

The next day, on Friday the eighteenth, Mikaela and my aunt flew back to Greece. That morning, Prof. H visited me during morning rounds. He examined my leg and told us that everything looked fine. He wanted to check the CRP count because he had noticed it was a little more elevated than expected. We talked a little bit about my leg, the recovery process, the bending potential, and the chances of the paralysis being reversed.

A quick medical talk is important for this to make sense; The endoprosthesis that replaced my knee and most of my tibia bone in my leg (where the tumor was), gives patients the ability to bend their silver knee about 90 degrees. This is also known as flexion. Normal flexion is about 140 degrees. When it comes to knee extension, patients with this endoprosthesis have an even bigger problem. Because the extensor mechanism of the knee is reconstructed during the surgery, most are never able to achieve complete knee extension. So basically this all means that post-operative rehabilitation with a tibial endoprosthesis as big as mine, is very long, very painful, and very uncertain.

In a nutshell, the answer to all questions about the recovery was, "We don't know. We *can't* know."

Different patients had different results, and frankly, you just cannot know what the future holds. That's where, I think, faith and determination come in. They're the best weapons to fight against uncertainty and the best way to live and grow in it.

Prof. H saw that I was really worried about the paralysis, so he told me about another case of a young girl who'd suffered similar nerve injuries after a similar surgery. She'd not only recovered, but had also become a surgeon, who was now working in the hospital. That story was all I needed to hear to find the inner courage I needed to be brave and to keep trying. During this entire hospitalization, I was tempted by the unbearable pain to give up, multiple times, and yet God always found ways—through people, conversations, and stories—to remind me why I had to fight. In the subtlest of ways, He gave me strength to endure.

Moreover, the story of that surgeon, had much more than a short-term effect on me. Along with giving me short-term motivation to deal with a short-term difficult situation, it did something much deeper, more purpose-filled, and meaningful. It turned the spark in my heart that had been lit in that hospital waiting room on the day of the graduation into a small flame. That flame would slowly and gradually turn into a wildfire raging in my soul and lead me down the path of medicine. What started as a spark would evolve into an undeniable passion to become a doctor myself and help other people in similar situations.

This flame is proof of the power of a story. Your battle can be someone else's greatest source of motivation. There's a message behind every mess—if you just have the right mindset to unlock it. Seeing how meaningful a story of suffering could be, how much healing it could provide, gave me hope that maybe, one day, my scars could become a source of strength for somebody else too. And if they ever did, I knew the pain that created them would instantly be worth it. What a beautiful thing it would be if the very thing that made me weak made somebody else strong. What an honor it would be to be a witness of the incredible transformative power the darkness of the night had to turn into the brightest light of the sunrise.

A couple of hours later, Prof. D visited me as well. Her coming was a very pleasant surprise for me, since her office was in a completely different building on the other side of the very large hospital campus. Her visit meant a great deal to me. When she walked in, we were trying to get the pain under control. She asked me how I was doing and was happy to see me. I told her the pain made everything difficult but that I was hanging in there. She understood how worried I was for the pathology results.

"We hope for the best," she told me. "Fingers crossed," she added, crossing hers.

I smiled. I'd just received a significant and powerful transfusion, a transfusion of hope. It is such conversations, such moments of raw human connection that become transfusions of hope. "Fingers crossed." I nodded and crossed mine too.

"You have to stay strong now OK?"

"I will," I told her and smiled.

That moment was exactly what I needed to keep going.

On Monday the twentieth, I was scheduled for a leg x-ray early in the morning. Before that x-ray, however, an anesthesiologist came in and asked me about my pain levels. By the tears streaming down my face, she understood that the pain was still very strong. Unfortunately, the nerve blocks had started causing nerve damage, which was why she'd advised decreasing the dose of the medication that had paralyzed the nerve. Soon after we decreased it, however, the pain got significantly worse. I was screaming, feeling like my leg was being electrocuted every other minute. It was a nightmare.

During morning rounds, the ward doctors told us it was time to remove the catheters that were still left in my leg collecting blood that was leaking out. Removing these tubes was a very painful process, since they had to literally be pulled out, across the entire area of the incision site. That Monday was a killer. I was at the end of my rope. I had completely run out patience to endure the pain. I was lying still in my hospital bed, unable to move. But my heart was restless. I wondered how I'd made it through another day. I couldn't see the end of my pain. I couldn't see the end of having to take twenty pills to manage that pain and still failing to do so.

My mom could tell I had no strength to keep going. "Why don't you call Dr. Vasilis?" she suggested that night. "Maybe he could help you get a little bit of strength back."

As a surgeon at a very busy hospital back home, Dr. Vasilis would be on call most nights. That night, however, he picked up the phone instantly.

He asked me how I was doing, but I couldn't speak. I broke down sobbing. "I'm so, so very tired of fighting," I told him in between sobs. "I just stare at the empty wall across my bed, and it all just seems pointless. The recovery is exhausting, I just can't take the pain anymore. Nothing helps, not even the morphine. I don't know how I can hold onto hope."

I then told him all about my fears, and my worries about the pathology report, the waiting, the uncertainty, the nerve damage, and my doubts about running again. I let everything out.

After listening, Dr. Vasilis told me, "OK, sweetheart, listen to me. Hold on for just a little bit. Let me call you back. I want to go pray for you really quick, and I'll call you right back. I don't know if it will help, but I just hope it will. Can you wait and hold on just a few more minutes? Can you do that for me?"

"Okay," I said and wiped a few tears away. "I think I can."

After a couple of minutes, he called back, and we talked for a while. He told me that I had been so brave for so long, and I now was on the finish line. He also told me about how the risk for infection had decreased and somehow managed to restore courage in my heart and give me a sense of enthusiasm for the future, which I was in dire need of. For just a moment, as we were talking on the phone, I felt at peace. A strange calmness overtook me—a sunset feeling. I was once again motivated to get better, to learn to walk again. Dr. Vasilis promised that, once I got better, we'd go on photography trips together. That promise filled me with hope for the future. It was a lighthouse leading me toward its light and saving me from the crashing waves of the storm. Before we hung up, he told me he would pray for me every night to be in less pain. That meant the world to me.

Pain was my biggest opponent at the time. It was what released the demons of despair, depression, and discouragement in my mind. Pain was a master manipulator that always strived to steal my courage and challenge my faith. But at the same time, it was pain itself that made faith heroic and brave. In every story, it's the villain who defines the hero. It's the hardship that makes faith an act of strength and hope an act of bravery. The size of the challenge says much about the size of the courage that will be needed to face it. Struggle and opposition shine a light on resilience. In my story, pain was the villain, and he had an army of soldiers that came along in every battle. But the strength of pain only reveals the depth of perseverance. In other words, pain projects perseverance, suffering reveals strength, and desperation develops determination. Therefore, the pain that was made to hurt me would inspire resilience.

The next day, the two women from the physiotherapy and rehabilitation department came to my room to teach me how to walk again. That Tuesday would be the day I walked again, for the first time, without a tumor in my body. After sorting out and putting aside all the catheters, the physiotherapists helped me sit up. My mom held a cup of juice in her hand just in case I got dizzy. I felt like a professional athlete about to start a race. My mom felt like my coach next to me, giving me water and juice. These thoughts and parallels helped me push through and motivated me to keep trying. After I'd sat up for a while, the physiotherapists helped me put on my shoes, since I couldn't do it myself, and then tied and secured my paralyzed foot in an upright position. Then they held my hands and back and helped me stand up. I'd gotten good at standing up, as I'd found a way to push through the dizziness that was caused by a drop in my blood pressure.

After a few tries, I managed to get hold of the walker and stay standing. My mom held the bottle of juice next to my face and, using a straw, gave me some to drink. The physiotherapists took their positions, and I attempted to walk. At first, I didn't know how to. The physiotherapists helped me take my first step with my left leg by literally holding my casted right leg in position.

I tightened my grip around the walker and, for a moment closed my eyes. *Courage dear heart. Be brave.*

My mom saw me close my eyes and got worried. "Are you OK?" she asked me. "Are you dizzy?"

"No, don't worry. I'm all good," I told her. "I got this. Let's do it." I really meant it. I was *really* okay. I chose to be brave.

I stretched out my right leg and lifted it to take a step. A tsunami of pain rushed through the whole right side of my body. As I pushed the walker, I put my weight on it and on my leg simultaneously. That was it. That was my first step—the first step I ever took with my new leg, with Sebastian; that's what I'd named my prosthesis for fun. That first step was a milestone. It was the greatest and tallest mountaintop I had conquered during this hospitalization.

As I continued walking, the pain only grew stronger. But so did my determination. Every step was a miracle. A huge smile brightened my face. As I walked down the hospital corridor with the walker, my vision started becoming blurry. My eyes filled with tears—not tears of sadness though, tears of gratitude. I could not believe I no longer had a tumor in my body. I was still trapped in sickness and in pain, in a hospital, and in a body that could not do much. Yet as I was taking these first few steps, I felt so free.

As I lay back in bed, I kept thinking about these steps. That was when the eyes of my heart were opened to a profound revelation and understanding about life. If you think about it, life is exactly that—a walk across a hallway. We all get from point A to point B, and the path to get there is this thing we call life. A lot of times we're forced to take steps we're not ready to; often, we're forced to let go when all we want to do is hold on tighter. Life is a constant walking movement. It always brings change and integrates it in its fundamental building blocks. Life and change have become complementary terms, which, as a matter of fact, implies that moving on, letting go and keeping on keeping on are the key components to completing that journey successfully. A lot of people could argue over what "successfully" includes and indicates, however, the gist of the matter is that, no matter what happens in life, you just have to keep going; you have to keep walking. Giving up is not an option.

But what happens when you don't have the strength to keep walking? What happens when you're too tired and broken to even stand? That's where true bravery is revealed. In these situations, all you can do is be brave.

But what does it mean to be brave? Frankly, the most profound act of bravery is hope. Just as change is fused into life, risk is assimilated by hope. In other words, hope incorporates risk. Therefore, choosing to hope through the deepest times of hurt, choosing to trust and surrender to something greater in times of humbling pain is an act of true bravery. Holding onto hope means being bold enough to take the risk of embracing change and trusting it will lead to growth. That's how bravery connects the discomfort of change with the courage of hope.

Ultimately, hope rooted in the soil of unconditional faith was what made me brave enough to get up and start walking. And it also restored strength and courage in me to *continue* walking, even when I felt my knees giving in, even when my paralyzed leg gave out. Sure, the pain got stronger, but so did I. Even when I couldn't see it or sense it, even when strong was the last thing I felt, I was actually getting stronger and stronger. I was learning not only how to walk in the hallway of the surgical ward in a hospital in Essen but also in the hallway of uncertainty, doubt, fear, and worry. And by doing that, by being bold and brave enough to try and walk in these hallways, I was learning what true bravery was all about. I was learning how strength can only be born from weakness, how hope can be found in hurt, and how healing can come from gratitude. Learning to walk again was much more than that. It was a process of learning to live again—but in a very different way than I had before. Just like with walking, where I now had a metal endoprosthesis in my leg, when it came to living again, I now had a newfound understanding and perspective about life itself. Now, I was seeing life from a lens of faith, gratitude, and hope.

What's interesting is that just like the prosthesis was internal and supported me to walk and helped carry me from the inside, so did gratitude, hope, and faith. That was what my prosthesis symbolized for me—an inner support system, an inner rock that kept me steady and helped me walk and live again, differently, steadily and holding onto hope and faith. That, for me, was what it meant to be brave. And it's the very act of choosing to be brave, even when you feel broken, that allows you to walk in the face of uncertainty, to walk when your knees are caving in, and to go on when you feel weak. Through choosing to be brave, you get to understand what it really means to walk across a stage, to walk across a hallway.

I like being brave more than I do being strong. Being brave doesn't require being strong. Strength is overrated. You don't need to be strong enough to overcome adversity. That's what it means to be brave—that even though I'm not strong enough, I choose to keep going. Strength is possibly an advantage, but it's definitely not a requirement. You don't need to be strong to make it. All you need is to not give up.

Brave is not something you are by default. It's something you become by choice. Nobody is intrinsically brave, but anybody can instantly become. That's why being brave is only relevant in the context of broken.

Only when you're broken can choose to be brave.

Chapter 16

Perseverance through the Pain

The next couple of days were spent similarly in the hospital. On August 22, my grandma flew to Essen. I was overjoyed to see her. I didn't want her to get sad, so I tried to hide how broken I was. But it was impossible. My mom had to take her to the waiting room multiple times, so she wouldn't have to hear me scream in pain.

Two days after I started walking, I switched from the walker to the crutches. Since my leg was really swollen, my old running shoes, along with every other pair of shoes I owned, no longer fit. So my mom went out and got me a new pair of white sneakers. A significant detail that we'll encounter again in the future.

My grandma stayed with me for two weeks. During these two weeks, I grew physically and emotionally stronger, I learned to walk with crutches, I trained myself to eat lunch *and* breakfast, and I even climbed a set of stairs for the first time. Step by step. Little by little. Just like my mom had told me. What was so meaningful was that, even though the pain was getting worse, I was getting better. The depth of the pain was not enough to stop me from growing, to prevent my body and soul from slowly starting to heal. I still got dizzy every time I stood up, but now I was able to walk up and down the hospital hallway four times instead of one. I now was able to have a conversation sitting up, without passing out after the first minute. I now was able to smile again at small things and little moments, despite the heaviness that weighed on my heart. The pain did grow stronger, but so did I. Even emotionally and spiritually, I grew more than I ever had. I learned lessons about patience, surrender, and trust that humbled me. I still had really, really bad days. But even on those days, there were hidden details of hope.

If August was the month of *learning* to *be* brave in the broken, September would be the month of *choosing* to *stay* brave in the broken. Notice the difference. There's power in that choice.

On September 1, I was scheduled for my first round of chemo after the surgery. This would be my second block on the VAC protocol. I still had six more to go. I was exhausted and in pain, but I wanted to get it over with and be done with the chemo as soon as possible.

I was transferred to the chemotherapy ward in the children's hospital building. I was in isolation because I was extremely immunocompromised, and I also had a kidney infection, which was extremely painful. Little did I know how that infection would help me find peace in the future. Everything happens for a reason. The nurses and doctors had to wear hazmat suites, gloves, and two layers of masks just to enter my room. My mom wasn't allowed to leave the room. The chemotherapy completely knocked me out. I was sleeping twenty-three hours a day.

Thankfully, it also somehow decreased my nerve pain. *Chemo just did what even morphine couldn't. Interesting,* I thought to myself.

The night was difficult. But with the sunrise that came in the morning, light was restored in the sky, and courage was restored in my heart.

That Saturday morning, my aunt flew in from Greece for the weekend. She walked in the room wearing a hazmat suit and a mask, but I could still see her radiant smile just by looking at her eyes. Instantly, I took heart to get through the chemo. I found a little more courage to hold onto.

Two days later, I was transferred back to the surgical ward. The side effects of the chemo—mixed with the extreme pain, the suffocating anxiety over the pathology report, and the emotionally draining exhaustion from constantly holding on—pushed me to my breaking point. Just like a thin, fragile, vulnerable piece of glass thrown to the ground, I felt broken, beaten, in pieces. But I still pushed through. I tried to persevere, to hold on, and to seem strong. I was scared that, if I let myself feel the fullness of the depth of the pain, I wouldn't be able to bounce back.

In my mind, fighting was the least I could do for God to thank Him for keeping me here. I felt as if God had done His part. Now it was time for me to do mine. But I was so wrong. God never asked me to fight by myself. He never wanted me to repay Him or to carry my cross alone. Instead, He carried it for me. He walked with me and by me. He stood beside me and lived in me. I thought the bravest thing I could do was keep fighting no matter how broken, torn, or powerless I felt. I thought the bravest thing I could possibly do was act stronger than I felt, hold back the tears, and push through. But I was so, so wrong. In reality, the bravest thing I could possibly do in that moment was *let go*. The bravest act of strength was trust. If I could be brave enough to give my worries, fears, and despair to God and trust in Him through them, then I would truly discover what bravery was all about. Vulnerability is so brave. Pain, however, had blinded me. Just like a veil, it had distorted my vision, and I couldn't see this revelation about the nature of bravery. Yet God knew exactly how to remind me and how to show me. To notice the truth behind the light of bravery, I first had to experience utter darkness, utter despair. That morning was the start of what would turn out to be a very long, dark, yet incredibly cathartic night.

Not eating nearly enough for multiple weeks mixed with incredibly high pain levels made me extremely weak. I developed a severe iron deficiency and became extremely hypotensive. I couldn't even sit up for over half a minute before getting dizzy to the point of passing out.

That morning was no different. My mom and my aunt stood by me and tried to convince me to eat. "Do you want some chips maybe?" my mom asked.

"No," I replied, my head bowed low.

"What about that fitness bar you liked?" my aunt suggested.

"No," I whispered.

"What if I get you an ice cream from the hospital cafeteria?"

"No," I replied again.

Each no was even weaker and quieter, my voice fading. I was exhausted.

"What do you want then?" my mom asked, upset.

I stayed silent.

"You have to eat something. Don't you want to get stronger? You need the energy to be able to do physiotherapy and walk and get better," my aunt tried to explain.

I stayed silent.

"Katerina, what do you want?" my mom asked again.

"A hug," I whispered and bent my shoulders low.

"What was that? I'm sorry, dear. I can't understand what you're saying," my mom said, worried.

"A hug," I repeated, with an even quieter voice.

"Sweetheart, speak louder. We can't hear what you're saying," my aunt said.

"A *hug*," I screamed out and broke down crying. "I just want a hug. Nothing else. Just a hug."

Pain was so heavy.

My mom and my aunt heard me this time, and I felt their heart break. They both hugged me tightly, as tightly as they had the day of the biopsy.

That's when it hit me. That's when I truly realized the depth of the power of vulnerability. Exposing my desperation and my brokenness was the ultimate form of deliverance from it. Doing that, being vulnerable and asking for help or for a hug was true strength; that was true bravery.

After that hug from my mom and my aunt, I felt courageous enough to crawl out of the pit of exhaustion I'd fallen into. I'd start with baby steps. So I agreed to lunch. That included strawberry yogurt, a juice, and a few crackers.

The next day, during morning rounds, a surgical resident came to my room to remove my stiches. The process overall wasn't really painful; since my nerve was damaged, I had no sensation whatsoever in my leg. Some areas hurt just a little, but I stayed strong. My mom was holding my hand. At some point, my nerve pain kicked in, and I felt extremely powerful electric shocks run down my leg.

"Stay brave for a little bit longer. We only have this bottom part left," the surgeon told me at some point.

The next day was pretty much the same—only way more painful. I was exhausted. I knew I could find hope all around me, but I was too tired to fight for it. When my mom woke me up, I didn't open my eyes. I kept them closed, tightly. I didn't want to open them. I didn't want to wake up to another day of this torture. I was done. I would wake up, cry, and scream. Doctors would come in and check my leg. I'd do some physio, be discouraged thinking of the path of recovery ahead of me, and then sleep.

Then I'd cry again, scream, cry, suffer. And eventually I'd go to bed again in agonizing pain. Every day, it was always the same. Nothing changed. Nothing got better. The opposite was happening, rather. As the doctors weaned me off my nerve block and morphine, the pain just kept getting worse. I was at my lowest point ever. I'd lost every last bit of courage to simply open my eyes in the morning. And yet I did—every day.

I had to persevere.

Chapter 17

Climbing up a Star

On September 6, I woke up in pain. What's new, right? After about an hour, my mom rushed into the room and hugged me. At first, I was worried that something bad had happened. But then, when she pulled back, I saw her smiling like I hadn't seen ever since I got sick. "It's all great, Katerina," she told me and teared up. "We got the pathology results back. It all went perfect."

I was speechless. I hadn't realized what she had just told me.

My mom showed me an email from Prof. H she'd received that morning: "The tumor is completely resected and has shown complete response to neoadjuvant chemotherapy. Congratulations!"

As I read it, my eyes grew blurry. My hands shook. I'd never experienced such a feeling of relief before. Once I read it, I broke down. My head fell low, and I started crying—tears of joy. It just didn't seem real. The heaviest weight of fear was literally lifted off my shoulders for the first time in eight months. For the first time in eight months, I finally felt like I could breathe. With my head still bowed and tears still streaming down my face, I closed my eyes and took the deepest breath I'd ever taken in my life. I felt *free*. I knew I wasn't yet *cancer* free. But for the first time ever, I felt as if I was going to be. I felt as if I wasn't trapped in this painful disease. I felt as if I could finally breathe again.

The pain wasn't over, the chemo would continue, and we'd receive more bad news in the future. But that day, September 6, and the news of the pathology report gave me courage to endure and get through all the challenges the future held.

Later that morning, some of our family friends, Philip and Jay visited me with their parents in Essen. I was thrilled to see them. They were too. We were all ecstatic about the pathology results. They had to wear hazmat suites, gloves, and masks to come in the room, but it didn't really matter. Nothing could take away the joy of that day. They brought me a banana cake their grandma had made. It was the only thing I was excited and willing to eat. My mom was elated to see me eat solid food again. It was a step that brought me closer to the finish line. What's significant is that it was our family friends who brought me that cake. One symbol brought the other. Hope brought home. My friends visiting was one of the greatest sources of hope and determination for me at the time. Philip, who was also in my year at school, told me all about things back home, school, and the summer. For a moment, I felt as if I were there with my friends, healthy. I desperately needed to feel that way. I needed to remember. I needed to glimpse what life would be like after I crossed the finish line of the race against cancer. And these casual conversations and inside jokes and school talk showed me—hope in the details.

After talking for hours with our friends and doing my physiotherapy session, I was exhausted. But I couldn't fall asleep that night. My heart was overwhelmed with gratitude. I closed my eyes and prayed. Just thinking about how grateful I was made me break down. I made a promise to God that night. I knew I didn't deserve the gift of life more than someone else who didn't receive it. But I wanted to *earn* it. I wanted to *make it count*. I wanted to make every breath I took and every moment I got count.

So that night, as I prayed and thanked God, reflecting on the purpose of adversity and staying brave despite the unbearable pain, I made the most significant promise I'd ever made in my life. I promised God and myself that, if I got better and beat cancer, I would *live*. I would live fully, passionately, purposefully. I would make my life mean something, something way greater and bigger than me. I promised I would make the most out of every moment I got, and I would choose gratitude every day, no matter how I was feeling or what my situation was. Gratitude isn't circumstantial. It's unconditional. I promised to count every blessing and to cherish and live in the moment.

But what does it mean to live in the moment? For me, living in the moment simply means acknowledging the moment and being grateful for it. Simply noticing the details of life and appreciating the little things makes every moment infinitely valuable and precious. That night, I promised myself that I would make it my life's goal to embody the light that had saved me from the darkness, through any way I knew how. I promised I would always try to be that light for other people. I'd been given the greatest gift of life. Time. Life itself. I didn't want it to go by unappreciated. I didn't want to waste it.

The next day, my dad and Amalia flew to Essen for my dad's birthday.

When they walked in the room and saw me, they give me the tightest hugs. I knew they needed this dearly. We all did—especially now. What a powerful force love is.

During morning rounds, Prof. H visited me. He walked in with a huge smile on his face. "We did it! Congratulations!" he said and smiled even bigger.

Smiling is contagious. That's why it's so powerful. As Prof. H sat in a chair next to my bed, he gave me more information about the pathology report. The news was great. We also talked about the paralysis in my lower leg. *This* news wasn't good. But I remembered the doctor he had told me about. Her story gave me strength. I then thought of the results of the pathology report and the promise I made last night—perspective.

A few hours later, our friends visited me in the hospital. In the afternoon, I finally got discharged. As soon as I exited the hospital, passing through the main door in my wheelchair, I teared up. I'd doubted I would every leave that door so many times. And yet I was. I felt the wind on my face again. The sun touch my skin. Light had won this battle.

That car ride home, however, was torture. We put a bunch of pillows, blankets, towels, and gauze below my leg to reduce the jolting effect of the bumps on the road. Unfortunately, though, all these efforts were in vain, since, with the tiniest bump, an avalanche of pain streamed down my entire leg. Arriving home, however, made it worth it.

When we entered the apartment, I celebrated another detail. Lying on the couch, I celebrated yet another. Every usual insignificant activity I used to do before would now be a huge milestone of an achievement. Celebrating details was such a humbling thing to do. It made me appreciative and, at the same time, aware of how fragile, weary, worn out, and vulnerable I was.

At home, Amalia had baked a cake to celebrate my dad's birthday. It had a layer of cookie dough and a layer of brownies. I loved it. It made me feel at home. Maybe home's in the details too. That's a thought for later though.

At night, our friends came over, and we all watched a movie, played board games, and enjoyed dinner together. My dad stopped by that Italian place next to our house and brought us all steak and pasta. I couldn't really eat a lot, but I enjoyed being around a table with loved ones. I was in a tremendous pain all throughout the night, but I didn't say anything. I pushed myself to fight it. Philip and Amalia told me all about school starting next week, and we all discussed future plans. I told them I was going to go to medical school, something I used to never dare say. It wasn't that I had doubts about becoming a doctor, but I did have doubts about getting better. That day, however, after the recent pathology results, I felt hopeful enough to share that dream out loud.

Tuesday, September 11, was the day everyone went back to school. That morning, I woke up in pain. It was too much to handle. I was crying desperately, screaming, and breathing rapidly. After that pain attack passed, I reflected on the situation. I thought of all my classmates who were in school, catching up, meeting new teachers, and laughing—whereas I was a mess. The pain had gotten out of control. Morphine could no longer help. Swollen and paralyzed, my leg was a wreck. And so was my soul. I was weary of fighting. In review, however, the pain of that morning would be a profound source of perspective. The potential transformation of pain into perspective on life ultimately gives pain *itself* a different perspective, and redefines it.

That night, just like every other, was unbearable. The constant shocking pain made me restless. I lay in a pool of tears, my mom sitting next to me, holding my hand. My oncologist suggested starting me on a medication to help me sleep. At some point, we increased the dosage of one of the pain meds I was taking so much it caused tremors, trembling, and tingling sensations all over my body. Decreasing the dosage, however, meant more pain. Every option was equally draining. I was so done. I didn't want to fight anymore.

Every night, my mom would give me my meds, hold my hand, hear me cry, hug me, and tell me I could get through this. I'd look at her and tell her I couldn't take it anyone. Then she'd hug me and tell me to just hold on a bit more and stay patient. Every night it was the same conversations, the same desperation, the same connection, and the same vulnerability. Then I'd watch an episode of a show my sister and I used to watch with our grandparents when we were little. It gave me comfort. The memories of pain-free times held my scattered heart together and gave me hope for the future. My mom would often sing me to sleep and rub my back. On some days, the meds worked, and I fell asleep to my mom signing lullabies. However, on most days, I'd lie there restless, in pain. On most days, she'd fall asleep first. On most days, my tears and screams would wake her up in the middle of the night. She'd jump up and sit beside me on the couch and hold my hand.

"Will it ever get better, Mom?" I asked her that night when I woke her up at 4:00 a.m. "Will it ever stop hurting? Will I ever make it out of this?"

My mom hugged me tightly. "Of course it will," she told me and smiled—a smile of hope. "You'll see. It will all get so much better. Have patience for a just a little while longer. Everything's going to be OK. *I promise.*"

I don't know what I'd do without my mom during these long nights.

Two days later, we were back at the hospital for more tests and appointments. On Friday the fourteenth, two of my closest friends, Dimitris and Ourania, flew to Germany to see me. They were going to spend the weekend with me. I needed to see them so much. I needed to remember what happiness felt like again. I needed to sit down with them and talk about school, to watch a movie with them or get dinner. I needed to do the things I used to take for granted before being sick.

That morning, I woke up excited. My mom drove to the airport to pick up my friends. I was nervous to see them too. The pain was uncontrollable, and many times, I'd scream and cry helplessly. I didn't want them to see me like that. I didn't want them to know how much pain I was in. I didn't want them to worry. When they walked through the door, I got emotional. They ran toward me and hugged me. I felt at home.

We spent the day catching up, playing card games, and watching movies. We talked about teachers, school, and memories from summer. At night, we got dinner from that Italian place near our apartment. They even helped me do my daily physiotherapy, which was walking up and down the living room and trying to climb a set of stairs. After moving around, I was in great pain, but I didn't want to let it ruin the moments I had with my friends.

The night, however, was even more difficult. I couldn't sleep. My leg was killing me. I started crying. My mom hugged me tightly. Ourania woke up, came to the living room, and sat next to me. Dimitris was still asleep in the other room. I didn't want to wake him. Ourania held my hand. I hated that she had to see me like that. I knew it was difficult for her. I remembered the last time she'd seen me cry like that, back in January during that physics class incident. I saw her eyes. They were red again. She hugged me and told me it would get better. The constant pain prevented me from being able to believe her. I was broken. But giving up was not an option. I had to be brave. I had to endure to keep fighting for it. I knew there was much to hope for and much to be grateful for, but pain can mask all that and steal your breath. I had a choice to make. I would either believe what the pain in my leg was telling me or trust what the hope in my heart was showing me.

The next morning was much better. I woke up later than my friends because I hadn't slept for most of the night. My mom made us pancakes and waffles, and we all had breakfast together. I'd lost a lot of weight from the surgery and the chemotherapy, so my friends and my mom joked around and tried to make me eat more by filling my plate with pancakes and my bowl with cereal. It is these little moments of laughter, these small details of hope that I'll treasure forever.

My friends left on Sunday morning. They had school on Monday and a lot of homework to catch up on. I wished I could go with them. That was all I wanted—to escape and to be set free from the chains of pain and the burden of suffering. I wanted to go back to school, to be able to walk again, and to laugh again. I gathered all the courage in my heart to stay brave, to hold on. Before they left, I hugged them tightly. So tightly. I didn't want them to go. But I trusted that, soon, I would be back with them.

"I promise, I'll visit again soon," Dim told me before leaving.

His words filled me with hope. Spending that weekend with my friends infused with courage to try and get better as soon as I possibly could, and it reminded me of what life would feel like once I was back home.

Two days later, my brother visited me from London where he was studying. We spent the day taking photos around the house and then watched a space-related movie while eating ice cream. I was grateful for that night. The pain was just as strong; my heart was still bruised, broken, and dark, filled with exhaustion and hurt. But that night, many stars lit up the sky, so many little details of joy. Making jokes with my brother and eating ice cream covered in blankets on a rainy fall night was so comforting, special, and wholesome. It made me smile. Here's an extremely simple, powerful yet underrated lesson cancer taught me about life: Do more of the things that make you smile. Read that again if you need to.

On September 22, I hit my breaking point. The pain levels skyrocketed, and on top of that, I started running a fever. One of the pain meds I was taking, specifically for the nerve pain, caused me to hallucinate and gave me chills and tingling sensations all over my back and neck. We called Dr. Thanos, who is a neurosurgeon, and he told us it was probably because of how high a dose I was taking. I had just gone through a light withdrawal from reducing the morphine a little bit too quickly, and so the idea of having to reduce that dose as well scared me a lot.

The next morning, my mom contacted Prof. D, who advised us to reduce the dose of that medication and consult a pain specialist. The details of that day made it a little bit better. Amalia asked me to help her with some homework for school, and I got the chance to write her essay for her. I was so grateful to have the strength to sit at the desk and write that essay. It instilled motivation in my heart to try and get better so I could get back to school and write such essays for myself.

The next day was chemo day. When we arrived at the hospital, I was admitted to K3. Usually, we would have to wait for four to six hours to get a room. And many times, especially during VIDE blocks, there was no room available, and we had to postpone the chemo. This time, however, since I was in isolation, thanks to the postoperative kidney infection I still had, I was given a room within the first two hours of waiting. The chemo itself was difficult and tiring. Usual stuff. On the second day, however, something happened that would stay with me forever. A conversation that, just like a small white dot on the night sky, promised hope for the sunrise.

After I was discharged, a nurse came in to remove my port needle. But it wasn't just any nurse. It was nurse M, my favorite nurse. She was young and spoke English fluently. She was like a best friend to me. We always had conversations, and she always gave me strength. She had a smile of hope. I could tell. That night, as she removed the needle, we started talking about my leg. My mom was in the parking lot loading our bags in the back of the car. So, nurse M stayed with me to keep me company. She asked me about the rehabilitation, and I told her that, as soon as I recovered from this chemo, I'd be able to start the rehab and work on bending.

She was really excited for me. "Are you in pain right now?" she asked.

"A little bit," I said and bowed my head. The truth was, I was in a lot of pain. But I didn't want to show it.

"It seems to me that you are in a little more than a little bit," she said.

I didn't say anything. I just nodded. A few tears ran down my face and fell on my leg. Nurse M knelt and sat on the ground next to my bed. "Do you want me to bring you something for the pain?" she asked.

I shook my head no. "It's the nerve pain," I told her and showed her the wound. "It radiates back to my calf."

"That's a very cool scar," nurse M told me and smiled.

"I don't really like it" I replied. "I know it symbolizes a lot. I appreciate it. But I don't really like it."

"It's part of your story," she said. "It shows how much you've overcome."

"I know." My voice trembled. "It's just that … some days, I don't really like my story." Tears flooded my eyes. I felt a lump in my throat.

Nurse M took my hand and held it tightly. "You will," she said and smiled. "One year from now, I promise you'll like it, and you too will think your scar is supercool."

She showed me her arm. A faded scar ran across her forearm, leading to her elbow. "I was in a car crash a couple of years ago," she told me. "I broke my arm here. And it left me with this scar. I know it's smaller than yours, but I didn't like it at first either. But now, I think it's cool. I realized it adds to the list of things that make me special. It reminds me that I survived that accident. That's something worth remembering, right?"

Little did I know that last sentence would change my perspective forever.

"It is. I guess it is," I replied, and a smile of hope replaced my tears.

Ever since that morning before the graduation, I had embraced my scars. But the scar from the surgery was so graphic. It was traumatizing to look at every day. I couldn't understand how that was my leg. There was dry blood all over, discolored skin, patches from the skin graft, random bumps of muscle from the muscle flap that had been performed to cover the prosthesis, so it didn't touch the skin directly. That conversation, however, changed my perspective of that scar completely—and forever. It did indeed remind me of all I'd overcome. It did remind me of all the sleepless nights filled with excruciating pain. It reminded me of the tumor that used to be there and of the endoprosthesis that replaced my bone. But most importantly, it reminded me that I'd overcome all these things. It reminded me that I'd come out of every of these battles a winner, that I'd stood stronger and I'd chosen to be braver. It reminded me I hadn't given up—ever. I'd persevered and fought and prayed. I'd believed and hoped and won. I had won. I was still alive. I was still there, fighting. I had won. And that was—and is—something worth remembering.

September 26 was a big day. Early in the morning, we went to the orthopedic clinic in the hospital and met with my surgeon. Since my surgery, I'd been wearing a cast that allowed no movement in my leg at all. That morning was the day the cast would be removed, which meant I could start the process of bending my knee. Since a third of my leg had been replaced by a metal endoprosthesis, I had to learn how to bend my knee again, how to extend it, and how to walk—literally how to use my leg. I knew the rehabilitation process would be difficult but had underestimated the depth of that difficulty. Once Prof. H removed the cast, he asked me to lift my leg. I couldn't—not only because of the excruciating pain, but also because I just didn't know how. Normally once you think about moving a part of your body, you're able to do it. But in this case, I tried lifting my leg, and it just didn't move one bit.

"It's normal," Prof. H said. "You have to work on this. It looks good."

After we got home, I lay back on the couch. I was discouraged—not because it was impossible but because it felt impossible. I knew the road up the mountain of gaining back the function of my leg would be one of the most difficult, long, and exhausting roads I'd ever need to climb.

I downloaded a protractor app on my phone that allowed me to measure the degrees at which I managed to bend me knee. I was excited about the future. Yet I was scared. I was scared that I might give my all to this rehabilitation journey and it would fail anyway. I was scared I'd fall apart. But I let faith rise in my heart and made the choice to try anyway—to hope anyway and to fight anyway. That wouldn't make it easy. Progress would still be slow. On some days, there would be no progress at all. On some days, discouragement would prevent me from even trying. Bad news would hit me like waves. Exhaustion would suffocate me. But somehow, somewhere between drowning and swimming, I would still catch a new breath—a breath of hope, faith, and courage.

Day 0. Bending reached—12 degrees. Pain level—unbearable.

The next day, I started physiotherapy. The clinic was in Werden, near our apartment. The physiotherapist, Mr. Dimitris, was Greek too. God's in the details.

Day uno of physiotherapy. Bending reached—20 degrees. Pain level—unbearable. I'm hoping I can get full nerve and muscle function back. I'm scared. But determined. I know God's got me. Somehow, I know it. It's all scary and exhausting. Pain's not decreasing either. But I'll make it out. I have to make it out. Now heading to the bae's place to get the goods.

That's what I wrote on my notes app that morning, referring to the physiotherapy and going to Starbucks after to get a cool lime. As I waited in the parked car for my mom to come back from Starbucks, I looked outside the window. It was a sunny morning. The day was smiling. I did too. Details. It's all about these details. I was out of the hospital and able to see and take in the warmth of the sun that transcended the glass window of the car and covered my face. That day felt like a warm, comforting hug. I took a deep breath. I felt it reach down my lungs. I was okay. I was going to be all right. Even if nothing else was okay, *I* could be. I could find joy in the pain. I could be *brave in the broken*.

On the way home, my mom stopped at a local store close to our apartment. She bought a few fall decorations, which we then put up together. I wanted to help decorate the house so badly. It was a way to make it feel like home. It was a detail of love, laughter, and hope. We put up fall stickers of leaves on the windows and decorative fabric cutouts of leaves and squirrels on the walls around the TV. My favorite fall decoration, however, was an orange, green, and brown garland with fabric cutouts of squirrels. I named one of them Daniel. Daniel would soon become an inside joke for the whole family. Joy's in the details.

Later that day, I bought myself a lens with some money I'd saved. Shortly after starting chemotherapy, back in February, I'd promised myself I would buy a specific camera lens as a gift to myself for getting through VIDE blocks and multiple major surgeries. Getting that lens didn't just make me excited about the photographs I could take with it; it made me determined—it symbolized a milestone I had achieved in my life. I knew that every time I would use this lens in the future, I would be reminded of all I'd gone through and all it symbolized. I also knew I would be reminded to look at life through this lens and these difficult memories that had taught me so much—memories that embodied faith, courage, and determination and that showed me what it means to be brave.

The next couple of days looked dreadfully similar—recovering from chemo, daily injections, tons of meds, unmanageable pain, physiotherapy, exhaustion, tachycardias, and lots of crying. Yet, despite all that darkness, there was light. In every single day, there was light. Crepe sandwiches for breakfast, Starbucks after physio, listening to my "motivation" playlist, watching the sunset, painting, and drawing on random afternoons, watching videos that made me smile, or even making jokes and puns with my mom in the car—light's in the details.

Think about what makes stars so bright. It's their size. You see, the smaller a star *seems* to be, the brighter it *actually* is. The smaller you see a star to be, the farther away in space it is. Yet, despite the unfathomable distance between you and that star, it still shines, and it still reflects. Just imagine how bright it would seem if you were up close. Details are just like stars. The smaller you think a moment is, the more meaningful it can become, the more joy and hope it can give you. No matter how distant some stars might be, how far a goal, a dream, or a wish seems, it can always feel close if you just notice the light this small little dot in the sky reflects. Even if healing seems far away, it can start to feel closer if you start appreciating the little moments of hope, joy, and purpose.

> Day two of physiotherapy. October 2. No progress still. The pain is too much. But I know there will be better days. I don't know how. I don't know when. But somehow, someday, things will get better. They always do. Even when it seems impossible, hope is near. And it transforms. There will be better days.

Chapter 18

The Bathroom
Floor Prayer

That night, at around 8:00 p.m., I decided to take my first real shower. My mom would help me wash my arms, legs, and body with a wet towel daily, but I still hadn't been able or allowed to take a proper shower and get my leg wet. As the water touched my leg, I broke down crying. I couldn't feel it. I couldn't sense it. The nerve damage was so extensive that it had affected both sensory and motor function of my leg.

As tears started filling my eyes, I wondered what else I wasn't feeling. This past week, I'd been feeling so much pain I'd been numb to feeling anything else. I took a deep breath. Releasing it all, I wondered what "water" was trying to clean me, to wash away my pain. What water was trying to offer healing that I just couldn't sense? That water was trust. I knew I had to trust God and His timing, but I couldn't feel His presence. I was numb to that strong and courageous faith. The pain and the discouraging words from doctors concerning my nerve had made me numb to that kind of trust. As I sat on that chair in the shower crying, I wondered whether the damage and numbness would be permanent—both in my nerve and in my trust. I wondered if I'd be able to fully surrender and find the bravery to truly trust God again. I wanted to, with everything in me, but I just didn't have the strength. I didn't have the courage. My nerve had been paralyzed from the surgery, but my soul and trust had also been paralyzed from the pain—the never-ending pain. I took another deep breath. I leaned my head back. I took another breath. I released all the hurt that was in my heart.

It was in that moment that I realized that, even though I couldn't feel the water, it was still touching my body; it was still cleaning me and washing away my pain. Likewise, maybe I couldn't feel God's presence since it had been masked by the pain, but He was still there, holding me, crying with me, wiping away my tears, keeping me safe at night, hurting with me, and helping me get through the suffering. God was right there. He was with me, by me, beside me, before me, within me, and all around me. I might have been so broken that I couldn't sense Him, but He was still there, in my brokenness, in my mess, in my lack of trust and faith, in my crying, and in my desperation. He was there—every second. I was not alone.

For a moment I thought, *Well if God is here and sees me suffer and cry and be in agonizing pain, why doesn't He just fix it? If He loves me, why doesn't He just make the pain stop?* I didn't understand. But as the warm water touched my body, it washed away these thoughts. It gave me comfort. It gave me a sense of protection.

There is purpose in every suffering, in every tear I shed. That purpose is so profound that I couldn't understand it back then. *Well, if God is so powerful and loves me so much, He would reveal this purpose without the pain,* the voices of doubt and depression told me.

But they couldn't rattle me. It was *because* God loved me, that He didn't remove that painful situation. It was *because* He loved me that He allowed this pain to overwhelm me. Most people don't like that idea, of love being expressed through pain. But I think it's true. God knew He could bring out the greatest testimony from the most difficult test. He knew He could bring the most meaningful message out of the most broken mess. He knew He could reveal the most profound purpose out of the most overwhelming pain. I didn't understand the logistics—the how and the why. But that's what faith is all about. It's trust in the absence of understanding.

I soon started feeling dizzy, and purple and red spots appeared all over my legs. As I got out of the shower, I looked in the mirror. I was pale, thin, and broken. Suddenly, I felt as if I couldn't breathe. My heart was tired and heavy. I sat down on the floor to catch my breath, and I caught a glimpse of the scar on my leg. It was so graphic. It tore my heart in half. It hid so much suffering. I was broken on the floor, crying with my elbow over my mouth to keep from making any noise. I was exhausted. I didn't want to go through this pain anymore. It was too much. I hadn't slept in weeks. I wanted to fight with everything in me, but I was too tired, too weak, too broken. I didn't want to give up. I didn't want to feel so helpless, so lifeless. I wanted to get up and walk and get better and sleep at night and go back home and go to school and escape this darkness, this pain, this nightmare. But I was just *too tired*. I leaned my head against the wall and took a very deep breath. I closed my eyes, held my fists tightly together, and prayed.

Oh, God, I thought and instantly broke down crying even more. *Find me here. Find me in this place—in this brokenness, in this mess. This pain is too much. I just cannot keep doing this. I don't want to hurt anymore. It just doesn't get better. The pain is agonizing. It's draining. It breaks me, and I'm so broken. And I can't sleep. I can't find peace. I need courage. I really do. I'm so tired. God, pull me out of this wreck of pain. Make it stop hurting. Help me sleep. All I ask is for this to stop hurting, even if just for a moment. God, I have hope. I do. But it hurts. God, it just hurts so much. Oh, God, give me just enough strength to make it through. Tell me I'm not alone. Just please tell me I'm not alone. Promise. Promise me I'm not alone. Please. Because honestly I feel so alone. So broken. The pain is too much. It's just too much God. Please, take this pain away, even for just one moment. Give me just one moment without pain, one moment of peace. Just one. Please. Only one. I'm desperate. I'm desperate for just a moment of peace.*

Tears and sobs finished that prayer. For a moment, I just sat there on the floor—waiting. I felt tired. I was tired of constantly waiting for things to get better, tired of fear, of hurt, and of being in pain. I was tired of taking morphine that didn't even help, of the hallucinations from the pain meds, and of waking up at night with electric shocks running down my leg. I was tired of getting tachycardic and dizzy every time I sat up and of feeling so nauseated I couldn't even swallow and tired of trying to smile. I was just so tired.

But then, I felt God speak to my heart: *I got tired too*, He said.

I placed my hands against the floor; *stay brave*, I told myself and tried to get up. A sharp pain rushed through my body. But I *still* got up. My hands *still* held me up. The same hands that had desperately wiped away the tears a couple seconds before now helped me rise again. Suddenly, there it was—in the deepest place of my heart, making its way all throughout my body—a sunset feeling. A strange sense of peace—a peace that exceeds all understanding and coexists with fear and exhaustion and restlessness. It was confirmation that I was not alone.

That sunset feeling helped me realize that maybe it was okay that I was not okay. Maybe it was okay that I broke and cried and hurt and fell. Maybe it was okay that it all got a little too much on some days. Maybe it was okay that doubt and worry tore me up inside. Maybe it was okay that I was weak, that I was weary, that I was scared, and that I was tired. Because, I was not alone. The One who holds the stars was holding *me*. I didn't have to fight on my own. No one has to fight alone. No one has to walk alone.

With a subtle but deeply rooted smile on my face, I called out to my mom to help me change into fresh clothes. I was too weak to do it myself. But I didn't care. I'd just realized, only a moment ago, that being vulnerable was the greatest source of strength. Surrendering and asking God for help, being open and raw about my brokenness was the very thing that delivered me from it and comforted me in it. That experience taught me that asking for help is not a sign of weakness but one of bold courage and bravery.

My mom helped me get dressed and changed the bandages on my leg. She brought in the chair and held my leg up as I wheeled my way to the couch. I lay down, and she tucked the blanket in around me. I then called my sister on FaceTime, and we talked for a while. That's all it takes. Those small details of light are enough for me—enough to give me courage to keep fighting. Distance means nothing when someone means so much.

On October 3, my mom and I had an appointment with a doctor who specialized in postoperative, nerve damage-induced pain. He was the specialist of the specialists, as you can tell. To break it down, he basically was an expert in pain caused by a nerve injury that happened during or after an operation. He was Dr. Thanos's classmate in med school, and Dr. Thanos had advised us to visit him.

The pain specialist's clinic was in a town about two hours east of Essen, so we woke up at 4:00 a.m. to make our 8:00 a.m. appointment. The town was beautiful and peaceful. After the doctor examined me and performed some tests, we were given the results. The news wasn't good. He basically told me the nerve damage was most likely irreversible and that there were potential surgical ways to regain some motor function, which unfortunately carried significant risk.

Nonetheless, there was a tiny star of hope. He'd seen a case where, even though it seemed irreversible and a nerve transplant had been scheduled, just a day before the operation, the nerve had started working. That story gave me hope. The doctor, however, told me that, statistically, given the extent of the nerve injury I'd suffered, if my nerve ever started working again, it would do so after twelve to eighteen months—at best. That felt like a punch to the stomach. He gave us some patches with a local anesthetic that could help alleviate the pain and told me to be patient and keep doing the exercises.

On the car ride home, I was a wreck. I was devastated. But hope's in the details. And it's always there. Often, we can't see it because it doesn't look or sound the way we expect. But Hope's still there—in a different form, hidden under different words. The question is, Can you notice it?

That day, I did. I did notice it. It looked way different than I'd imagined if I'm being honest. I was expecting hope in the form of a good prognosis for the paralysis, yet instead hope came through an email. Later that day, I received an email from Mrs. B, my grade 9 Modern Greek teacher:

Katerina,

I wanted to tell you a huge Bravo for all that you've accomplished so far and for all that you are fighting for. Once more, I would like to tell you how proud I am, that you were my student. I want to dedicate to you, some verses from a poem by C. P. Cavafy who is my favorite poet.

Wise as you will have become, so full of experience,

you'll have understood by then what these Ithakas mean.

Don't ever stop fighting for your Ithaka.

That was hope hidden in the details. In the poem, Ithaka was a symbol of the destination. The destination is the whole purpose of the journey, right? But is the destination at the end of the journey? Maybe the journey itself *is* the destination. Maybe the destination isn't something you get to but something you discover along the way. Was healing my destination? If yes, what did healing mean? Did it just mean clear scans and a good prognosis? Was hope my destination? Was it peace? What if it was adversity itself?

Ithaka was also a symbol of home. But what was home? What did it mean to be at home? Was home just the place you grew up in? Was home even a place? I didn't yet have answers to these questions. I was too busy surviving. I hadn't taken the time to process. But I would—at the most unexpected times and in the most unexpected ways. All these questions would be answered soon, and the significance of that email would be revealed. There's purpose behind timing. Twelve to eighteen months. Remember that estimate.

The next day, Grandpa Nick visited me in Essen. He stayed with me for five days. I felt grateful to be surrounded by a loving family. It didn't make fighting easier. But it did makes it worth it. And that was all that mattered. My grandpa and I played multiple games of chess. I won the first three and lost the last two. Eventually, my mom called us for dinner. We got steak from the Italian place near our house.

The next day was pretty much the same. In the morning my grandpa went to the Greek restaurant across the road and bonded with the owner, who was Greek too. At around noon, he came over to the apartment and woke me up. We played some more chess, and then we went to physiotherapy. He came too. He was excited for me to learn to bend my knee and walk again, and his excitement was my source of motivation.

> **Day four of physiotherapy. October 5. No improvement today. But that's OK. Patience is the key to perseverance. And perseverance is the key to progress. My grandpa helped me do some exercises for my leg at home. Let's focus on that. On the process. Maybe progress will only come once I embrace the process. Maybe. I don't know at this point. The pain is too much. But ... patience. How? Through trust. Trust supplies the strength needed to practice patience.**

The night was difficult. The pain was extremely strong. I couldn't take it. I kept crying out, and my mom sat by my side and held my hand. I took some morphine and a medication to calm me down and help me sleep.

I fell asleep while watching a movie with my mom. But only an hour later, the pain woke me up. It was unbearable. At some point, after weeping and shouting in agony, I looked at my mom and whispered, "Mom, I don't think I can take this any longer."

My mom hugged me tightly. "I know, sweetheart. But hold on. It will get better. It will soon get better. You can't see it now, but I promise. I promise, it will get better."

For the next few hours, I would fall asleep for a few minutes and then be woken up by the pain. The same thing happened over twenty times. It was exhausting—for my mom too. She didn't sleep. She stayed next to me on the couch and watched over me like a guardian angel sent from God. I had so many guardian angels in my life. That gave me courage.

After about four hours, I finally fell asleep. My mom did too. But the night wasn't over yet. The next time I woke up was at 5:30 a.m., drenched in sweat and overtaken by a numbness across my whole body. I had seen a dream—a dream that changed me forever. I don't remember specifics, but in the dream, I was standing in front of a dark brown, wooden door. There were no walls, just a door and a white blank space. Behind the door was a staircase—a white staircase with black handles on the side. I was left in this white area and walked up to the door. When I opened the door, I instantly felt my head drop low. I was blinded by light. I'd never seen a light so bright. I couldn't even look up.

Yet I tried anyway. And when I did, I saw the figure of Christ. He smiled at me and placed His hand on my shoulder—just like I had pictured in the mirror the day of graduation. Only this time, it wasn't me consciously imagining. This was a dream. But it didn't feel like one. We all have dreams that we wake up from surprised because it just felt way too real to be a dream. This was one of them. As soon as I saw Christ put His hand on my shoulder, I physically, in my body, felt an unreal sense of heaviness and a force of gravity rush from my shoulders to my toes. It was like the feeling of awe had taken a physical form. I do know that was a dream. And it's something I can't explain. Maybe it was all just chemicals and my subconscious mind had created this dream. Maybe it was simply random.

225

Or maybe it was neither. Maybe it was the answer to the bathroom floor prayer. I really don't know. I *can't* know. But I do know that it gave me strength. Whatever it was, even if it was just a dream, it gave me courage. But it wasn't the kind of courage that gets used up during a battle with pain or hurt or hopelessness. It gave me the kind of courage that can't be rattled, that remains steadfast and perseveres, that is unconditional. That doesn't mean I didn't break, cry, or hurt. But even when I did, I always had this deeply rooted inner courage that pulled me out. Somehow. Someway.

After receiving the discouraging news about my leg, I had let go of hope. I didn't see a point to going to physiotherapy or doing exercises and isometrics for the paralysis at home. I'd convinced myself I would not walk again. I kept telling myself I just had to accept the situation, but what I thought was acceptance was actually hopelessness. Through this dream, God broke the chains of hopelessness and gave me courage. When I saw Christ place His hand on my shoulder, I felt an overwhelming sense of protection. I felt determined to try, because I knew He would catch me if I fell—just like I believe He did during the graduation ceremony as I climbed the stairs, just like I believe He did as I was taking my first steps after the surgery in the hospital corridor, and just like He did *after that bathroom floor prayer.*

The next day, my mom came in the room holding an envelope. I opened it and saw that it was from Make-A-Wish. Hope came when I needed it the most, after getting the bad news about my leg. I find it fascinating how hope can hide in small moments, exist in so many different forms, and shine through so many things. All you have to do is notice. Stop and stare.

That night brought me to my knees. It destroyed me. The nerve pain was unbearable. I was screaming. It's strange to think how tidal life is. One moment I was filled with hope, writing out my wish or laughing with my mom, and the next I was crying out desperately as the unbearable pain rushed through my leg. I just waited it out. I had to keep going. I was broken. But I was learning to be brave.

The next day, my physiotherapist, Mr. Dimitris, put on some music for me to listen to as we worked on my knee. The songs were familiar—a warm hug of comfort. They were all Greek songs I used to listen and sing to with my friends every summer. I missed home. But I was fascinated at how God always found ways to bring home to me—subtle ways, details showing me what home was really about, what it truly meant. I wasn't ready to see and receive this revelation yet though. There's purpose in timing. There's purpose in the tides. Tidal joy. Tidal hope. Tidal pain.

On October 11, my mom and I stopped to get brunch after a long, tiring day of clinic and follow-up tests. We went to a new restaurant that only had waffles and enjoyed *the best* waffles I'd had in a very long time. Waffles are such a childhood memory for me; my grandparents would take us to a waffle place close to their house every summer after the beach. That detail that morning gave me comfort. It felt like a warm familiar hug.

Later that day, I practiced my knee flexion at home.

Day fifteen since bending begun. Degrees reached—25! I managed to put two towels today under my knee. The bending reached 25 degrees. What? I'm excited. Slow progress is still progress.

The next day at the end of my physiotherapy appointment, I tried to cycle. But I failed. *I am getting there*, I told myself. Patience is the key to perseverance.

Later during the day, Elena flew to Essen. Elena has basically been our nanny ever since we were little. She's family. She was going to spend the next two and a half months with me in Essen. I was ecstatic.

The next day, I woke up in pain. What's new at this point, right? My mom helped me take my meds and gave me a big hug. She hugged me for a while. I was in so much pain, yet somehow a simple hug from my family could make me feel safe. It didn't take the pain away, but it was a safe place for my tired soul to rest—even if just for a moment. That was all I needed—a moment of rest, of peace.

What's really fascinating about peace is that it helps you fight. It's ironic, yet incredibly beautiful how peace and fighting are not contrasting but complementary. One doesn't cancel out the other; rather, it completes it. The existence of peace is what fuels perseverance to fight. You can be fighting but still be at peace—on the inside. That morning, on the outside, I was in unbearable pain. I was beaten down by sudden, stabbing waves of pain that rushed across my leg. Yet even though on the outside I was bruised and broken, on the inside, I felt whole. There was something else that was filling me up. It wasn't material objects. It wasn't a temporary situation. It was the only constant, unfailing, everlasting force—Love.

When pain emptied my strength, drenched my courage, and left me broken and lifeless, love made me whole, restored the pieces of my heart, held them together, and got me through the night. Love sheltered me, made me brave enough to hope, and made me boldly courageous to have faith. Love helped me persevere. Love held my hand as I cried and hugged my scattered soul as I hurt. Pain ripped me apart, yet love put me back together. However, the most beautiful observation is not the power of love but the *potential* of pain. Think about how meaningfully impactful pain can be. The purpose of pain hides behind its potential to project and portray the power of love. Without the presence of pain, the power of love wouldn't be glorified. Similarly, the presence of adversity creates the need for hope and sets the foundation for faith.

Let's look at the metaphor of the sky to better understand this idea. I'm sure you've heard the saying, "Stars can't shine without darkness." Well, that's not really true. In reality, stars intrinsically shine, whether the sky is dark or not. The darkness, however, gives us the power to *see*. Ironic isn't it? Beautifully so. In reality, the darkness gives us the ability to see the light the stars intrinsically reflect. The darker the sky, the more stars become visible. Difficulties and struggles work just like that. They act as a backdrop that intensifies the contrast of the stars, the brightness of the light, the significance of the details.

That morning, I decided to focus on the stars and try to pinpoint the details of light that could be intensified by all the darkness of the pain I was going through. Thus, I spent the day making a fall bucket list. A simple list of details—that was a detail in and of itself—was suddenly going to bring a splash of color into my life and somehow, in the smallest and most unexpected ways, make it brighter.

One of the items on my bucket list was catching up with school. So, I reached out to Dimitris, and he sent me photos of all his chemistry, biology, and social sciences notes since the beginning of the year. Just the fact that he took the time to do this for me meant so much to me.

I spent the day copying notes into my notebooks. It made me feel at school. It made me feel healthy. It was a way for me to practice hope—to choose to be brave, even in the broken.

Chapter 19

The Garden with the Roses

On October 14, we went on an adventure. I found a pumpkin field outside Cologne, and we decided to visit. It was on my fall bucket list too. Going there, even if just for a short time, reminded me of what normalcy felt like. Before I got sick, I used to be the most adventurous person ever. I always wanted to go on hikes, walks, road trips, and any other kind of spontaneous adventure. I used to plan trips in my free time and explore random remote locations for sunset, stargazing, or sunrise missions. Adventure gave me the sense there was something more than me, that life had a greater purpose. Little did I know, the biggest, greatest, and most meaningful adventure I would ever go on would not be on an island, on a mountain, or in some foreign country. It would be on a hospital chemotherapy ward. The adventure of cancer is very different from the adventures I was used to going on and loved so much. For the longest time, I thought of adventure as a noun, "an unusual and exciting or daring experience." Going through cancer, however, I realized that adventure isn't a constant or stable situation but, rather, an action, a process. The verb, to adventure, means to "engage in daring or risky activity." With cancer, I wasn't going on an adventure, I was adventuring. I was taking a risk every single day, with every new breath—the risk of hope. With every breath I took, I chose to trust in the purpose of the path I was walking on—and keep going. With every needle poke and prod, I chose to be brave—even in the broken. And that's the riskiest activity I'd ever engaged in.

We spent the day wandering around the field, taking photos of pumpkins and seeing all the farm animals. The llamas were my favorite. They were hilarious to me and made me laugh a lot. It was that innocent, pain-free, insignificant laugh that I used to take for granted. But now it was like the treasure chest of the whole adventure. I brought my camera and took many photos. Walking with two crutches made the photography process a bit more challenging, but it also made seeing the photos turn out nice more rewarding. After a few hours on the field, my leg started giving in, until it completely collapsed under pain. My mom helped me get to the car and got me a waffle stick to make me smile. Waffles symbolize family to me. I've told you why. Love's in the details.

The next day, we went to the hospital early in the morning for blood tests and an appointment with Prof. H. Progress was slow, and the pain didn't seem to be getting any better. But I took heart. I had to be brave.

The next morning, my aunt flew to Essen to visit. She visited me every month and a half. We spent the day together at the house. Later, we drove to a city in the Netherlands called Tilburg. There, we attended a concert of one of my favorite bands, Why Don't We. I was in a wheelchair, which made me feel insecure and sad. Yet it was *because* of that wheelchair that I was able to go in first and sit in the first row. That simple experience proves that perspective is the single most important tool to fight adversity. It's all about the story you tell yourself, the angle you choose to view your situation from, the mindset you decide to have. Joy isn't circumstantial but a *choice*. Authentic joy and deep gratitude can't be rattled by difficulties or situational setbacks. Rather, they flourish *in* them, giving them meaning and are glorified *through* them. The darkness can't cast out the light. It only intensifies its brightness.

Attending that concert with my aunt, signing at the top of my lungs, and releasing all anxiety and pain for just a moment was therapeutic for me. Going on this adventure with my family was a special gift before the next block of chemo. I got to meet the band and tell them how much their music had helped me throughout the blocks of chemotherapy. They gave me a hug and told me to keep being strong—and *brave*.

It's details like that—small moments of light amid darkness, conversations and hugs of hope amid pain and sorrow—that make life *matter*, make suffering *worth it*, and make fighting a *privilege*. At night, my mom got us quesadillas from a taco place nearby, and then we drove back. I was in a lot of pain, but I was also smiling. And the pain couldn't change that, even if it tried. My mom and my aunt were both thrilled to see me smile again. I could see it in their eyes.

After getting about four hours of sleep, my mom woke me up to get ready to go to the hospital for block 4 of my phase two chemotherapies. When she left to bring me a set of chemo clothes, I sat on the couch, cuddling a teddy bear and thinking about how much I didn't want to go to the hospital. I'd had so much fun these past few days, finally feeling somewhat well enough to go outside. And now I had to go back for chemo. It seemed as if it would never end. I was trying my very best to stay above water, to be brave, to fight it, to study, to do things I'd normally do, and to practice walking and bending my knee. But for what? Every twenty days, a huge wave came crashing down on me and pushed me back in the ocean, just as I was starting to see the shore. And then I'd have to pick my broken pieces up and swim again, try again, and get better again. It was *exhausting*. But as my mom walked out of the bedroom and sat by my side on the couch, she held my hand, and I realized something about trying to get to the shore. It was worth it. No matter how many times I was pushed back in the ocean, swimming to the shore was always worth it. It wasn't easy. It seemed impossible at times. But that's what bravery is all about. Even when your boat is broken and its pieces have scattered all over the ocean, you can always choose to be brave enough to hope and be bold enough to act on that hope and keep fighting, keep trying, *keep swimming*.

On October 19, my mom and I carved the pumpkins we'd bought at the field a few days ago. I was still sick from the chemo, dealing with the side effects, but this activity brought me joy.

A few days later, on October 21, my mom and I had dinner at Zwolf Apostles. Our waiter friend was there. When he saw me, he gave me the biggest hug. He could tell I was recovering from the chemo, so he placed an order for a mango mint as soon as he saw me. It was through people like him, my doctors, my teachers, my friends, and my family that I could experience the profound power of love. Having people in my life who could make me smile, bring me hope and joy, and offer me a shoulder to cry on was the greatest gift I'd received.

A day later, my grandma flew to Essen to spend the next two weeks with me. Every time my grandma visited, so did home. She brought home with her. How? Through the lullabies she'd sing to me, through the homemade traditional Greek food she prepared every day, and through the prayers she would say over me every night. She brought home to me, by bringing love. And that love was shared through memories and details.

On October 23, we were back in the hospital for appointments and follow-up tests. The ladies at the lab gave me a ladybug plaster just like every time. It made me smile. Later that afternoon, I went to the physiotherapy clinic. I had three to four physio appointments per week, but because of the chemo, we often had to call off some of them.

Two days later, we were back in the hospital—yet again—for more tests and an appointment with my surgeon. As we drove home, I stared out the window and thought. I'd gotten used to going to the hospital. For the past almost year, I'd spent more days in the hospital than at the apartment. It was scary how much life had changed. As I reflected on all I'd endured so far, the heaviness of grief for the pain I'd experienced overtook me. Yet there was another feeling that these thoughts and reflections created—a feeling deeper and more profound. It was a feeling of gratitude. The fact that I was able to reflect on all the battles I'd fought these past months meant that I had survived them. I had overcome them. I was nowhere near finishing fighting the war, but I had survived all my past battles, even the ones I hadn't thought I could endure; that realization gave me comfort and filled me with gratitude and courage. I couldn't give up.

Later that day, my mom went to the airport to pick up Amalia, who'd flown to Essen to spend the long weekend with me. As she walked through the door, I got so emotional. I had missed her so much. I hugged her tightly—just like that time at the airport. My mom went back toward the door. As soon as she opened it, I saw my friend Ivy walk in. I was shocked.

"Surprise!" she said with a smile.

I was beyond happy. I needed this so much—more than words can describe. I hugged Ivy tightly. I hadn't seen her since graduation day. We spent the day playing card games, catching up, and making jokes around the dinner table. Happiness is simple.

The next day, we went on an adventure, exploring Essen's countryside. We took photos at a forest and then went to Zwolf Apostles for a hot chocolate. The waiter who'd become my best friend was there too. He was happy to see me smile. He prepared a pastry for us to celebrate. Love's in the details. At night, we carved more pumpkins (because why not?) and then watched a movie. It was so much fun. I was laughing the whole day. I had completely forgotten what that felt like.

The next morning, we had pancakes, waffles, and donuts for breakfast. Healthy stuff, you know? We were pretty extra as a family, as you can tell. But that breakfast table somehow made me smile. It made me feel at home. Maybe home wasn't really about a place. Maybe home was the destination, but the destination wasn't a place. Maybe my Ithaka had been around me all along.

After breakfast, we took Amalia and Ivy to the airport. That weekend had flown by so quickly. Seeing them leave and not being able to join them was difficult. But I chose to be brave.

The past week, I'd felt well enough to try and study for school. One day, Amalia had told me about an English class assignment to write a short story with "time" as the theme. I was excited and motivated to write such a story too. I spent all night thinking about the plot and the characters and developing my idea. I was exhausted at physiotherapy the next day, but it was totally worth it. A day later, I pulled another all-nighter and wrote the story. It turned out bigger than I'd expected. Let me tell you about it.

I gave it the title "Beating Time," and it was about a woman who was going on a mission to space. The idea was that this woman tries to find a way to beat time, just like she has promised her father she will, before leaving for space. After a sudden diagnosis of heart failure, while she's still in space, her father decides to give her his heart as soon as they return to Earth.

I added many details, a lot of scientific information and specifics, which I'd studied due to a passion for space that I'd developed these past few months. The message of the story was that the only way to beat time is through love. I could really relate to that story. Cancer often felt like a race against a running clock. But here's the beautifully meaningful irony about this race for life. You win the race by slowing down. Normally, you have to speed up, rush, and go faster to win a race. But not this one. This one, the more you slow down, the more you win. The more you pause, step back, and appreciate each individual moment you get, the more time you win. Cancer taught me to stop and smell the roses in life. Let me tell you what I mean.

Let's say you're on a train, going to a famous train station known for its beautiful garden. You haven't seen it but have heard plenty about it. You're so excited to get to that train station and see the garden that you spend the entire train ride on your phone, googling and learning all you can about the garden. Once you get there, you realize what you thought would be a beautiful garden is actually a gallery of images and paintings of other gardens. As you ask around, you discover that these are all photos people who get to that train station have taken of the garden the saw while getting there. "Where is this garden then? At which train station?" you ask. But it's not in a train station. It's on a train ride. Beside the train, as you were moving, the garden was all around. All it took for you to see it was to look. All it took was to notice, to pay attention. All it took for you to see it was to look.

Isn't life the same? We think happiness is this great garden found in a train station. But here's the thing about happiness. It's not a station; it's a ride. Here's the thing about gratitude. Here's the thing about hope. Here's the thing about joy. It's not a destination. It's a journey. We think it can be unlocked only in the absence of problems and pain. We think we can be grateful only when things go our way or be happy when life is easy. But happiness is not a garden found at the end of the train ride. It's a garden found alongside the train, amid the ride. Gratitude is found in the small individual roses, the individual moments and details of everyday life, of the journey. It's these flowers, these details, these little things that compile the beautiful garden we all want to see. And all we have to do is look. Notice the small moments. Stop looking at our phone, stop rushing through life, only caring about getting to the destination. Instead, open the window and smell the roses. Notice the garden all around you. Capture the flowers you see along the ride. That's your garden. That's what life's all about—appreciating the journey, making the most of this one ride we get.

The next morning, I submitted the story on our class online page and went to the hospital for some follow-up tests.

A couple days later, my mom informed me that she had some very exciting news to give me. "I received a phone call from Mrs. Q a few days ago. She loved your story so much, and she asked me to ask you if you'd like it to be included in the school's magazine."

"I'd love to, but I think the teachers are the ones who select one of the stories. I don't know if it's going to be mine," I replied.

"They already did. And they chose yours."

I was so excited. A couple of days later, I started communicating with Mrs. Q through email. She was my English teacher that year. Little did I know how meaningful of an impact she would have on my life. We worked on a few corrections on my story and finalized it. She'd send me updates about what we were doing at school and give me homework I could do if I felt well enough in between chemotherapies. I loved it. She made me feel as if I were a part of the class. Sometimes, she would give us online class discussions for homework, in which I could participate. She even included me in class group presentations.

Getting to work on school stuff with Mrs. Q felt like a gift God had given me, to remind me of my end goal and to motivate me to keep working toward it. Having received the bad news about the nerve damage on my leg, I'd lost all motivation and courage to try and get better. I didn't want to work on my physiotherapy exercises or put in any effort to reverse the paralysis. I'd given up, not because I was bored, lazy, discouraged, or tired. I'd given up all effort to get better because I was *scared*. I was terrified of bad news and constantly being let down and hurt. But through the tiniest of details, like a reading comprehension question that Mrs. Q would assign for homework or positive feedback she'd give me on my overall effort to keep up with the class, she could somehow give me hope that things would indeed get better. Through these small details, taking the risk of hope was worth it.

I always got excited whenever I came home from chemo to an email from Mrs. Q. It would make me smile and motivate me to try my best and recover from that chemo as fast as I could, to get back to school stuff. Studying helped me picture a healthy me, and it encouraged me to keep fighting to get to that version of myself. It gave me another reason to stay brave. I found hope in such details, in email conversations with Mrs. Q.

On November 5, I was scheduled to start the fifth block of the second chemo phase. Everything had been going according to the doctors' expectations. Time was passing. Slowly. But it still was moving forward. And yet, for some reason, that night, it all got a bit too heavy. As I lay on the couch, I stared at the dark ceiling. I was weary—a wreck. I didn't want to go through another chemo block. I turned to the side and checked the time on my phone—5:25 a.m. I fell back down. As thoughts rattled my courage and pain tore my strength, I closed my eyes and took a deep breath. A tear escaped my eyes and ran down my face.

God, take this load off my shoulders. Please just take this weight off my heart. I'm so grateful that I can enjoy small moments every day, that I can smile here and there. But every night, it all gets heavier. It gets scarier. Desperation gets louder. Pain gets stronger. I keep crying out, but…. Please, give me peace. Oh, God, please give me just a moment of peace. Make me brave. I thought my shoulders were strong enough to carry this weight. But I've grown weary. My hands are too weak. I'm so tired—all the time. How I need you, God.

As I released all my exhaustion, I remembered that dream I'd had about a month ago. That was all it took. I knew I wasn't carrying the weight of pain and fear alone. God had His hand on my shoulder. And that was visible through the details.

The next morning, we got to the hospital early. I got my regular preadmission finger prick blood test, and the lady in the lab gave me the classic green plaster with the red ladybug. The blood tests, however, were really discouraging. I had been on GCSF injections for almost ten days, and even a month after chemo, my bone marrow had not bounced back. As I was sitting in that waiting room, I heard someone speak to me. I lifted my head and saw the girl I'd shared a room with back during block 6, in June. I hadn't seen her since. She gave me a small box, and her mom told me it was for me. When I opened it, I got emotional. It was a necklace with an angel. She'd been keeping this box with her, waiting to give it to me, even though she had no idea when or whether she would ever see me again. God's in the details. I felt so loved, so grateful. I was so moved.

When we got called in, the ward oncologist informed us we couldn't go ahead with the chemo. She started me back on the injections, and we made an appointment for later during the week. At home, my mom made me fresh orange juice with ginger to try and boost my immune system. It was our new thing.

Eventually, my blood values increased, and I was admitted for the fifth round of VAC chemo. It was tough compared to the previous ones. The nausea was severe this time around. But *the only way out was through.* By faith, I believed that things would get better. Somehow, some day, things would get better. And that made every one of the side effects absolutely worth it.

At night, I would walk up and down the apartment with my crutches, and somedays, I would even climb the stairs from the garage up to our apartment. The pain would usually get much worse after walking or moving, so I would then take my pain meds and go to bed—to the couch to be exact.

The last time my dad visited, he brought me my boxing gloves. Why is that important? Let me give you some background information. My physiotherapist, Mr. Dimitris, always believed in me and found ways to motivate me. Before I got sick, I used to kickbox weekly. I loved it. After the surgery, however, Prof. H told me I would never be able to kickbox again. He told me I could try to pick up boxing instead. But here's what's cool about the details. That's where God is found. Mr. Dimitris perfectly coincidentally, or not coincidentally at all, happened to be a professional boxer. He told me we could practice together. He wanted me to keep pursuing the things I loved. He was always able to somehow make me smile. He really was a best friend to me.

From then on, during every physiotherapy session, we would spend ten to fifteen minutes practicing punches and targets. I would first work on my knee flexion and extension, I would do isometrics for the muscles on my leg, exercises for the paralysis, and then we'd do some boxing. It was our thing—just like photography was our thing for Dr. Vasilis and me. God's in the details. He was bringing people in my life who could give me reasons to smile, to feel excited, and to be motivated to keep fighting. Simple conversations with such people were like pit stops in a race against time, a race against disease, pain, hurt, fear, agony, and suffering. Those pit stops gave me moments of peace and rest while simultaneously recharging my batteries, changing the worn-out tires in my car, and prepping me to continue the race. And they were accessible through the details. It's almost as if all the small moments and little things in life compiled a road map that led me to the pit stops—the needed sources of courage, strength, and hope.

November 13 was a day of smiles. In the morning, a package was delivered to our apartment. It was a Harry Potter Lego I'd bought on Amazon. I know what you're thinking. *Katerina, you are literally a fifteen-year-old spending your money on a Harry Potter Lego?* And my answer to that is yes – yes I am. It was one of those moments that brought me back in time, made me feel at home, and gave me a reason to smile, while also keeping me busy. That night, we had a "Chinese feast." That basically meant we prepared traditional Chinese food for dinner. Nothing fancy, but it was fun. Elena made her signature noodles. My mom even got us those fortune cookies you usually break after eating to read the message inside. The message on mine read, "A smile is worth a thousand words." I think that sentence summarized the day.

> **Day 28 of physio. November 14. Physio was really cool today. I cycled, did some boxing with Mr. Dimitris, and worked on walking, balance, flexion, and extension. Cool stuff. I'm excited for the future. No improvement on the nerve paralysis. But I'll hold on to trust and push through. Let's focus on the good.**

A day later, we were back in the hospital for follow-up checkups and blood tests. As I sat in the waiting room, I saw that hospital volunteer, who I was friends with, walk in. We talked for a while. She so excited to see me get better and learn how to use my leg again. That conversation made my day. Her excitement intensified mine. Joy's in the details.

On November 22, Dimitris flew to Essen to spend the weekend with me. We were going to celebrate Thanksgiving together. We spent the days exploring Essen, watching Harry Potter movies, and playing cards. On the twenty-fourth, we had a custom makeshift bonfire in the living room, using a candle instead of a fire—not exactly your typical bonfire, but flexibility leads to happiness. We roasted marshmallows and made s'mores while watching movies. We challenged ourselves to watch all seven Harry Potter films in three days. We planned it all out. However, our plans fell through, since we both fell asleep after the first movie.

Before our living room bonfire, we had our Thanksgiving dinner. My mom and Elena spent the entire day preparing the food, while Dimitris helped me understand some chapters in chemistry. At night, my mom went to Zwolf Apostles and brought home a perfectly cooked Thanksgiving turkey. Our waiter friend even gave us two mango mints to take home. Love's in the details. Compassion is too. After setting the table, we all sat around it and enjoyed the food. We talked about school, gratitude, turkeys, chocolate, fear, and hope. That night was full of meaning, just like our stomachs were full of delicious food. Nights like this made it all worth it—nights when gratitude was truly celebrated, and details were noticed. That's what makes life meaningful—noticing the little things. How much more beautiful would life be if we stopped once in a while and just stared? Stared at the flowers, the roses that are all around us? Pay attention. Notice the small details of color and light.

As I fell asleep that night, I reflected on the meaning and message of Thanksgiving. Looking at my situation from the outside, you wouldn't see things to be thankful for. At that point in my life, I was on chemo every three weeks; my leg was paralyzed; I'd been diagnosed with a heart problem, a neurological problem, and a pain problem that even morphine couldn't help; I had a chronic kidney infection; and I had cancer on top of all that. It almost sounds like a joke. What people don't realize, however, is that pain, hurt, and fear all are the soil that helps the flower of gratitude grow. A flower grows from the dirt, right? Well, in the same way, authentic gratitude, joy, hope, and peace grow in adversity. I challenged myself that night to turn every day into Thanksgiving Day. But I had some questions. *How can I celebrate gratitude every day, when some days go by with me lying unconscious on a hospital bed, waking up only to throw up and then passing back out?* I wondered.

I believe there are two types of gratitude—the superficial and the deep. Both are equally important. Let's break them down. Superficial gratitude is gratitude *for* something. Deep gratitude is gratitude *despite* something. Not every day could I be grateful *for*. But every day I could be grateful *even though*. Not every day could I be thankful for the big things. But every day, I could be thankful for the small things, *even though* the big things might not look like I thought they would or expected or hoped they would. And that's the kind of gratitude that we're called to have and to celebrate on Thanksgiving—the kind that celebrates the small things. Deep gratitude recognizes the value of a moment and appreciates the details. And it can be celebrated every day, as it's not circumstantial. It doesn't depend on your situation and your feelings; rather, it disregards them.

And that is how I could turn any day into Thanksgiving Day. That's how I could choose to celebrate gratitude every day—by noticing the details.

Chapter 20

Against All Odds

A day after Thanksgiving, Dim left. A few hours later, my dad arrived in Essen for the weekend. I was thrilled to see him. That night, we decorated our apartment for Christmas. There were so many moments during this past year when I'd doubted I'd get to decorate another Christmas tree. And yet, there I was, limping my way around the tree, placing ornaments on its branches. Everyone knows that the hardest part of decorating a Christmas tree is putting up the lights. So this year, I decided to do this part all by myself. I challenged myself to do it. It was exhausting, and it caused my leg to swell up and start hurting, but it was totally worth it. *Celebrate the small mountaintops.* At the end, I placed the star at the top of the tree and made a wish. It's something we've always done in my family.

On November 26, I went to the hospital for more cardiac tests. I was scared. But I chose to be brave. After dinner, my dad and I watched a Christmas movie. Battling fear and pain, I couldn't fall asleep that night. So, I started taking photographs of our Christmas decorations instead. I thought of Dr. Vasilis. I was excited to show him all the photographs I'd taken this past year.

The next morning, my mom made me waffles for breakfast, and I spent the rest of the day copying notes and catching up on schoolwork. Studying by myself was difficult, but I called Dimitris in the afternoon, and he answered some questions I had on some chemistry chapters. At night, Elena and I baked gingerbread cookies. Little moments like that brought me joy and made me feel at home.

December started off with a miracle. After physiotherapy, I gave my mom the crutches and tried to walk for the first time without them. At first, my knee was trembling and shaking. I felt it giving in. I could feel the prosthesis slightly moving within my leg. Adequate scar tissue had not yet formed. I was scared to take that step. What if I couldn't do it? But I wasn't going to let fear win. I turned my what-if to an even if, and I chose to be brave. And that simple choice released a miracle. After taking that first step, I took another one and then another one and then another one. Before I knew it, I had walked across the parking lot. I had just done something that, even a week ago, had seemed impossible. I remembered all the days I'd doubted I would ever walk again. I remembered the days after the surgery, the fear, doubt, and discouragement. Turns out, impossible is just an opinion.

A few days later, I was admitted for chemo block 6. It was a tough one. Every round was more and more difficult. But as the side effects grew stronger, so did my resilience. I had to be brave—even in the broken.

I spent the next weeks at home recovering. I pushed myself to do more physiotherapy exercises, and I worked on school stuff with Mrs. Q. I was so thankful for this pocket of peace, this detail of hope. At some point, Mrs. Q sent me an email. One of the things she wrote in that email was, "You have been so brave and tough!"

That small detail. That simple phrase. "You have been so *brave*." It felt like a tight hug. And I really needed it.

I was given this incredible gift of love through people like Mrs. Q, the waiter at Zwolf Apostles, Nurse M, or even the lady at the lab and that flight attendant who'd anointed me with oil as we were flying back to Athens for the graduation. Through these people, who came into my life for only a short while and for a specific purpose, God was showing me a love that was profound and a hope that was powerful. It was a source of courage. Despite the failure in the recovery process after the surgery, despite the discouraging news and the fear about my heart, despite the tiredness and the exhaustion from all these months of treatment, somehow, the simple act of doing English homework with Mrs. Q brought the joy of normalcy back. It made me believe things would get better. *I* would get better. It gave me hope and courage in resilience—even for just a moment, a split second. That was enough. Light entered my life—through the details.

On December 10, my mom and I went to the hospital to meet with Prof. H. I had my first x-ray since the surgery to check the healing process and the overall state of the prosthesis.

"Looks perfect," Prof. H said as soon as he saw the x-ray films. "Now, the game begins."

"Can I get back to cycling?" I asked, full of excitement.

"It's completely up to you. For me, now it all begins."

That small conversation with Prof. H meant so much to me. Just a few days ago, I'd been lying on the couch crying because of how discouraged I was. The nerve paralysis showed no improvement, and doing exercises for it was emotionally draining. In theory, I knew it was supposed to help my leg, but there was no sign of progress. That simple conversation with my surgeon, however, was a star I could reach and hold onto. A reason to fight harder.

After leaving the hospital, we stopped at Starbucks for a coffee—a sunset feeling in a cup. At home, we made *kourabiedes*, traditional Greek Christmas cookies. It was through such details that love made our house feel like home.

Love brought home *home*.

A day later, we got the results from my Holter heart test. It showed intermittent negative T waves. Not the best news. We weren't yet sure what these results meant. I was scared. My cardiologist scheduled me for a heart MRI. She held my hand and told me everything would be all right. That small moment gave me courage—details.

On the seventeenth, I woke up more excited than ever. We were finally flying home. It would only be for a week, but still. We hadn't told anybody because we wanted to surprise my family, especially Amalia. Prof. D had really fought for this trip to happen, as my immune system was terribly damaged from all the chemo. She put me on double-dose GCSF and some other meds. She knew how important it was to spend the holidays with my whole family at home.

When we landed at the airport in Athens, my dad picked us up. We drove to his house. I hadn't been there in over a year. When we arrived, my sister was sleeping. The surprise was unfolding perfectly. I walked in her room and sat by her bed. I didn't wake her up immediately. At first, I took a moment to just sit there with her. She had no clue I was there. She was asleep but had gone to bed thinking I was—and would continue to be—in Germany. Difficult thoughts crossed my mind. If I didn't make it and went up to heaven, would it feel like this? Would I be sitting next to her without her knowing it? Would I be standing by her side, trying to find ways to communicate with her? Would she ever have a feeling I was near? What if this was how it was with God and me? What if God was just sitting there, on the edge of my bed, next to me, watching over me as I slept? What if He was there, sitting next to me every time I cried, but I was just "asleep" to his presence?

Suddenly, my mom walked in. "Aren't you going to wake her up?" she asked me, excited.

"Yep," I said. "I'm on it."

Waking her up was the funniest thing ever. She was still loopy from sleeping, and I could tell she was wondering whether this was a dream or reality. The day ended with laughs, hugs, and happy tears. As Amalia hugged me, tears filled my eyes. I remembered hugging her at the airport when we'd first left for Germany. I remembered my prayer that day, asking God to keep my sister safe while I was gone. Gratitude and grief battled in my heart—grief for all the hurt that we had endured as a family but gratitude that God had brought us through it. All these thoughts and feelings because of a simple hug.

The next day, my dad drove me to school to pick up my friend Mikaela, who was going to leave early so we could grab lunch together. As we were waiting, we were parked outside the school gate. That one gate was separating me from going back to school. I wanted to just run inside and see all my friends, surprise everyone. But I couldn't. A tall gate stood between me and that dream. What did that gate represent for me? Was it doubt? Was it fear? Maybe it was something physical, like the treatment or the immunosuppression. I couldn't really identify what it was yet. I just knew I had to cross that gate, to walk through it. And to do that, I needed to be brave.

When Mikaela walked out, we both started laughing. I hadn't seen her since August. We went to a local bakery and grabbed some snacks and smoothies. The next day, my dad and I went to the hospital. I had some scans to check the state of the prosthesis. The doctor who reviewed my scans was shocked.

"Who did the surgery?" he asked me. "Did you have this surgery in Athens?"

"No", I replied. "I had all treatment in the university hospital in Essen, Germany. Why?"

"This is a miracle", he said shocked. "It's perfectly placed. It's a miracle."

I remembered the night before the surgery. That prayer. Asking for a miracle. Because of the nerve damage and the unbearable pain that followed I hadn't always been able to see that miracle. But after that conversation, I felt so grateful for it. I felt so grateful for Prof. H and his team. I like to believe that that day God was on Prof. H's surgical team too.

The doctor then referred me to a neurologist at a different hospital for the paralysis in my leg, and advised me to have an EMG to check the nerve function, if any.

A few hours after I got home from the hospital, my mom came in my room and told me to put on some perfume. She was smiling. I was confused.

"What for?" I asked her.

"You'll see," she told me and walked out.

I thought my grandparents were probably coming to see me. I hadn't seen them in months, and I was excited. But when the doorbell rang and I opened the door, I stood speechless. Around fifteen friends of mine walked in and yelled, "Surprise." My knees collapsed. I teared up. I felt so loved. My friend Bill was the last one to walk in. He was holding a box—a big box. He gave it to me and told me it was a gift from everyone here to me. "Something to give you strength," he told me.

I gave him a tight hug—a hug of gratitude. What a surreal day. Just a few hours ago, I'd been crying because of how much pain I was in. Now, I was filled with happy tears of gratitude and love. I was with my friends, sitting around the living room, talking, and eating dinner together. God's in the details—just like love. And, oh, how powerful those details are. They make me brave. Even in the broken.

When I opened the box, I couldn't hold back the tears. First, I saw the Canon logo appear. It took my breath away. As I pulled a smaller box out of the big box, I saw that it was a brand-new camera lens. When I saw which lens it was, I felt my heart fill up with a gratitude so powerful it shook me to the core of my being. I remembered talking with my friend Bill about this specific lens a few days before and a few weeks after my big surgery. He knew how much I wanted this lens. I had been saving up to someday get it. But my friends got it for me. It wasn't just about the lens. It was about what the lens symbolized. I'd been trying to save up on my own, to fight this battle with cancer on my own. Yet my friends got it for me. My friends could help me fight; they could give me strength. I was not alone.

As we were talking, at some point, I caught a glance of my parents, staring and smiling. My heart ripped apart, yet it felt full of love at the same time. They hadn't seen me smile and joke with my friends in so long. I hurt for them. Yet I felt so loved.

Two days later, I went to see the neurologist I'd been referred to. The EMG was a very painful test. But that was only the beginning.

"There seems to be *no* nerve activity whatsoever," the neurologist said after completing the EMG.

I felt my heart being ripped out of my chest.

He went on to say that the nerve was permanently damaged and that the paralysis was not reversible. He also said I had severe neuropathy in all my other limbs, due to the chemotherapy. It was unsure whether the neuropathy would be reversible, so he advised us to do another EMG in six months to check for that. As far as the peroneal nerve was concerned, however, there seemed to be no hope. He suggested that, once the chemotherapy was done, we start discussing surgery options, even the potential of nerve transplantation. That sentence felt like a bullet through my chest.

At night, the weight of everything became heavier. I was happy to be back home and grateful for all my friends had done for me, yet the results of the EMG were so discouraging they masked my joy with fear and grief.

I want to fight this. But what if I'm not strong enough? What if I'm too tired to go on, too scared to be hope? What if I'm not strong enough?

What I hadn't yet realized was that I didn't *need* to be strong enough. Why? Because God is. God *is* strong enough—even when I am not. I can be vulnerable and feel the hurt and cry and break down, not because *I* am strong enough but because *God* is. And because of who God is, I can expose my fear, face my doubt, feel my hurt and my grief over my disappointment, and be weak. Through that weakness, God will make me strong. Therefore, deciding to feel the pain and let the hurt hurt hides hope—a hope that is unchanging and unconditional and set in who God is. Faith allows me to grieve, hurt, cry, worry, and embrace being overwhelmed by weakness, because *that* is how I am made strong. That is how I choose to be brave—even in the broken.

So, that night I let hurt overwhelm me. I lay awake in bed—arms stretched out, tears on my pillow. And I let myself cry. Then I sat on the floor by my bed, and I prayed. I told God everything. I talked about the discouragement, the doubt, the fear, the worry and about my weakness and weariness. I remembered that bathroom floor prayer shortly after my surgery. It was okay that I was not okay; it was okay that I got tired, because Christ got tired too. I was not alone. I then read the card my friends had given me once again. I was filled with courage. I took the new lens they'd gifted me, and I took photos of my Christmas tree. Oh, how beautifully did that lens bring out the intensity and brightness of the lights—just like love does.

The next day brought more difficulties. I developed a high fever and my mom rushed me to the ER. I was terrified. Within a few hours, I'd been admitted to an isolation room at the oncology ward in the hospital in Athens. My parents contacted my oncologist in Germany. The tests all pointed to a very advanced infection that originated from my port, possibly sepsis. I was started on extra doses of GSCF and multiple antibiotics.

At night, Amalia came to the hospital to visit. She brought me a hospital bag with all the things I would possibly need during this hospitalization—snacks, clothes, a teddy bear, magazines, cards, board games, movies, you name it. Love's in the details. I felt so grateful for my sister. No one fights alone.

The next morning, a team of doctors visited me and examined me. They told me I would have to stay for ten days inpatient to receive antibiotics. However, we were planning to fly back to Germany in five days. My team of doctors contacted my oncologist in Germany, and they all agreed to postpone the chemotherapy for two weeks. It was a risk, but my bone marrow was severely damaged.

I was crestfallen. I thought we'd come home to be at *home*. Instead, I would have to spend my time in the hospital. "This isn't what I'd expected, hoped, and prayed for. I don't understand. Why can't I have like three days of freedom from hospitals and pain, and suffering?" I replied when my nurse asked why I was sad.

She held my hand. "You'll get through this. You'll be surprised at how Christmas and home can be felt anywhere," she told me. "*Don't lose hope.*"

She was right. Little did I know.

That night, a young man walked in my room. "I'm sorry to disturb. I'm the guy from the room across the hallway. My son and I are here for Christmas too, and I just wanted to wish you all the best. I know these days it's even harder to be in the hospital, but I wanted to tell you that you got this and that everything will work out."

I teared up. This guy, out of nowhere, like an angel, delivered me hope in the most profound and unexpected way. We talked for a while. That conversation was a miracle. It was something I could observe and participate in, but I couldn't fathom the amount of empathy and pure human compassion it was based on. We talked about fear, miracles, the impossible, God, faith, hope, and Christmas cookies.

At night, the guy from the room across mine came back. This time, he was holding a small byzantine icon of Christ and Panagia. He gave it to me, along with some oil and a small black plastic cross. That small cross would turn out to symbolize so much for me. That action embodied human compassion. It felt like home.

A few hours later, my sister visited me, despite the fact that visiting hours were over. I loved how the nurses would sometimes bent the rules for love and family. My nurses and doctors, both in Germany and Greece, they all showed the type of doctor I too want to become; one who's human first.

Amalia brought me funky Christmas socks. I always made jokes about them with my doctors. It was a bet I had with my mom, that all the doctors would comment on my funny socks—and they all did. That was a small detail that brought me joy. At around midnight, spontaneity kicked in, and we decided to order Chinese food. Another detail of joy.

Three days later, I was discharged. I still had the infection. My immune system was still compromised. Yet the fever, was gone, my labs were a little better, and the doctors told me I could come to the hospital every day for my IV antibiotics and meds, rather than staying inpatient in the ward for another week. I was filled with joy. I went home. And as I fell back on my bed, I felt a rush of gratitude. I was home.

Little did I know, though, that I wasn't home because of my location. Little did I know that, even in the hospital, I was at home. Even in Germany, I was at home. I would soon find out. You'll see.

That night, we had a Christmas Eve dinner party with a bunch of family members and friends. As we raised our glasses to toast, I got emotional, and tears flooded my eyes. A flashback overwhelmed me. I was brought back to the night before we left for Germany, to that spontaneous dinner with friends and family, that moment I'd been filled with fear, uncertainty, and anguish and yet had chosen to *raise my glass anyway*. Without even realizing it, in that moment, I chose to stay brave. I chose to push through, to persevere. And now here I was, almost a year later, raising my glass again. Despite all the chaos, the trauma, and the suffering of that past year, I was *still* here, my heart was *still* beating, and I could *still* raise my glass *anyway*. And just the fact that I could do that meant I could *still* choose to *stay* brave in the broken, to fight back and against whatever came my way. Not because I was strong or tough but simply because the beating of my heart, the air in my lungs, and the glass I raised all symbolized the fire I *still* had in me that pushed me to keep fighting. We all have that fire, deep within. Sometimes all we need to see it is something to ignite it, and that something is always gratitude.

That's also where my hope came from. Hope is what best describes Christmas. A miracle of hope is there for anyone to witness. In reality, every day has the potential to be Christmas. Every day has the power to be celebrated through the lens of hope and guided by gratitude. For me, throughout the past year, this miracle of hope emerged through my ability to withstand affliction and push through. The sheer act of being home, enjoying dinner, smiling, and raising a glass to toast was the projection of God's presence and my miracle of hope. And all I had to do to receive this hope was to notice, to choose gratitude. So, that Christmas, I *was* hopeful. I was hopeful because I was grateful. For what? For the simple choice to *stay* brave. Having that choice meant I was *still* here. I could *still* fight. I never took that for granted.

I spent the next few days at home, enjoying time with friends and family. Every day, I would go to the hospital for a few hours for infusions, but I didn't mind at all. I loved being around my doctors and nurses. For some strange reason that I couldn't yet explain, I felt at home there, with them. That feeling kind of messed up my perception of home. But maybe I'd been wrong about it all along. I wasn't yet ready to answer that question—*yet*.

During the next few days in Athens, I focused on getting as much of my hobbies and passions back as I could—or tried to at least. I even cycled for the first time in the garage and played basketball with Thanos.

When I started basketball in fourth grade, I remember my dad asking me after my first practice whether I liked it or not. I told him I didn't really like it because it was tiring, and the coach was strict. Yet, the end of that first season, after playing and winning many games, my dad asked me again, "How do you like basketball?"

I remember clearly telling him that I loved it. I told him it was making me strong and fast, and I was able to do all these cool things because of it.

"Well, isn't it tiring anymore?" he asked. Isn't it hard and difficult?"

"I mean yeah," I replied. "But *it's worth it*."

"How so?" he asked.

"Because the difficulty of the sport only makes me better at it."

Chapter 21

A Special Raincoat and the Pockets of Home

The next day, we flew back to Germany. Leaving home was difficult. But were we actually *leaving* home? Was home something to leave? I felt more at home on the plane ride back *to* Germany than I had on the one *from* Germany. It almost felt as if I was filled with "home." How could that be? How could I feel at home when leaving home? These were questions I couldn't yet answer. During this final stretch of treatment, however, the answers would appear in the most unexpected, yet magically meaningful way.

On the fourth, we went in for my seventh round of the second phase of chemotherapy—thirteenth in total. Maybe that number has something to do with the fact that it got postponed. I don't mean that it's the number 13; I told you, I'm not superstitious. I mean that the number 13 is high, when it refers to multiple daylong chemo blocks. Even after fighting off the infection back in Greece, taking high-dose GCSF injections for weeks, and even eating lots of food, my immune system remained severely compromised—so much so that it was too dangerous to proceed with the next round. As a result, I went home feeling discouraged and tired.

Great. Chemo got postponed again. Plans canceled. I'll be stuck here till March. I'm so done. I just want to crawl up in a ball and cry. Thanks 2019. Looking great so far.

251

Looking back, I see my reaction as more of an overreaction. But back then, every slight delay meant more patience, more courage, more perseverance, more holding my fists together tightly and saying, "I'll go on," after every, "I can't go on." That delay hurt me so much that day.

But little did I know what was coming.

That same night, a miracle was awaiting—a miracle I'd prayed for, cried over, and stressed about. It was a miracle that nobody had thought would ever come. It was a miracle, however, that appeared in the most subtle and unexpected way, in a way that could easily be missed and go by unnoticed.

As I got ready to sleep at night, I adjusted my night cast to fit my leg properly. While doing so, I felt a strange tingling sensation in my toe. I thought nothing of it, as I blamed it on the nerve damage. That's when I noticed. It was sudden—instant and momentary. I could move my toes. I could only move them a few millimeters, but this was still incredibly significant. This was a sign of nerve regeneration, and it indicated there was some activity in my peroneal nerve and potential for the damage to be reversed. This was the impossible. This was the unattainable. I started bawling. I could not believe it. I thought back to that afternoon appointment with the neurologist, back to the countless nights that the pain had kept me up sobbing and screaming in despair. I thought back to the morning after the surgery, when I'd first learned that the nerve had been damaged. Reversing this damage was indeed impossible, but that night was proof that God is the God of the impossible.

I didn't know whether the nerve would get better or whether the movement had been only an involuntary spasm (though it didn't feel like it was). I chose to believe, to trust. I reflected on all the times throughout this past year that I'd been told something was impossible or the odds were against me. I was overwhelmed with abundant love and peace when I realized that God had used each of these situations to redefine the term *impossible* and bring me closer to Him. That night as I fell asleep, my body was still in pain, but my heart was full of gratitude. It was teeming with a sunset feeling that rushed through my veins and flooded my heart, just like a sunset fills the sky with its warm pastel colors. Light had overcome once again.

A few days later, my mom dropped me off in front of the cardiology clinic and drove to the parking lot. I went in and made my way to the MRI waiting room. It was empty. I chose a place to sit. I stared at my phone to check the time—7:18 a.m. It was early. The hospital corridor felt like a ghost town. I sat there waiting for my mom or the radiologist. I was alone. I found a moment to breathe. I felt the anxiety boiling inside my soul. A heart MRI was a big deal, it seemed. I rested my head back against the wall. As I stared at the ceiling, my eyes slowly lost focus. The quiet atmosphere faded away. I isolated my breathing. I felt air filling up my lungs. The sound of inhaling gave me peace. It offered comfort. I closed my eyes.

God, can you sit with me for a while? I've grown tired of all the noise, all the anxiety and pain. Can I sit by your side for a moment? My heart needs a friend, a place to rest. Only for a minute, before I have to go in for the scan. I want to sit by your side for a little while.

The sound of silence gave me peace. It was beautifully and meaningfully ironic how the absence of sound made me feel the presence of God. Maybe the noise was what was stealing my peace—the voices. It has been loud in my mind this past year. This morning, however, as I sat in that waiting room during sunrise, a sunset feeling gave me rest.

The MRI took longer than expected. I had an adverse reaction to the contrast dye, and we had to stop for some time. After the scan, Mom got me Starbucks for being brave. Love's in the details.

On January 8, I made the "official list of what to pack." It was exactly what it sounds like. It felt unreal. Hope's in the details. At night, my mom and I drove around the city blaring music. I was kind of sad about having to go back for chemo the next day, and she wanted to boost my mood. At night, we stopped at Starbucks.

"Nothing that a cool lime can't fix," she told me and smiled.

Joy's in the details too.

The next morning, however, after some blood tests, the doctors told me that chemo would have to be postponed yet again.

> Not enough white blood cells yet again. So many signs that my bone marrow is just done. Why do I keep having more chemos when my body cannot handle them? It's been almost five weeks since my last chemo, and even with daily GCSFs, my bone marrow has not recovered. I'm so over this whole thing.

Patience, however, is the key to perseverance. I felt broken. But I chose to be brave.

A few days later, I was finally admitted for round thirteen. Each round hit me harder, but I knew I was almost done. I had one more block left according to the protocol I was on. On the seventeenth, we went to the outpatient clinic for follow-up tests and an appointment with Prof. D. She showed me the post-treatment disease evaluation plan. I'll never forget that appointment, or the warm smile of hope that lit up Prof. D's face when I told her I wanted to go into medicine too. We talked about hope, working together, long-term side effects from the chemo, fear, relapse, life, happiness, oncology, and even Greek food. That simple appointment gave me more hope than all the test results that morning. I felt Christ sit by my side on the exam table, between my mom and me, carefully listening to the doctor, holding my hand, and smiling at me. In that room, during that conversation with Prof. D, hope was abundant, and so was love. Wherever there is hope and love, right there is God too—especially in the details.

"We'll give you some doping before the next round," Prof. D told me and smiled, referring to starting me on GCSF injections early on.

What looks and sounds like a simple insignificant inside joke between me and my oncologist was big enough to fill my day with joy and form a bright smile on my face. As we left Prof. D's office, I shook her hand with both of mine and thanked her. How could I fit all this gratitude, appreciation, and respect in one simple thank you?

I spent the next few weeks at home recovering from the chemo. I pushed myself to study more, and as a result I spent three to four hours a day just copying school notes and trying to understand them on my own. Physics made this very difficult, however. Thankfully, I called my friend Philip on FaceTime, and he explained it all. Kindness is in the details too.

February started with bad news. My bone marrow had not yet recovered. Amalia and my dad flew to Essen to be with me during my last round of treatment, but it got canceled. I was started on more meds and injections. It all seemed endless—even at what I thought was supposed to be the end. However, a bad morning doesn't mean a bad day, a bad chapter, or a bad story. That night, as we were eating dinner at Zwolf Apostles, it suddenly started snowing.

"A mango mint? With this cold weather?" my waiter friend asked when I placed my order.

I smiled. "Never too cold for a mango mint," I said.

Even though it was an iced beverage, it felt warm. It felt like home. Strange how a drink can feel like home. I was making steps forward on my journey to find home, but I was not close enough yet—*yet.*

At around midnight, my sister, my parents, and I all went outside for a walk. We did angel figures in the snow, played snowball wars, and laughed with each other's reactions to cold snowballs in the face. We went inside, changed into cozy Christmas pj's, and watched a movie.

At 2:00 a.m., my dad and I were the only ones still wide awake. I asked him if we could go outside one more time. I wanted to make the most out of every detail of joy life presented to me. He agreed. We went for a walk outside. It was snowing heavily. I didn't care. As the cold snowflakes fell on my face and touched my bare skin, I felt the warmest emotion of life—gratitude. I was so in love with life. Mess and all. Painful and all. Broken and all. Because if I bravely chose gratitude in the face of hardships and obstacles along the way, then that broken part of life would somehow become beautiful. And, oh, how powerful and meaningful it is to be beautifully broken.

My dad and I spent the next hour building a snowman. I then took a little walk across the street. I looked all around me and then looked up. The sky was pitch-black, yet small white dots were falling down. The motion blur intensified the bright white light emitted by these dots, contrasting the blackness of the sky. The air was crispy. My nose was red. My fingers were cold. But my heart was as warm as ever. Nothing else mattered, other than stopping for a while and being present in that very moment—taking it all in. What a peace. Who would have thought that the darkest night could create such a bright sunset feeling?

The next morning, we woke up to a winter wonderland right outside our window. The landscape, the trees, the forest, and even the houses were all part of it. I got up and made my way from the couch to the kitchen and made breakfast. I tried out a new vanilla brownie recipe. Details of joy. Later during the day, we decided to go explore the forest. We walked by the river, stepping on the powdery, dazzling fresh snow that covered our path. Every moment was treasured.

A few hours later, my mom takes me to physiotherapy, where I worked on my knee flexion and my walking with Mr. Dimitris. We talked about school, and he suggested I study in Germany. I smiled. A few months ago, I didn't dare have conversations about my future as something that was actually going to happen. It's so profound how just a conversation can hide a precious yet easily missed miracle.

My dad and my sister left the next morning at 5:00 a.m. There was ice on all roads, and we didn't have winter tires on the car. We drove slowly across the completely empty streets to the airport. It was magically peaceful and incredibly therapeutic for me—a landscape and moment so simple yet so significant.

A few weeks later, I was admitted for my last round of chemo. For a moment, I was alone in the room. My mom was at the office for international patients getting my admission papers ready. I still had about half an hour before chemo started—half an hour of peace and reflection. I was in room 112—again. I'd been in this room so many times for so many different reasons. I'd cried, lost hope, hugged my parents, thought about death, and faced it too, all in this very room, in this very bed. I stared outside the window, getting flashbacks every other second. It was a lot to deal with. Gratitude, fear, grief, and joy battled in my heart—gratitude for what I'd overcome, fear of the uncertainty the future held, grief for the trauma I'd experienced this past year, and joy for what was beyond the horizon. What-if goes both ways.

The chemo was a tough one. But I was filled with courage. I counted down the days, the hours, and the minutes. After a difficult round, the clock reached zero, and a doctor walked in to give me my last dose of chemo. "All right! This is the last one!" he exclaimed.

As he injected me with the drug, my taste changed, my throat burned, and I got hot flashes; then suddenly I was shivering. I repeated his words in my mind. I fell asleep. A few hours later, the nurse woke me up. It was very late at night. With a smile on her face, she handed my mom my discharge papers. I felt a huge weight lift off my chest. *That's it. It's done. Chemo's done*, I told myself. Tears flooded my eyes.

"I'll go to the parking to bring the car, OK?" Mom said.

The nurse took the antibacterial solution and sprayed three times on my port. "Are you ready?" she asked me after removing the bandages around it.

I paused for a second. That question. It brought me back to the big surgery, to that warm summer morning when I lay on that cold operating table and Dr. M asked me that same question. I stayed silent as a thousand thoughts hindered my answer.

The nurse placed her hand on my shoulder. "Hey," she asked again, "are you ready?"

I was never ready—for any of this. But that's why it had made me brave. "okay," I said and smiled.

A simple "okay" can go a long way. A simple "okay" is all it takes for bravery to exist in brokenness. And just like that, just with that simple "okay" the port needle was out.

Chemo was done.

I thanked the nurse, and she wished me all the best. As I walked out of the ward, I stopped, turned around, and watched that K3 door close behind me. That's it. I didn't ring a bell, didn't throw a party, didn't have balloons like I had planned to with my sister or dreamt of as I imagined this day throughout this past year. Yet that simple moment of closing the door of the chemo ward behind me—that was the most profoundly meaningful and impactful act of closure I could have done.

The door was clear, made of glass. You could see the ward even when it was closed. Likewise, I might have closed the chapter of treatment and chemo behind me that day, but I would always be able to see it—to look and to remember. Cancer was and would always be a part of me. And I'm grateful for that.

People always told me, "Cancer doesn't define you". Yes it does. *Beautifully* and *powerfully* so. It defines my faith, my hope, how I stayed brave. It's a part of me that I'm proud of. It's a part that left me traumatized and yet changed me forever, for the better. That part of me showed me what matters in life, how precious it is. It helped me get to know God a little better, to love myself a little deeper and to live life a little fuller.

The next few weeks went by in a flash. I spent most of the time recovering from the chemo, doing cardiac scans and checkups, working on English homework with Mrs. Q, and going to physiotherapy. These weeks all felt so normal. It was strange how I'd become familiar with this life that, from the outside, looked anything but normal. Maybe normal was never something I had to get back but something I had to find and create.

I had my last physiotherapy session. Goodbyes were difficult. Mr. Dimitris has become family. I'd miss seeing him every other day, joking about living in Germany, and talking about school and boxing and physiotherapy. But I'd see him again soon. This wasn't a goodbye, just an "I'll see you in four months."

Two days later, our apartment was empty, and big cardboard IKEA boxes were spread all over the living room, just like when we'd first moved in. Our suitcases were packed, and a taxi was outside waiting to take us to the airport.

I was the last to leave the apartment. I felt like I was saying goodbye to a big part of my life. I remembered the first time I'd ever walked in. I remembered all the nights I'd cried in my mom's arms because this house didn't feel like home. And yet now it did. This *was* home. How meaningful that moment was. It was in that moment that I realized something very profound about home. Throughout my journey of cancer, God had shown me the true meaning behind things I'd thought I knew. He'd taught me what it means to have faith, to trust, to surrender, to hope, to be brave. And now—now He was teaching me what it means to be at home.

Home was never about a place. Home is a sum of details, routines, and little things that give you a sense of peace, comfort, rest, protection, and love. That's what it means to be at home—to be surrounded by the details that make you feel safe even when your life hangs in the balance. At first, our apartment in Germany was just a space surrounded by walls. But now it was home. It was full of such details, such pockets of peace.

This is my favorite way to describe what home means to me. I like to think of it as a metaphor. See, I view home as this big, puffy, warm raincoat. It has many layers, and it feels really cozy. It also has a ton of pockets—so many of them. We all have a puffy, oversize raincoat. Let's dive deeper. A raincoat is designed to protect you from the rain. But this is not your typical raincoat. This one's special. It has specific qualities and characteristics. Firstly, it's warm, just like home. Home is warm even when the world is cold. This special raincoat is also oversized and puffy. There's always extra space, extra room, just like at home. The size or the condition of the house doesn't determine the size of the home. The smallest house can become the biggest home. The raincoat of home also has many layers. It's designed this way to maximize the protection it offers. Home is just like that. It shelters you from all the pain. Somehow, even though it can't make pain disappear, it can disregard it. It can give you comfort and courage, a piece of the wrecked boat to hold onto and catch your breath. It can also give you a peace that surpasses your understanding. The last characteristic of this unique raincoat is that it has countless pockets. Most of them are hidden, but there's a pocket for everything. Home is just like that. It's full of pockets of peace and pockets of love, joy, courage, and comfort.

Here's the thing about home. It's in the details. Home is in a hug. Home is in a smile. Home is in a prayer. Home is in the cozy feeling of watching a movie covered in a blanket. Home is in the late-night cereal bowls. Home is in the pillows drenched in a pool of tears at 3:00 a.m. Home is in the vase with yellow tulips that Mom bought to add color to our day. Home is in the boxes of doughnuts my dad brought me before every surgery. Home is in the FaceTime calls with my sister as the day turned to night. Home is in the jokes I made with Dr. S, and in the times she held my hand, as I lost hope and cried. Home is in the daily videos my aunt used to send me to cheer me up and encourage me. Home is in the smile of hope from Prof. D as she saw me bend my knee to ninety degrees. Home is in the mango mints the waiter at Zwolf Apostles would prepare for me and the ice creams we would share together after dinner. Home is in the smell of the dirt after the rain as my mom and I would drive with our windows down, across Essen's countryside. Home is in the hug my mom gave me as we watched the sunset next to the flower field. And it's in the hug my dad gave me in the middle of the hospital corridor because I was too weak and lifeless from the chemo to remain standing—physically and emotionally. Home is in an email from Mrs. Q telling me she's proud of me for all the work I'd been doing. Home is in the Tupperware with my grandma's food that my aunt brought me every time she visited.

Home is in the afternoons I spent with my grandpa playing chess. Home is in the peaceful sunsets I'd spent drawing. Home is in the songs I'd listen to at night before bed. Home is in the lullabies my mom would sing to me to make me feel safe when I screamed and cried out because of the excruciating and unbearable pain. Home is in the random yellow rubber ducks my aunt and I placed around the house to prank my mom. (Joy's in the details too.) Home is in the waffles my mom made me for breakfast to cheer me up and get me excited to eat. It's in the 3:00 a.m. conversations with my dad on the couch, the 5:00 a.m. hilarious toilet runs due to the Lasix I was on at the hospital. It's in the Greek jokes my physiotherapist made at every session. It's in the cards my friends at school had given me. It's in the French fries my sister and I would eat whole bowls of every time she visited me in Essen. It's in the two-hour phone calls with Dr. Vasilis, talking about faith, hope, resilience, volcanos, photography, and airplanes.

Home is in the funny comment the clinic doctor made about my funky Christmas socks. It's in the warmth and coziness of my bed and the cuddles with the teddy bear I'd had since I was a little kid. It's in the souvlaki anyone who came to Essen would bring me. It's in the hours my sister and brother spent trying to teach me how to solve math equations. It's the Harry Potter movie marathons with Dimitris, even though he always fell asleep first. It's in the FaceTime call with my class on my birthday when I was in the hospital. It's in the "I love you" my parents said every time I apologized for throwing up. It's in the jokes my sister would make every time I had to take the "cotrim" antibiotic. It's in the firm handshakes with Prof. H after every clinic visit. It's in the conversations with nurse M, or with that guy across the hallway in the hospital in Athens. It's in the sunset feelings that hugged my heart as it broke, as it got tired, as it gave in to pain and yet chose to stay brave.

Home is not a house. It's not an apartment. It's not a place. Nor has it ever been about a place. It's a feeling. Home is a sum of details—a sum of small moments of comfort, a collection of sunset feelings and smiles of hope.

When we left Athens and first flew to Essen, I thought I was leaving home behind. For my first couple of months in Germany, I felt far from home. Yet I hadn't left home itself behind. I'd left my perception of home behind. And I'd boldly embarked on a journey to find what it really meant to be at home. The real thing. The true essence.

That was then. Now, Essen felt like home too. The hospital felt like home too—not the building but the community of people in it. But this time, as I was leaving, I knew what home was.

Home is a veil that covers everything in it with love, reverberating compassion and deep empathy while evincing kindness. As I walked out of the apartment, I knew, this time, I wasn't leaving home behind. I was taking it with me. Even if I tried, I could never *leave* home. Because home was never a place that *I* was in. *Home* was in *me*.

Chapter 22

Airport Hugs and the First Sign of Sunrise

As the airport gate opened, I walked out and saw my family waiting for me. Dr. Vasilis was there too, and so were two of my friends, Dimitris and Mikaela. As I hugged Dr. Vasilis, I broke down crying. I thought of the hug he'd given me before my biopsy, the one at that same airport a year ago before I'd left for Germany, the hug as I'd counted down from ten, and the one in the summer when I'd stopped by the hospital he was working in to see him. As I thought of all the hugs of hope he had given me, I felt a rush of gratitude flood my heart. God had brought this person in my life as a guardian angel to protect me, to keep me company despite the distance, to plan photography trips with, to take my mind off of things, to encourage me in my faith, and to love me like a best friend.

"We did it," he told me, and a laugh of hope escaped his heart. "We did this!"

"Together," I told him.

Love's in the details.

When we got home, my aunt had decorated the house and prepared a cake for us. We ordered Greek food, and all enjoyed our first dinner together. It didn't feel real.

"We're home, Mom," I said that night as she tucked me in to sleep in my own bed.

"Yes, we are," she said with a chuckle and a deep smile.

Over the next few days, I got ready for school. I tried to catch up on as much of the material as I could, and I asked my friends for the class notes. At the same time, I started my postoperative rehabilitation program at a facility across town. At first, there was no progress at all, but patience is the key to perseverance, and perseverance always leads to progress.

March 5, 2019

I bought a new pair of sneakers today. Ever since my operation, I had been wearing the same pair of white sneakers that my mom had got me, once I learned to take my first steps with the crutches after the big surgery. That pair of shoes had been with me through the whole recovery process of that operation, through the whole second phase of my treatment. But now, it's time to let them go. It's time for a new step. I'm so excited to put my new sneakers on. I've never felt so grateful for simply putting on shoes before. Perspective.

March 18 was Clean Monday, a national bank holiday. My family and I went to my grandparents' village for the day. After lunch, we stopped by the graveyard to light a candle at Grandpa John's grave. As I sat by his grave, tears filled my eyes. "I did it, Grandpa," I told him. "I did it."

A smile shone across my face. It hid love and grief. Some say they're the same thing.

"I'm going back to school tomorrow," I added. "I wish you were here, Grandpa." Tears ran down my face. "You would have been really proud. But I know you're watching from heaven. The view is nicer from up there. I hope you're proud of me. I know I am. I hope you know that your pain wasn't in vain. You showed me how to fight, Grandpa. I don't know if you're listening, but if you are, give God a hug for me. He really helped me this past year. He kept me safe. I miss you—a lot. All I want is to celebrate with you, to run to your arms and tell you all about school and going back. But maybe this way, instead of me just telling you about it, maybe now you can experience it with me."

At night, we drove back home. I lay in bed but couldn't fall asleep. I was too excited for the day that followed.

The next morning, I got up at 6:00 a.m. I was way too impatient to stay in bed any longer. As I sat on the edge of my bed and pressed my feet against the ground to get up, I felt goose bumps all over my body. It was a Tuesday morning. I was getting up to get ready for school. The last time I'd done that, I had fallen in pain. Little had I known *that* Tuesday, what the months leading to *this* Tuesday would be like. That Tuesday morning as I tried to get back up, I fell. But this Tuesday morning, as I let my weight fall over my knees, they were able to hold me up and lift me up. I didn't take that for granted. Once I stood up, I stayed there for a moment. I didn't take another step. I first wanted to appreciate the moment. Full circle. Purpose behind timing.

I then walked toward my desk, where I had already laid out what I wanted to wear. As I dressed, I caught a glimpse of the scar on my leg. It filled me with gratitude. I remembered that conversation with Nurse M about scars and stories. Staying brave—that was something worth remembering.

After getting ready, I went to the bathroom to brush my teeth. I stared at the girl in the mirror. I was so proud of her. I remembered the girl who had stared back at me in that same mirror after getting the diagnosis and before the graduation—how much had she gone through, how much had she'd endured. Yet she was still standing there—beautifully broken yet beautifully brave too. Besides, she had now realized that bravery is only significant in the context of brokenness. I smiled at her, and she smiled back at me. Suddenly an image started playing in my mind—a scene. I was transported to a different place. It seemed familiar. I looked around and saw the old me. Fourteen-year-old Katerina was wearing her white graduation dress. Yet she was not in her bedroom but, rather, attached to medicine poles, lying lifeless in a cold hospital room. She was staring me, trying to smile, struggling to hold on. I wanted to tell her about all that I was getting the chance to do now, about going back to school. I knew it would give her courage to fight. But before I got the chance to do so, I snapped out of this vision, and I was back in my bathroom, staring at the girl in the mirror.

On the drive to school, we blasted my favorite songs. Ami and I argued jokingly about whose playlist we were going to listen to. I'd missed these silly arguments. Home's in the details. We arrived at school very early. Almost nobody was there. I walked in with Amalia and got in the elevator.

As the door closed, I bent down and took a breath. "Aaaahh! I'm so, so nervous. But so, so excited," I told her with a shaky voice.

We joked about people's reactions, and before we realized it, the elevator doors opened again. I felt butterflies. Every step I took was for the girl I'd seen in my vision this morning, for the old me.

I stopped walking right before going in my classroom. The hallway was empty. But someone was in the room.

"OK, I'll go first. You wait and then jump in," Amalia told me, excited.

"All right OK," I said and took a few deep breaths.

She walked in. I heard her greet her friends. I took another breath. I felt it reach my lungs. I then took a step, turned, and walked in the room.

"Good morning," I said, and the biggest smile covered my face.

My friend Kat was the first to see me. Her reaction was priceless. She was speechless. She hugged me tightly in complete shock and asked me how I'd been. We started talking and then planned out how we were going to surprise everyone. I sat by the teacher's desk, which was across from the classroom door. Anyone who walked past or entered saw me instantly. I'll never forget people's reactions. There were so many hugs and so many smiles and even a few tears—happy ones. I hadn't seen most of my friends in eight months, some in a year and half. I took in every hug and appreciated every smile. I locked them all in my heart.

After about ten minutes of catching up with my friends and laughing over their reactions to seeing me, our teacher walked in. I approached her and introduced myself. She instantly recognized me. I saw a smile of hope on her face. She seemed very excited to meet me. When the bell rang, I sat down at the first desk next to the door, so that I could surprise anyone who walked in late. Mrs. A, our language teacher, began the class by giving me the warmest welcome. She was emotional. She began a beautiful conversation about gratitude and appreciating what we have. The whole time she was talking, I thought of the me in the hospital, flashbacks of where I'd been just a month ago and, much more so, a year ago filled my mind.

She was still talking when a knock sounded at the door. It was Miltiadis. He walked in but didn't see me at first. The class started laughing. Someone gave him a hint, nodding that he should look down at the first desk. His reaction when he saw me was the best gift.

After taking some moments to realize what was happening, he pulled out a bag full of hats. He gave me one and told me that there was one for everyone in the class. He explained that they were organizing a surprise for me.

"We were planning to surprise you, but you got us first," he said and laughed.

I took the hat in my hands. "A3 full house" was written on it in gold letters.

"Class A3 is finally full again," he told me and smiled.

"So is my heart—full of gratitude and love," I replied, and my voice cracked.

Mrs. A continued the conversation on gratitude. She referred to me a few times. I didn't mind. I appreciated it a lot. We spent the whole class talking. When the bell rang, I walked out to greet some friends I hadn't seen yet.

I then saw a lady walking toward me. She approached me. I didn't recognize her—not yet at least.

"I'm Mrs. Q," she told me, her voice emotional.

Gratitude and joy took over, and without saying anything, I rushed to her and gave her the tightest, strongest hug. "Thank you for all that you've done for me," I told her, without letting go. My voice cracked and my eyes got blurry. A few tears streamed down my face. "Thank you *so much*."

My heart was flooding with gratitude.

The rest of the day was just as exciting as the morning. I met most of my teachers and saw my friends; had beautiful conversations; and, most importantly, took in every moment. During some classes, my leg was really hurting. But I couldn't let it get to me. If I'm being honest, I struggled a bit to feel like I belonged back in school. Throughout this whole day, for some reason, I kept getting the feeling that this wouldn't last, that soon I'd have to go back to Germany, back to treatment. I was also scared I'd missed out on too much already. School was such a novel environment for me. I'd been in hospitals or isolated in an apartment for so long that going back to my routine and school felt profound. I had changed so much that past year, and most of my classmates and friends had no idea. I was scared they would expect me to be the same person I'd been before. But trauma changes people. For worse of for better—that's up to each person to decide.

After school, I went to the rehabilitation center for my knee. I talked with my physiotherapist about school, and we laughed as I narrated the story of the first day. That helped me appreciate it more and ignore the fears and anxiety that tried to steal my joy.

The night, however, was difficult. I lay in bed tired and in pain. Within the first ten minutes of closing my eyes, I broke down crying. I was angry at myself for crying. The day had been one of the happiest and best days of my life, yet I was crying. Throughout this book, I have openly and vulnerably exposed the truth behind my battle with cancer. PTSD is something I did struggle with. Lying in bed that night, I feared I would never be able to overcome the emotional burden of the past year, that I would never be able to fully catch up with everyone else. I feared that I would never be able to fully go back to normal. But maybe that was the goal. Maybe that was for the better. Maybe normal was never something to get back to, but something to create and redefine. There's purpose in timing.

Oh, God, what a beautiful day today was. I had forgotten what it felt like to smile so much. Yet there are now tears in my eyes. I'm scared all the time. Today at school, someone mentioned something about applying to college, and the first thing I thought was the what-if of relapse. Instantly, a dozen scenes from memories of similar fears flooded my mind. Why am I chained to this fear? And then there's this other thing too. I feel like everyone thinks I'm all OK now, but dealing with trauma is a constant battle. There's just so much on my mind, and I'm so overwhelmed. I'm still grieving over all that has happened. I think it's important to feel that hurt.

It's like when soldiers come home from war, you know. While in battle, all they cared about was surviving, yet once home and safe, the reality of what they went through starts to hit. That's me right now, God.

But I'll stay brave. I'll cling to gratitude. I prayed for this—to be back at school. It was all I thought about. I didn't expect to be dealing with flashbacks and fears and trauma, but I'm at school. I'm alive. There's a beat in my heart. There's air in my lungs. I stood up this morning. Like what? Fourteen-year-old Katerina could never believe it. God, I'm here. Still. That's all that matters. So, I'll choose gratitude. I'll choose to notice the small miracles all around me.

And I'll choose to make my fear weaker than my thank you. So, God, thank you. Thank you so much for today. Today was a miracle.

The next day at school was equally exciting, happy, yet exhausting and mentally and physically draining. I was still dealing with many side effects from the chemo. And being at school, I kind of forced myself to hide the discomfort. Yet I chose gratitude. In the afternoon, Grandpa Nick picked me up from school and drove me to the physiotherapy clinic. The drive there took about an hour, and usually I took a nap to help with the after-school exhaustion. This time, however, I didn't.

As we were driving, my phone rang. I didn't recognize the number. I picked up, and a female voice on the other line, said, "Hey, Katerina, I'm calling from Make-A-Wish."

Little did I know what that phone call would be the start of.

The lady on the phone asked me what my plans were for Easter. I told her about school and physio, and then she paused for a moment.

"Weeeell," she continued, "You know, about thaaat … You'll be in LA this Easter. Your wish is happening."

This was the answer to my prayer a night ago. This was what hope sounded like. Pure joy. Powerful impact. Another miracle in the making.

Chapter 23

The Yellow Notebook
above the Clouds

"Ladies and gentlemen, the captain has turned on the fasten seat belt sign. Please stow your carry-on luggage underneath the seat in front of you or in an overhead bin. Please make sure your seat back and folding trays are in their full upright position."

It's Wednesday, June 20. We're on the plane flying back to Germany. It's been a while since we were last up there. I'm going back for my first post-treatment evaluation since coming home. I have to have scans every two months, alternating between Athens and Essen.

"In the event of a decompression, an oxygen mask will automatically appear in front of you. To start the flow of oxygen, pull the mask toward you. Place it firmly over your nose and mouth. Secure the elastic ..."

As the plane takes off, I stare outside the window at the clouds. My mind is racing. I'm suffocating in anxiety. I reach down and grab a big yellow notebook, pulling it out of my bag. I call this notebook "Packaged Joy Journal." It's filled with small journal entries describing small moments of joy and light from these past few months I've spent home. I open it up and start reading.

March 21, 2019

I went to school today. That's it. That's the highlight of my day. I woke up, got ready, grabbed breakfast, and went to school. Wow—unreal.

March 27, 2019

I shouldn't be here today. It's been exactly twenty-one days since my last chemo. I shouldn't be here. I should be getting admitted for chemo. I woke up at 7:00 a.m., just like I used to before going to the hospital. Yet today, instead of getting ready for chemo, I got ready for school. Instead of packing a suitcase, I packed a schoolbag. Instead of sitting in the wheelchair, I stood up and walked. I washed my face and felt the cold water on my hands. No neuropathy. I had breakfast. No nausea. I sat in a classroom, not in the waiting room. I made jokes with my friends, not with my doctors. Don't get me wrong. I love joking with my doctors, but something about ordinary normalcy makes it unique. I shouldn't be here today. Yet I am. What a miracle. I'll make the most of it. I won't let a moment slip away.

April 5, 2019

My brother and I went on a long drive in the mountains. We were listening to music with the windows down. I remember doing that in Essen before every chemo. Life feels unreal. Through little moments like this, gratitude shines the brightest. It's in the details, after all.

April 16, 2019

We just came back from a two-day school trip. It was so much fun. I couldn't walk much, but I tried my best to follow.

After walking all day, my leg got really swollen, and the pain got really bad. Thankfully, however, my roommates, Vicky and Ourania, helped me get some ice to put on it at night. Love's in the details.

We laughed a lot. We got to sit at a local Greek restaurant there and have lunch all together. Such small details, like lunch with friends and walking in the rain without an umbrella and getting ice cream while it was freezing outside, is where light is hidden. That's what life is all about. And I'm never taking them for granted again.

April 17, 2019

I've been having lots of flashbacks recently—nightmares too. I was at school today, and my leg started hurting. I'd forgotten to take one of my meds in the morning. I started feeling shocks run down my leg. I felt helpless. I panicked. I hurt so much. I wanted to scream in pain. Instantly, memories from the past fall flooded my mind. And for a moment, I was back. I was back in that dark place, in the prison of pain.

"Make me brave, God," I whispered under my breath. I didn't want people to know I was in pain.

Mrs. Q could tell. She asked me if I wanted to go to the nurse. I told her I was fine. In reality, there wasn't anything that anyone could do. Once the bell rang and class finished, I went to the bathroom and put on a lidocaine patch. I cried a lot. Then, I walked out of the bathroom like nothing had happened. Pain feels lonely sometimes…

I left school earlier because I had physiotherapy scheduled at the clinic. Grandpa Nick got me a juice and a fitness bar, so I could eat something during the drive. Love's in the details. And it's through love that God lets me know that, even on difficult days, I'm not alone.

April 18, 2019

Today I drank three smoothies. Nothing special about it. But it brought me joy. Combining different fruits and trying out different things. Joy through the details.

April 19, 2019

Today at school, we had a basketball game for charity. I was the official photographer. Dr. Vasilis would be proud. I'll call him tonight to tell him. It's not volcanos yet, but it works for me.

Something surreal happened during that game, however—a small miracle, a detail of hope and purpose. Mr. G, my ninth-grade gym teacher came up to me and gave me a cross bracelet he got for me on his trip to Jerusalem. I was so moved. We had a very meaningful conversation—one full of hope, light, and courage. I pictured God smiling. It's all in these details.

April 22, 2019

Today I went back to the hospital for tests. They had to access my port to heparinize it and add a line for the contrast dye. I was nervous. There I was, back in the waiting room. It seems as if I can't ever fully escape it. There it is, that fear—hiding, crippling me from behind, ready to take over. But it's worth it. It doesn't matter. Life's worth it. Those moments of pure joy and gratitude make it all worth it. Two months post-chemo and the scans look good. Fingers crossed and prayers sent for them to stay clear. But regardless, I'll make the most out of every new day I get.

April 24, 2019

I witnessed a miracle today—one that could have easily been missed. But I noticed it. I captured it. And I'm grateful for that. So, for the past few weeks, I've been organizing a visit to the children at the oncology ward in my hospital here at home. I wanted to give back, to spread hope, to help them in any way I could. So, I got them gift bags I customized for each kid and organized a few Easter activities for them, like painting eggs and coloring Easter books.

When I got to the hospital, I started handing the bags out. At some point, I was left with two extra bags. But there were no more kids inpatient, on treatment. There was one little girl, however, in the outpatient clinic. She was with her mom and her best friend. She was crying. Her mom was too. As they came out of the exam room, I noticed their eyes. I knew the hurt they hid. I was reminded of the graduation day, when I sat in that same waiting room, across two other grieving, hurting parents. They'd had the same look in their eyes—the same redness, the same pain. I also recognized the look because I had seen it in the mirror. I had seen the same suffering. I had felt the same unbearable weight.

As I saw the little girl's mom sit in the waiting room, I approached her and gave her the two bags. She smiled through the tears and thanked me. It really meant a lot to her. Before walking away, I placed my hand on her shoulder and told her, "I know it hurts right now, but I promise it gets better. It truly gets better."

She started crying. She told me she was afraid. I teared up. I told her about my story, about losing hope and finding it again. She was so emotional. I could see how much strength that story gave her. God's in the details.

I then saw the little girl walk toward me. Her mom told her about me and the Easter bags. The little girl looked at me and, with tear-filled eyes, fell in my arms. She hugged me for a while. She didn't let go. And that brought me to my knees. I teared up and felt a lump in my throat. I saw myself in her. I saw the old me, a little girl, terrified of the pain, scared of suffering, afraid of enduring. I held back a few tears and told her, "I know you're strong enough to do this. You can do this. And I believe in you."

She was sobbing in my arms. Her mom was standing next to me, smiling through her tears. That was one of the most profound moments of my life.

After everyone wiped away their tears, we all sat down in the play area of the ward and colored eggs and Easter books. We spent so much time on these projects. Before leaving, she gave me the egg she had colored and decorated. "It's not that nice, but it's my thank you," the little girl said, and her voice cracked.

Little did she know how much that plastic Easter egg meant for me.

I wished I could do more for her and help her as a doctor. That's all I wanted to do. But I couldn't—not yet. There's purpose in timing.

April 26, 2019

I can't believe this is actually happening. We're landing in LA in an hour. I'm scared I might have caught an infection because my WBCs were low pre-trip. But that's OK. This is going to be the best trip of my life—not only because of what we'll get to do, but mostly because of all that it symbolizes. It warms my heart knowing there are people who care enough and love enough to bring so, so, so much joy and hope to children who desperately need it. I can't believe this is life right now. I said the same thing last year; only last year I couldn't believe how difficult and hopeless life was, but this year ... man is this year different. This year, I cannot believe how much gratitude my heart can hold. God's amazing—not because good things are happening but because he has brought me through the worst of things and stood beside me in the process. I wish I could share this gratitude, give back this hope.

Little did I know that day that I would dedicate my life to giving back this hope—through any way possible. I would give back through medicine in hospitals, through speeches on stages, and through love by simply giving someone a hug when they need it the most. We can all share this hope. That's how darkness is defeated.

May 2, 2019

We've been on a plane for most of the past two days. Time difference struggles. This trip to LA was life changing. I smiled so much. I noticed every detail. I took in every moment. I made the most of it. On the flight back home, I started crying. I was so sad to leave. I wished I could stay. I have traveled to so many places, but never have I felt so connected to a place. Maybe it's the memories, the symbolism, or simply the smiles. Either way, what a blessing this trip was. Made it all worth it. My heart is flooded with gratitude.

May 3, 2019

We landed late at night. After we got home however, we decided we wanted to get dinner. Ami was way too tired, so it was just Dad and me. I told him all about the trip. We talked about Germany too—about gratitude, about fear, and about stories. "If you have a story to tell, why not write a book about it and tell it?" he told me at some point.

A book? No way I can do that.

After dinner, we made an hour-long drive to the center of Athens, where we rented electric scooters at 3:00 a.m. and explored the empty streets for over an hour.

May 12, 2019

Tonight, my dad told my sister and I to get ready. We were all going out for dinner to celebrate our birthday which was a few days ago. Dad found a random excuse for needing to first stop by Mom's house. I bought it though. My sister did too. As we went up the elevator, we heard voices.

When the elevator door opened, I saw fifty kids jump up and yell, "Surprise!"

I felt my knees collapse. My heart felt so filled with love. My friends had organized a surprise birthday party for my sister and me. I went in and hugged everyone. As my sister and I were blowing out our candles, everyone was singing.

Suddenly, all the noise fades into the distance. I am alone in my thoughts. I'm alone with fourteen-year-old me. I stare at her blowing her candles out in the hospital. She is about to become fifteen, doubting she'll ever get to sixteen. Her body is weak and weary. She is bald, skinny, and pale, and her eyes are red. She was crying just a few hours before because of the pain she's been feeling. I approach her, in my mind, and as she rests her head on Amalia's shoulder, I place my hand on hers. She smiles. In that moment, I feel as if she is proud of me—as if she knows, she sees, and she holds on because of who I have grown to be and will grow to become.

A few seconds later, I snapped out of it and saw my friends again, surrounding me, singing, and smiling. I smiled too. I held on to fifteen-year-old me in my heart. I took a deep breath, and I blew out the candles—with her, *for* her. Sixteen. I pictured her smiling. God too.

At night, Dimitris, Mikaela, my sister, and I all went to the rooftop. We ate a few leftovers, talked for hours, and stared at the stars. Lying on the rooftop, looking up, and laughing with my friends—that's what life is all about. Thank you, God, for this day. And thank you, fifteen-year-old Katerina, for fighting. Today was because of you. Today was *for* you.

May 23, 2019

Today was a perfect day. It was a simple day. I've learned that, through gratitude, these two words become synonyms. I made myself some breakfast, went down to physio for an hour with my grandpa, and then studied for my finals. Dimitris came over, and we had a study group session with my sister. Today felt like home.

I remember before cancer, I used to say, "I have to study", or "I have to go to school". But I don't anymore. I don't have to. I get to. I get to study, I get to go to school, I get to walk, breathe, love. I get to give, I get to laugh, I get to cry even. I get to live. What a priceless gift perspective is.

June 1, 2019

Happiness—that simple words best describes tonight. My friends Dimitris and Mikaela surprised Amalia and I with a special dinner for our birthday. Dinner in the sky. We were running late, and there was so much traffic. The taxi ride was the funniest thing. Dinner was amazing, and the view was breathtaking. I thought of fourteen-year-old Katerina. I'm sure she's so excited I get to do this stuff. Throughout the entire drive home, we couldn't stop laughing. I am so grateful to remember what happiness feels like. I'm so very grateful.

June 6, 2019

Today, after my algebra exam, I gave a speech at a global conference for Make-A-Wish. Then I went to the hospital to get my port heparinized. The speech was about the power of hope—the choice of hope. I think this is the start of something big. I don't know where this path will lead, what the future holds, or what it could become. Yet, whatever the end point, this is a journey I am passionate and very excited to embark on—sharing my story, using my scars as a source of healing, just like I wished that Easter in the hospital. Purpose in the pain.

What does purpose in the pain mean? Let me give you an example that I think explains this idea best.

Let's look at a glow stick. It's created to emit and reflect light. Yet if it doesn't first break, if it isn't first placed in the darkest room, it can never fulfill its purpose. Without being painfully broken first, it can never do what it was created to do or be what it was created to be.

There's a purpose behind the pain. There's a message in the mess. The struggle is a setup.

June 14, 2019

Today I went to the hospital for scans. I saw that little girl again, the one I'd seen when I visited the kids before Easter. She looked good. When she saw me, she instantly recognized me, even though now my hair has grown a little more, and she ran toward me and gave me the tightest hug ever. We talked about school closing, summer holidays, and dreams. God's in the details.

I haven't seen that little girl since. I never even learned her name. Yet somehow, I always carry her with me—in my heart. I always remember the hug she gave me. It gives me strength. It fills me with motivation, lighting a match in my heart, and turning the spark of my desire to become a doctor into a raging fire.

June 16, 2019

My dad and I went on a long car ride to the mountains to watch the sunset. We first stopped by Starbucks and got the classic goods—a cool lime. Details of home away from home. At night, we got Thai food. I'm really grateful for sunsets, my family, and being able to walk today.

June 20, 2019

It's super early right now. I can't sleep. We're leaving for Germany in a few hours. I'm scared. Battling "what-ifs." Breathing feels heavier. I don't know how I'll manage to go back in the hospital. I don't know if I'm going to be strong enough for that. But God made me brave when I felt broken. The results have to be good. I can't leave yet. I have so much more to do, to feel, to give, to experience. Dear heart, please be brave.

"On behalf of the captain and the entire cabin crew, I'd like to thank you for joining us on this trip, and we are looking forward to seeing you on board again in the near future. Have a nice stay!"

I close the yellow notebook, put it back in my bag, and place my hand on my heart. I feel it beating—as if it's promising to be brave, as if it too is saying, "okay."

Chapter 24

Stars and Swimming Lessons

As I walked back in the hospital, a numbness rushed through my body and paralyzed me. I was back in that dark, lonely, broken place in my mind—at that room I'd tried to burn down but never with any success. Trauma has a way of shadowing hope and purpose. It can become louder, deafening, just like the magnet of the MRI.

Lying there, I felt powerless, humbled. I had no control of the situation. No matter how I'd lived these part four months, no matter how much orange and ginger juice I'd drunk, how many hours of sleep I'd gotten, or how much physiotherapy I'd done, nothing could affect the results. Nothing I did could ever control what that MRI film was going to show.

Cancer doesn't care. It never did, and it never will. It doesn't care about who you are, what you do, what your dreams are, or what you're scared of. It doesn't care if you love others, if you're a kind and good person, if you laugh weirdly, or if you first pour in the milk and then the cereal at breakfast. Cancer doesn't care. It doesn't care if you have a family, people who need you to be here, ambitions, and a future to work toward. It doesn't care if you're happy, grateful, and hopeful. Cancer doesn't care.

Then why do I? I wondered. *Why do I try so hard to fight it? Why do I try so hard to win and take in every single second of freedom and joy it gives me? Why do I put so much work and effort and hope into something I cannot and will not ever be able to control? Why does it keep me up at night, why do I care so much, if cancer doesn't?*

Because *life is worth it.* That's why. That's why I fight. That's why I endure. Life is worth it.

Lying on that cold CT scan table it was difficult to remember how to fight. But when I was in the car singing along with my favorite songs at the top of my lungs, when my sister gave me a hug, when I got the chance to sit in class and see my friends, when I lay on the rooftop with my arms stretched wide thanking God for keeping me alive, when I finally walked again without crutches, when my brother and I spontaneously ordered pizza at 3:00 a.m., when my mom told me she was proud of me, when I got to travel by a plane to a faraway country, when I got to laugh uncontrollably with my friends over nothing, I was reminded why life is worth it. Every single morning I get to get up and stand up, take a breath, and feel that breath I am reminded why life is worth it.

Fear might have been louder as I lay on that exam room waiting for the scan results. But it was not loud enough. It was not loud enough to silence gratitude, to silence love. And it could never be.

As we spent more and more days in the hospital, I remembered what it was like to practically live in it. At first, I hated being back. But then my oncologist smiled at me, my favorite nurse high-fived me, and that lady who used to visit me during chemotherapy to play sports and games with me asked me if I wanted to play football with her. And just like that it hit me; I was home. I had always been home. This was home—not the building or the wards but the people and the emotions in it.

"Your chest CT looks clear," my oncologist told me with a smile.

My dad got emotional and teared up. I did too. Gratitude. Humbling gratitude.

Being back in Essen was an undeniable source of light for me. It really felt like home, especially in the summer. My dad and I went on different road trips across Germany and the Netherlands. We explored the forests and drove with the car roof down across the country roads and the grassy fields. We even went to a concert of my favorite artist. That was one of the most fun nights of the summer. The next day, we went on a road trip to Amsterdam and perfectly coincidentally—or not at all—that artist was having another concert there that night. Embracing spontaneity, my dad and I decided to go. Little did I know that, at that second concert, not only would I sing out all my fear, but I would also meet another girl, Breg, and create a friendship that would bring light into my life and always make me smile.

Over the days we spent in Essen, we went to Zwolf Apostles multiple times. My waiter / best friend was always there. His reaction when he saw me was priceless, engraved in my heart forever—just like my oncologist's smile after seeing my progress, my family and friends' reaction when I went back to school or Dr. Vasilis' words about being brave. How powerful compassion and love are! My waiter - best friend brought me two mango mints and sat with us as we enjoyed lunch outside, accompanied by the sound of the river flowing and the leaves of the tall beautiful green trees rattling to the summer breeze. This was why life was worth it. That lunch. That mango mint. That conversation. That hug. *The details.*

A day after we got back, I started my summer internship at the hospital. When I got home, I opened my yellow notebook. This is what I wrote that day:

> *Just a day ago, I was in the hospital as a patient. And today I was at the hospital as a future doctor. Yesterday, I was looking to doctors for hope; today I held a patient's hand and gave her hope. Yesterday, I was wearing a hospital gown; today I was wearing a white coat. Yesterday I was vulnerable, scared, and powerless. Today I was passionate, determined, and confident—all because of a white coat. Just like that white dress at last year's graduation. They both symbolize the same thing—hope. Each are hope, not as a feeling, but as a piece of clothing, hope, not as a temporary emotion, but as something that hugged my scarred body and clothed it in white, in peace, in trust, in faith, and in resilience. Just like that white dress, this white coat was proof of the power and the presence of hope. It symbolized a hope that perseveres, that stays steadfast and brave, that holds on, that fights time and time again, that never gives up. Whenever I wear a white*

coat, that's what I'm clothed in—a hope that motivates me to fight, a hope that makes me brave.

A day after finishing my internship, I flew to the states with my aunt. We spent three days in Washington and then drove up to Baltimore, where she dropped me off at Hopkins. I spent the next two weeks there, at the hospital and university, where I participated in a medical school summer course. That summer experience was a ray of light. It filled me with countless incredible memories. From simple things like getting coffee from my favorite place in DC to big things like getting my CPR certification and completing my first patient history and intubation in the SimLab, that trip was one for the books.

A day after coming home, I got my yellow notebook out of my bag, and made this note:

July 18, 2019

We're leaving for vacation tomorrow. I'm so excited. Last night as I was packing up my camera bag, I teared up. This was what had pulled me through chemo block 2—the thought of packing up lenses and cameras in a bag, fitting everything in small compartments, and getting ready for a photography adventure. Such a detail. Yet I doubted I would ever do this. But I just did. Wow. Gratitude's in the details.

In the beginning of August we went to Paros Island. Something surreal happened on the boat. We were casually crossing the sea, when, suddenly, a storm broke out. The waves rattled the boat and pushed us side to side. Bottles fell off tables, people who were walking were pushed to the side, and surprised gasps and sounds were heard from the lobby.

I sat back in my seat and held Amalia's hand. She was asleep. She didn't notice. But love made me feel safe.

After a few hours, we arrived at the island safely. As we drove to our house, I started thinking about that storm we'd gone through earlier and noticing the similarities between it and the one I'd gone through just a few months ago.

I was on a boat going through a storm, and the ship was breaking. It was broken and sinking. How could God let me go through the storm with a broken ship, a stumbling courage, a heavy heart? Why would He want me to be in so much pain? How could He see me suffering and do nothing? Well, because the only way out is through. And because He loved me too much to let me be stuck where I was. God was taking me where I was meant to go, just not through the path I expected. The pain was a path to purpose—and a path *of* purpose. There was a purpose for the broken. I just had to be brave—in it and through it. Because the only way out is through.

On the night of the fourteenth, I stayed up. I couldn't fall asleep. I sat on the front porch and watched the night sky. It was peaceful. It was quiet. There was no noise. No voices of fear, no screams of pain, and no silent sobs broke the calm. It was completely and beautifully quiet. As I stared at the stars, I reflected on the darkness of that day just a year ago when, like tonight, I'd stayed up, unable to sleep. The voices in my head of anxiety, fear, doubt, and worry had been deafening. It had been a quiet night, yet nothing about it was quiet. In reality, it was the loudest of nights. Yet I was at peace. I felt the abundance of a peace that surpassed my understanding overwhelm me. It was the darkest and loudest it had ever been, yet I was still filled with peace.

Gazing at the stars and the dark sky, I took a deep breath. I felt that breath reach the lowest point of the lower lobes of my lungs. The only sound that could be heard was that breath. I lay down and looked up. Maybe the stars were the source of my peace. Or maybe peace is the constellations the stars form. Maybe it's the sum of all these details that shine a light, painting the darkness with courage and bravery—simply by reflecting light.

That night, as I let the stars brighten the sky, I also let them brighten my heart and fill it up with gratitude. I thought of the stars that had been revealed to me during the darkness of cancer. These stars were the details of everyday life, the small pockets of peace and comfort that could be found each day.

One such star that shined the brightest is love. I've realized that love doesn't always sound like, "I love you." Sometimes it sounds like: "Do you want another Zofran?" "I said a prayer for you last night." "Don't worry; it's going to be OK." "Take your medicine; it's already noon." "Don't forget to do your leg exercises." "Soon things will be brighter." "I made you pancakes for breakfast."

Other times, love doesn't sound like anything. It's not expressed through a sound but through an action. Love was in the cool lime my mom bought me after weekly checkups in the hospital. Love was in the tight hug my sister would give me every time she saw me. Love was in the two-hour phone calls with Dr. Vasilis in the middle of the night when I couldn't sleep. Love was in the high-fives with the clinic oncologist when my white blood cells increased. Love was in the minute-long videos my aunt would send me every night. Love was in the IKEA runs my parents went on, trying their hardest to make our house feel like home. Love was in the smiley faces Mrs. Q would send me in every email. Love was in the smile on my waiter friend's face once he saw me drink the mango mint he'd prepared for me. Love was in the times my sister would fall asleep next to my hospital bed, sitting on a chair, resting her head against my knee. Love was in the encouraging words Mr. Dimitris would tell me, to motivate me to keep going and improve my knee function.

Love was in the flowers Dr. S brought me to cheer me up. Love was in the surgical masks my dad would spray with his cologne so I wouldn't have to smell the chemo. Love was in the photography trips my brother and I took whenever he visited. It was in the late-night text messages with my older sister, Ageliki, as she was trying to convince me I would walk again. Love was in the photos I would take with Dr. Vasilis's camera. It was in the hugs from my friends when they surprised me for Christmas. It was in the inside jokes and carpool karaoke's with Amalia. It was in the yellow roses my mom would fill up our apartment with.

If there's one thing that made cancer worth it, it was love—the love I experienced. It was the love of people that either were in my life or entered for a certain time and purpose. Among them were teachers, classmates, doctors, nurses, the ladies at the lab, my physiotherapist, my waiter / best friend, and even strangers I shared a room with in the hospital or the flight attendant who gave me the oil from Jerusalem. Through all these people, I experienced a love so authentic it could offer me a hand to hold when I wanted to let go.

What a bright star love is. Yet, somehow, the unimaginable, blinding brightness its light can reflect is intensified only in complete, utter darkness. Through this characteristic, it has the power to not only defeat the darkness but also redefine it and use it as a background instead of a cover.

The next day, I woke up excited—not anxious like last year but full of gratitude. We all enjoyed breakfast together, the whole family. My mom had flown to Paros island to spend the fifteenth of August with me and celebrate as a family. My breakfast a year ago was a pill to help me relax before the surgery. And now, it was a table full of food and smiles.

I put on a dress I really liked, and my mom took me to Ekatodapiliani, a church at the port of the island. I lit a candle and walked around. The name of the church means that it has a hundred doors. It was given this name because of how many rooms it has.

As I walked around, exploring some of them, I turned right and entered a small, hidden room. I approached the iconostasis and sat at a chair in front of it. I closed my eyes and prayed. What a special moment that was. I couldn't hold back the tears. Overwhelming gratitude made me tear up because of how unfathomably meaningful that day was in my heart.

As I got up to leave, I approached an iconography of Christ and Panagia and saw two white flower blossoms. It felt as if they had been purposefully left there for me to find. They weren't just any flower blossoms. These were jasmines—the most beautiful white flowers. Tears ran down my face. These beautiful white flowers reminded me of the white graduation day dress that, as if it were hope itself, had clothed my fear and hurt. They reminded me of the white gown I wore before and after my surgery a year ago. And lastly, they reminded me of the white coat that covered me with determination and passion during my first medical internship as a future doctor in the hospital, just over a month ago. These white flowers meant so much to me.

I picked them up and held onto them tight. When we got home, I gave one to my sister. Hope multiples the more you share it. By giving it away, you get more of it. She smiled.

At around 8:00 p.m., my mom and I went on an adventure. I was grateful to spend this time with her. A year ago, she was holding my hand in the ICU, hearing me scream and cry out in pain and then fall back down, giving in to the remaining anesthesia. And now, we were driving around Paros with the windows down, singing to my favorite songs. She was still holding my hand—just like she had last year in that cold, dark, loud ICU room. Yet now, there were no tears, no machines beeping, no morphine, no fear, and no suffering. Love overcomes.

As we drove, I saw a small church at the top of a mountain. "Can we go there?" I asked my mom. "The view must be awesome."

"I don't know, sweetheart," my mom replied. "I don't know if there's a road that leads there. And even if there is, I don't think we can find it."

That conversation reminded me of when I was sick. I searched for hope, just like we were searching for an adventure that day. But hope was just like that small white church. There wasn't a dedicated road leading to it, a specific known path to get there. And even if there was some deserted road leading to it, there was no certainty as to whether I would find it. But was that enough to stop me from searching for it? No.

"That's okay," I told my mom. "We can still try to get there, and even if we don't end up finding the road, or even if that road doesn't lead anywhere, we can still make the most of the journey and enjoy the ride."

My mom smiled and made a left turn. To cut a long story short, we got lost, and for forty-five minutes we tried to find a road. We were stranded and lost on some sand roads that led nowhere. But we didn't give up. We didn't drive back. And I believe, because of that, eventually we made it up the hill to that small white church. By the time we got there, the sun was already setting behind the horizon, where the sky met the sea. The view from that church was breathtaking.

"Maybe we got lost, only to find the road and come up here at the best possible hour. If we would've been up here two hours ago, we wouldn't have gotten to experience this magical sunset," I commented as we got out of the car.

How powerfully beautiful was that realization. We first had to get lost to see the sunset—almost like how the sun first has to set before the stars can appear.

As I got up to the church up on the mountaintop, I realized the door was locked. Even when you find hope, you can't always access it. But I didn't give up. I didn't leave. I walked around the church and saw that the window was open. I climbed up and got in. The church was abandoned. Inside were two wooden chairs. They were old, dusty, dusky and somewhat dilapidated. I sat down on one of them. I pictured Christ sitting on the other chair next to me. Holding my hand, He told me, "We did it. We made it through, together."

That simple moment of just sitting there for a while, talking to God, thanking Him, and feeling tears run down my face at that small white church filled me with peace. I felt at home. Getting lost was worth it, all for that moment. Enduring pain, suffering, and feeling alone were worth it, all for that simple afternoon, that conversation with God, the overwhelming, abundant gratitude I felt in my heart.

After half an hour, I climbed back out through the window. My mom was sitting outside, taking in the sunset. How magical the colors were. The landscape seemed taken out of a movie—out of a fairytale.

Looking at the sunset filled me with peace—a strange form of peace that overwhelmed my whole soul and hugged me tightly. Maybe the presence of peace amid the battle proves that there's purpose behind the battle itself. Maybe the beauty of the sunset, the colors, the brightness, and the splendor proves that transition can be meaningful, and that change can be graceful. The presence of color and the presence of peace as light faded away, made me think that maybe the sunset wasn't a proper goodbye to the light, but a proper hello to the night. Maybe it was a preparation for the majestic constellations of stars that the darkness would reveal. Maybe this abundant peace, this overwhelming sunset feeling foreshadowed the significance of the details of joy, love, and gratitude that can shine right through pain and hurt.

At night, we all went to a restaurant by the sea and enjoyed a family dinner. We laughed around the table, reflected on our vacations, talked about school, and most importantly celebrated life and victory with grateful hearts. And now—now I was home.

Now, I wasn't attached to a chemotherapy pole. Now, I wasn't poked and prodded daily. Now, I wasn't woken up every night by a tumor pressing against my knee. I was still immunocompromised. I still dealt with fear, pain, and long-term side effects. But it didn't matter. Chronic pain, fear of relapse, and dilated cardiomyopathy were all things I could learn to live him—exactly because of the last part of that sentence, *live* with. Nothing else mattered. I was given a second chance at life. And I'd promised myself I would make the most out of it, every day, with every new breath.

When we got home, everyone went straight to bed. It was pretty late. But the sunrise was in three hours, and I decided to stay up and watch it.

As I stared at the horizon, shortly before 6:00 a.m., I saw the color pallet of the sky gradually shift. Pastel teal and pink splashed across the sky. The sun was rising. I stared at the landscape in front of my eyes and let it sink in. I saw the mountains. I reflected on *my* mountain—on the small mountaintops I had conquered. And now, there I was, at the top. And the view made it all worth it. That sunrise made it all worth it.

I looked down at the sea. It was peaceful—calm, still, quiet. There was an abundance of peace in the atmosphere—a peace stronger than a simple sunset feeling. It felt like that first breath of relief after a panic attack. It felt like lying in bed after a long day. It felt like the first ray of sunlight after a dark night. It was peaceful. The storm had passed. The night had ended. And I was still on my knees. Still wounded and scared, I was still broken by trauma and pain. Yet I was made whole in the most unexpected ways. Light had inhabited my heart and glued its pieces together. I felt at home. I felt a sense of relief, protection, gratitude, and joy that I hadn't experienced before. This was a *sunrise* feeling—peace *after* a storm.

But you see, to experience a sunrise feeling, you first need to be overwhelmed by a sunset feeling. It first has to get dark; you first have to watch all your hope come crashing down for it to be built back up, with peace as its foundation and gratitude as its building blocks. It first needed to get dark. And it had. It had gotten dark, and it had stayed dark for such a long time.

Yet even though life had been so dark, light was all around. Light was hidden and reflected through my doctors and my friends and through random people in my life like my waiter friend, my physiotherapist, Mr. V, or even that little girl at the hospital before Easter. Light was reflected through everyday conversations, emails from teachers, long FaceTime calls with my family, messages, and my sister holding my hand. There was so much light. Some would even argue that the night is brighter than the day. But its light is hidden, making people believe it doesn't exist. Once you start noticing, you'll realize that, in reality, *the night is brighter.*

When I was younger, my dad told me it was time for me to learn how to swim. We went to the sea, and he walked with me in the sand, holding my hand until we got to the water. I was scared to get in by myself, so my dad got in the water with me. As I started swimming, I felt confident because I could see and feel my dad next to me. But as I went underwater, into the deep, fear took over. I could no longer see my dad. Nor could I feel his hand holding onto me. There seemed to be no sign he was still there, no proof. Yet I knew. I was sure. How? Because I knew my dad. I knew who he was and how much he loved me. He wasn't going to let me drown; he wasn't going to abandon me. I didn't see him there. I didn't feel him near. And yet I could still trust in him because I knew him. I didn't need to feel his hand holding me to know he was still there, because I had already felt his love in the past, and I knew that, because of that love, my dad wasn't going to leave me. He just wanted me to learn how to swim—all out of that same love.

As I went underwater, I felt scared. I felt as if I was suffocating, drowning, sinking deep. I was scared because I struggled to keep my head above water. *Isn't Dad going to help me, to save me? Why isn't he saving me? Why doesn't he pull me out of the water?* I began crying out. Nothing seemed to be different. Nothing seemed to change. I got so discouraged I stopped trying to swim. But as I began sinking, I fell onto two strong arms that hugged me and kept me from drowning. I realized my dad had been holding up his hands, stretched out, all this time, waiting to save me, waiting to catch me. He wanted me to learn how to swim. He hated seeing me scared. But only through overcoming fear could I learn how to swim. Only if I faced that fear could I also experience his love and protection in a way I hadn't before. And even though swimming was difficult and painful and scary to learn, the feeling of finally swimming, once I learned how to, was unbeatable. Swimming trains your body, making you stronger. Perseverance does the same. It trains your soul, making you complete. If my dad loved me that much, how much more did God?

God let me fall into deep waters, but just like my dad had, He jumped in the water with me. And just like my dad, He had His hands underwater, below me, ready to catch me and lift me up if I started sinking. At some point, I got tired of swimming. Yet God was there to give me peace when I was scared, when pain kept me up at night. He was there to transform the tears I cried and make them clean my eyes and open them to the beauty and the power of gratitude, love, and hope. He was there to hold the pieces of my heart as it broke from pain and disappointment. He revealed to me the power of the details and turned vulnerability into strength. He made his light shine through my scattered and tired soul. He carried my pain; took up my weakness, sickness, and fear on His shoulders; and helped me walk up the mountain. He was there when I almost drowned, and He was there when I learned how to swim. He cried when I cried and smiled when I smiled —all out of love, out of perfect, never-ending, unconditional, unfathomable love.

The wind was against me; the waves were surrounding me. God didn't always stop the wind. He didn't always stop the storm. Instead, He taught me how to swim through it. He walked by my side. He carried me when I got tired. He held me up when I fell. He kept my head above water when I could no longer swim. It takes faith to stay in the storm when you can't see the shore.

As these thoughts filled my heart with gratitude and peace, the sun peaked through the mountain. Light shone across the sky. The night was over. Darkness was defeated. The sun rose again. A new day had begun. Light overcame.

Dear God,
thank you for teaching me how to swim.
for showing me the stars.
for making me
brave in the broken.

Epilogue: Stay Brave

It's now October 2020. I'm on a plane going back to Essen for my post-treatment scans. It's been twenty months since I finished treatment. Life hasn't been easy. The past two years, I've faced more challenges than I had in all the rest of my life. Although life has been difficult, however, it has also been undeniably beautiful and incredibly meaningful. These past twenty months have been the most purposeful of my life. I've experienced miracles, smiled, cried, loved, received, and given. I've lived life to the fullest. I've kept my promise. I've made the most of every moment and in every space I've found myself. I've truly lived.

As I'm sitting on the plane to Germany, fear raging in my mind, I flip through the pages on my yellow notebook, my Packaged Joy Journal. Staring out the airplane window, I notice the ambient golden light shining through the clouds, and I reflect on the words that fill the pages in my journal. These ones stand out:

February 25, 2020

Tonight I experienced a miracle. Tonight I gave a speech at a Make A Wish event. I talked about the power of gratitude—how to be grateful even when pain is more abundant than joy; how to be grateful simply for the choice to hope. The event was hosted at the school auditorium. Over a thousand people were there. I was a little nervous. A few moments before getting on the stage, I took a moment to pray.

293

"Oh God... How far you've brought me... I remember being on the other side of this stage a little over a year ago, praying before getting up to receive my junior high school diploma. As I walked across the stage, across impossible, it was just you and me. And now... it's still just you and I God. I'll keep my eyes on you. Give me the words. Speak through me. Touch people's hearts. Make this night mean something far greater and bigger than me."

And God did.

Tonight, hope took a physical form and literally lit up the whole auditorium. In an effort to conceptualize and depict the power of gratitude, the lights were switched off and I asked everyone in the audience to light up a flashlight that had been given to them. As more and more flashlights were pointed to the sky, beams of light overwhelmed the room. It was magical, surreal. I felt so small. It was such a humbling experience, such a purposeful and powerful moment. It was so, so much bigger than me.

August 14, 2020

As the sun was setting; as the mountains and the clouds were preparing for the night, preparing for the stars, and awaiting for the sunrise; and as light was beginning to fade, the chains of impossible were broken. A sunset feeling overwhelmed me as I prayed and asked God to help me sit up and surf, just before the boat begun pulling me. Two years ago today, a few hours before my surgery, I was told I would never be able to surf again. A year ago today, I was told it was impossible; that the endoprosthesis in my leg could simply not handle it. But I think it all comes down to a choice. Would I stay trapped in what's impossible, or would I stay brave and overcome it?

I chose to stay brave. And today, I crossed "learn how to wake surf again" off my list with my post-operative goals. Today, God showed me yet again, that there's no such thing as impossible. He carried me and made my knees strong enough. He made me brave through the sunset whose colors flooded the sky and through the sunset feeling whose peace filled my heart.

Here's something cancer taught me about life; it's tidal. It's full of waves of fear, waves of joy, waves of pain, waves of gratitude. But here's what's really cool about the waves. You can either give up and drown, or you can be brave and learn how to surf. The choice is yours.

That's what I have to do, I then think to myself as I close the yellow notebook and put it back in my bag. I have to *stay brave*.

Two days later, I find myself sitting in the waiting room of the Ambulanz, the outpatient oncology clinic at the hospital.

That morning, my dad woke me up early. I couldn't have breakfast because I was scheduled for scans throughout the day. I got dressed and went to the bathroom to brush my teeth. As I stared at the mirror, I noticed my hair. It was long. It reached my shoulders. I smiled. As we drove to the hospital, I pulled out my phone and started typing.

"Who are you texting this early?" my dad asked jokingly.

"Just getting some thoughts down," I replied.

These are the thoughts I typed into my phone journal:

Same dread. Same gut-wrenching feeling. It almost feels as if nothing has changed. That final stretch before entering the hospital campus makes fear's chains tighter. Stalling—a traffic light, a missed turn, the guy in the front car driving slowly. In these small moments, time slows down, and I get to breathe again. But then the stopped car continues. Traffic spreads out. The red light turns green. And just like that, we make the turn to the hospital parking lot. And just like that, fear steals that same breath. Does it ever get easier?

So here I am now, sitting in the waiting room. My heart's beating out of my chest, my palms are sweaty, and my mind's flooded with what-ifs. The room is quiet. It's just us and another family—a mom and her daughter.

As I look to my side, I see the young girl, and I experience something so strange, straight out of a movie. She's skinny, pale, and frail. She's wearing a pink chemo cup to cover her bald head. She looks just like I used to. As I sit there, it feels like I'm in a time machine capsule, watching a flashback—to when I'd been where that girl was, sitting in that waiting room with my mom, waiting for chemo to start. It feels as if I'm in the waiting room with myself, in some strange parallel where time is warped and two different moments, years apart, connect and intertwine.

As I try to process my thoughts, I get emotional. I picture myself sitting there, two years ago. I picture *that* Katerina. All I want is to talk to her, to tell her all that I've lived through and all the miracles I've witnessed, and to thank her for all that I've experienced because of her fight. And then I start thinking. When I was going through treatment, in *that* moment in time, as young Katerina was sitting there, she had no idea of all I'd get the chance to live through, of who I'd become, or of what I'd achieved. She had no idea of all she'd get to do if she kept going. Yet, even without knowing what the future held, she kept fighting for it. She chose to be brave. Maybe I could do the same. I could choose to *stay* brave.

The next day, I'm scheduled for a PET scan. I'm greeted by my favorite radiologist, who instantly recognizes me. We chat and make a few jokes, and then he asks me to change into surgical scrubs for the scan. In every other hospital I've been to, they give you a classic white hospital gown for all kind of procedures. But not in this one. In this one, you're given actual surgical scrubs. I love that. It's a hope for the excitement of what can be, that helps me push through the fear of what is. Such a small detail gives me a glimpse of a future in medicine that, during a scan, I'm doubting will come. It reminds me of my why and my goal. Life, although difficult and scary, is full of such details of hope. You just have to notice.

The scan soon begins. Fear—it's something I deal with daily, yet on that scan table it becomes so loud. I guess the right question is not, Why do I have to face this kind of paralyzing fear? Rather, the question is, In a battle with fear, how can I win?

A couple of weeks ago, I was in class, and I was talking with someone about our goals in medicine. At some point, he looked at me and asked, "Why are you in such a rush? I feel like you're doing so many things that you'll do in like ten years anyway. So, if you will get to do these things in the future anyway, why rush to do them now?"

"Out of excitement I guess," I said.

In truth, I lied. I don't live the way I do because I'm excited for all that I'll get to experience but because I'm *scared* for all that I might not. I read this quote somewhere that said, "Cancer's like walking around with a gun pointed at your head all the time." It's something I relate to a lot—not necessarily because of a high risk of relapse but because just the mere possibility it could happen changes everything. With my cancer, right now, if you relapse, you're looking at a few years at best. It's either this or nothing. It's either breathing or not. So me, I guess I kind of live on the two extreme ends. You have normal days, when you just sit in school and talk about the French Revolution, potential energy, and cell division; days when you write a college essay as if college is something you'll definitely get to experience; and days when you plan the future as if you're invincible. But then you also have those reminding days, as I call them, when you're lying on a PET scan table to see if the cancer's back.

As you lie on that table, nothing matters anymore. Goose bumps rush over your body. The room is cold. It's freezing. You're trembling, but you're strapped down. You can't move. Nothing moves—not even time. It feels frozen, distant, arbitrary. Enclosed in the deafening machine, fear paralyzes you. All around you, darkness. The space is so narrow light can't even get in. The what-if is suffocating. Loud noises feel like a thousand bombs going off one right after the other. All you ask for is a moment of peace. You're desperate for just a moment of peace. And then, suddenly, somehow, as it gets louder around you, it gets quieter within you. The noise gradually fades out. It's just you and your breath.

Every breath you take reminds you that tomorrow is not guaranteed, not even promised. Yet we all just assume it's going to be there. Maybe that's why we let moments slip away. We take them for granted. We think we'll somehow get them back or get to live them again. But when you know tomorrow's not guaranteed, you can be brave enough to make the most of today.

That's why I live the way I do. That's why I try to squeeze as much life as possible into each moment I get. Knowing that tomorrow's not guaranteed, why not write a book? Why not go on stages and speak to people about what I went through? Why not stay up till 6:00 a.m. just to watch the sunrise in an oversize hoodie? Why not drink five cups of coffee in a day? Why not randomly call a friend to tell them you miss them? Why not say thank you more? Why not remind people every day how much you love them? Knowing that tomorrow's not guaranteed, why not pursue your goals and dreams? Why not eat that donut at 4:00 a.m.? Why not hug people a little tighter? Why not laugh a little louder? Why not sing at the top of your lungs in the rain? When tomorrow's not guaranteed, why not make the most of today?

Why not *live* today?

The truth is, yes, I *am* scared. All the time. But I don't let that stop me. I choose to stay brave in the face of fear. Courage is not the absence of fear but the triumph over it. Fear creates the mountain; faith moves it. But without fear, there'd be no mountain for faith to move; it would be arbitrary. So, I *use* fear. I use it as a foundation of faith, a source of courage, and a reminder to choose brave. *That's* how I win. And that's how you can too.

After that PET scan, we went to our favorite restaurant, Zwolf Apostles. My waiter / best friend was there too. When he saw me, he gave me the tightest hug and something meaningful to him that I could keep with me forever. A little while after we sat own, Dr. S walked in the door. We all sat together for a coffee. I hadn't seen her in over two years. We talked for hours about those past two years, about medicine, hope, fear, dreams, role models, and angels. I'll never forget that conversation or the tears in Dr. S's eyes when I invited her to my high school graduation. It was a full-circle moment, hope redefined, hope embodied. We talked as doctor and patient, recalling the struggles of my treatment; as colleagues in the medical field, discussing my internal medicine internship that summer; and as two best friends, making jokes and laughing. Love's in the details.

The next day, I was scheduled for a full cardiac evaluation. As we walked in the Kinderklinik, I saw a doctor I hadn't seen in over two years. It was the doctor who'd sat by my side after giving me the bad news that I would not be able to travel home for graduation, the doctor who'd knelt and held my hand after my heart condition diagnosis. I waved at her, and she smiled at me. God's in the details. I then went to the oncology outpatient clinic. Just as I walked in, I saw a *patient* I hadn't seen in about two years. It was the girl I'd shared a hospital room with, back during chemo 6 in June. She'd given me the necklace with the angel back in November 2018. I thought I would never see her again. She smiled at me, and I smiled at her. God's in the details—and in smiles of hope.

On the last day of the trip, we had appointments set with Prof. H and Prof. D. At the surgical outpatient clinic, we were informed that Prof. H had an emergency to attend to, and our appointment would be postponed for two hours. My dad got nervous. We had to rush to the airport right after the hospital visit because we had a flight to catch, which couldn't be postponed because Germany was going on lockdown the next day – pandemic stuff.

We headed to our appointment with Prof. D at the Kinderklinik. She was very happy to see me.

"How are you doing?" she asked as I sat on the exam bed.

"I'm good," I replied, my voice filled with emotion. "I'm doing well."

"You look very good," she told me.

In the cancer world, this sentence is the greatest compliment and the most meaningful thing somebody can tell you. It doesn't mean that what you're wearing is nice or that you're pretty. It means that you look okay. You look healthy. You seem to be doing well. And in the cancer world, to be doing well means to be alive, to be breathing, to have survived. And, oh, how beautifully powerful it is to battle with death itself and see the one who helped you fight once you've survived.

"I managed to surf this summer too," I told her at some point as we were discussing how I'd been doing.

"Do you have a video?" she asked.

As I showed her the video of me wake surfing, she couldn't believe it. "And that's with an endoprosthesis," she said in disbelief, surprise, and awe. "*I* can't even do that," she joked. "Have you shown this to Prof. H?"

"We haven't seen him yet, but when I see him, I'll show him," I told her.

"Yes, show him," she said. "He'll be very proud."

299

Prof. H was indeed very proud when I showed him that video. I'll never forget that conversation with him. Hope's in the details.

As we left the hospital for the airport, my heart was full of gratitude. Fear still haunted my mind, as we still didn't have the scan results. Yet gratitude was louder. Hope was louder.

We were already late and nervous we'd miss our flight. At some point, my dad missed an exit on the highway, pushing us back half an hour. It was almost certain we'd miss the flight. God, however, had other plans. He needed me to get on that plane. And nothing—no traffic light, no wrong exit, no delay—could stop His plan.

We arrived at the gate just as our flight was boarding. As we sat on the plane, something felt familiar. But it wasn't yet time for me to find out what.

About an hour into the flight, I looked outside the window. The sky was filled with clouds. Through massive holes in the sky, light poured down. It seemed like heaven. *I've seen this before. I've been through this before. Why is it all so familiar? What do you want me to notice, God?* I wondered.

"Would you like anything to drink?" I heard someone ask me.

I turned and saw the flight attendant. "No, thank you. I'm all good," I replied.

And then it hit me. Then I noticed.

There's no way God. No way this is true. It's all in my head; there's just no way.

Yet a voice inside me kept whispering, *That's her. That's the flight attendant who anointed you with oil on that flight to Athens two years ago, when you were going back home for the graduation. That's the flight attendant who told you everything would be all right.*

Battling that voice, logic came in running. *No way that's her. She's wearing a mask. How can you recognize someone you only saw once, two years ago, for literally only ten minutes? How can you recognize her now, two years later, wearing a mask? You can only see her eyes. There's no way you can recognize someone you saw once, two years ago, only by her eyes. No way that's her.*

When the plane landed, I approached her nervously. "Excuse me, could I ask you something? This might sound strange and maybe I'm mistaken, but two years ago, I was on this flight going to Athens from Düsseldorf, and I think I remember you giving me some oil from Jerusalem and telling me everything was going to be all right. I was going through chemotherapy back then. I was sitting in the same seat as I am today, and—"

"Yes," she interrupted me surprised. "Yes, that's very possible. I always carry that oil with me. Are you okay now?"

I couldn't believe this was happening. Neither could she.

"I recognized you. I remembered you. Yes, now I'm okay. I'm doing well," I told her, my voice thick with emotion.

I saw tears fill up her eyes. We were both wearing masks, but that didn't hide the huge smiles of hope on our faces. Besides, remember, you can recognize a smile of hope only through looking into a person's eyes.

"I just wanted to tell you how much you helped me. I always anoint my leg with some of that oil before scans, and I just wanted to tell you that it has given me so much strength and courage throughout this journey."

She was speechless and emotional. She kept asking if I was okay now.

"It was as if you were an angel sent to give me hope," I told her before my dad called me.

All the passengers were already on the transport bus, and they were all waiting for me to get off the plane.

As I walked to our next gate for our connection flight, I kept thinking about what had just happened. How could it be that I'd recognized her simply by her eyes, two years later? How could it be that, out of all the flights, God wanted me on this one, to see her? I had been visiting Germany every four months. And there's only one direct flight. Yet, I'd never seen her before. During this whole entire trip, I'd been seeing people from the past – people that I hadn't seen in a very long time; people through whom I was able to see God's grace and love. It was a miracle I couldn't understand; I could only witness and experience it.

When we finally boarded the next plane, we took our seats. I stared out the window and saw the most beautiful sunset as I listened to my music. I turned and saw my dad crying.

"What happened?" I ask, worried.

He showed me an email on his phone. It was from Prof. D: "We just saw the images. Everything is perfect! No relapse."

My eyes blurred. I felt my heart burst. For the first time in so long, I could finally breathe again. I started laughing. I couldn't believe it. A huge weight of fear was lifted off my shoulders.

Thank you so much God, I thought and teared up. *Thank you.* Tears streamed down my face. *I'll make it matter. I promise.*

As the plane took off, I stared out the window and reflected on all the miracles I'd experienced these past twenty months. They're a whole other book on their own. Life hadn't been easy. But there had always been moments that were undeniably beautiful—even in the broken. It's these moments that make life worth fighting for.

I took out my yellow notebook and wrote:

Hey, Katerina,

This is the future you—or the future me I guess.

How are you holding up? How's chemo going? I hope it's more bearable this time around. But I know it won't be.

I've been thinking a lot about you lately—about all you're going through and about the way you fight.

I know it gets heavy. I know you're scared. I know you're tired. I know the pain is unbearable. I know you can't go on for a minute longer. But I also know you will. I know you won't give up. I'll know you'll choose to be brave.

I want to thank you for that. Thank you for choosing to keep going. Thank you for enduring, for fighting. I know you feel broken. But you choose to be brave. You choose to hold on. You choose to keep walking. And because of that choice you make every day, I get to be here today, to breathe, to walk, to laugh, and even to write you this letter. I'm alive today because you choose to fight. Thank you.

I wish I could give you a hug and take all your pain away. But I know you're surrounded by love - family, friends and guardian angels. I also know God is with you. He has never left you. And He never will. And lastly, I know that you're brave. You choose to be. With every new, painful, heavy breath.

I wish I could show you all the things I've experienced and achieved these past twenty months. You wouldn't believe it. But I know we're experiencing these things together. Besides, we're the same person, right? I can picture you smiling. I know I am.

Please don't ever give up. You're going to make it. I promise.

You're going to make it.

I won't give up either. You suffered through so much for me.

So I'll live just as much for you.

I promise to live – truly; whole-heartedly; meaningfully.

And for you,

I'll stay brave – brave in the broken.

About the Author

Katerina Karaindrou battled a rare and aggressive form of bone cancer and dedicated her life to impacting others. Through lived-experienced advocacy and public speaking she vulnerably and powerfully shares her story. Katerina is on a path to become a doctor and is dedicated to make a difference in cancer treatment. She spreads the message of hope and resilience to encourage people to overcome their fears and choose to fight.

Printed in the United States
by Baker & Taylor Publisher Services